# Hippo in a hairnet

## By Stewart Shale

# About the author.

Stewart is a 75 year old father of two, stepfather of three, and grandfather to 15. He obviously has a sense of humour!

After a varied lifetime, most of it in sales and admin, he and Diane moved to France in 2004 after taking early retirement. After living and working in France, they returned in 2010.

Stewart now works seasonally as a visitor attraction guide at a castle in the Scottish Borders, while Diane, happily retired enjoys gardening, crafts, and generally living the life of Riley.

# Acknowledgements.

First and foremost, I'd like to thank my wife Diane for living with me through thick and thin, while putting up with my lunacy. Then, my thanks go to family who helped and sustained us throughout this crazy period of our lives. We couldn't have done it without you.

Moving along, I must thank Oliver and Iona for their help in setting me on the right track. And finally, last but not least, a special thanks to Lady Jane Grosvenor, who found time in her busy life to support my efforts. Thanks to one and all.

# HIPPO IN A HAIRNET

## A French Adventure

## Prologue

Alone in that pitch black cave, I felt abandoned and helpless. It wasn't the warm, cosy darkness you'd experience in the safety of your bedroom. This was a complete absence of light. I'd never experienced anything like this before. With neck hair bristling and my other senses operating on high alert, I sniffed at the cool musty air. But apart from my own shallow breathing; the silence was absolute in that Stygian cavern.

Stumbling around in the dark, arms stretched out, I'd become totally disoriented. Confused and uneasy I stood listening, my heart pounding like a trip-hammer in my chest. Despite logic dictating that I'd be okay, the feeling that the walls were closing in on me was impossible to ignore. However, this was something I had to endure and defeat, otherwise that worm of fear would always linger in the back of my mind.

I stood it for as long as I could, then a draught of air brushed across my face, setting my mind racing. It felt like someone – or worse still some *thing* was in there with me.

Right, I'd had enough. Fumbling blindly, I switched on my cap lamp; its beam reassuring as it swept the limestone walls. Thank god, I thought, as the overbearing sense of danger began to subside. My surroundings were no longer threatening; and though I'd been left down here alone, I reckoned that by staying calm I could find my way back out. After all, many before me had entered these tunnels; and as far as I knew they'd all made it back to the surface safely. In fact, to some this was their everyday normality.

Shrugging tensed shoulder muscles, I looked around me. I was in a small gallery at the end of the long twisting tunnel, its entrance lost way off in the gloom. Branching randomly off from the main walkway, were side tunnels resembling eye sockets in a skull. Right then, they looked sinister and uninviting.

Okay, I'd proved to myself that I could handle a lamp-battery failure if it happened. But now what? A weight seemed to settle onto my shoulders. I'd arrived here at seven am, and it wasn't even eight thirty yet. Could I really do this?

It was my first day underground, and from the beginning I'd been out of my depth. Vehicles were rushing everywhere, people were shouting, machinery clashing and banging. Why had I allowed myself to be talked into this? Worse still, I may well have been an alien, as no-one spoke my language or could really understand me. I felt overwhelmed by it all. I'd been led here and dumped with the barest of information by the only person who I could communicate with. She'd warned me against getting lost in this underground system. 'Make sure your cap-lamp battery is always fully charged,' she'd said. 'If it dies you could become lost in the tunnels.'

Worried at her stark warning, I'd decided to switch it off to experience what it felt like. Never again, I thought. Breathing deeply I pulled myself together.

As my lamp picked out familiar features in the cave, my spirits began to rise. I was aware, that far off, through a warren of tunnels was safety. All I had to do was hold my nerve, accomplish my task, then find my way back out again. I mean, how hard could it be? ... I would soon find out.

# Chapter 1

## Long journey down

'Calm down? You're joking right? Christ, I'm just getting started. You've just told me we're lost in the back of beyond, and you're asking me to calm down? Well you're the map reader; if you want calm, do something about it.'

'What do you expect me to do,' Diane hissed. 'This map's been a pain in the arse since we bought it. And now, the damned village we're looking for isn't even shown on it.'

'Well isn't that just great? So now you're telling me you've lost a whole *village*? Now bear with me here. Assuming it hasn't been beamed up by aliens, it's got to be around here somewhere right? Let's face it; we've just paid for a new map, but it was shown on the tattered old thing we threw away. So where the hell *is* this place?'

'God only knows. But that signpost we passed back there said it was 25 kilometres away,' she said through gritted teeth.

'Yeah, but that was ages ago. I've already driven further than that. Are you sure you've got it right? I mean, there's absolutely nothing here. It's like that seventies movie Deliverance. You know, the one with the weird looking kid playing a banjo.'

'Right, I've had enough of this,' she snapped.

Oh-oh! I recognized that tone. 'Now look, I only meant ...

Oh, I know *exactly* what you meant. You meant I can't be trusted to read a simple map. Well there you go then Einstein; if you're so flaming perfect, you make sense of it.'

And with that, the laminated map-book shot at me like a Frisbee. Instinctively, I swerved to avoid it. 'Oh terrific,' I sneered, as it glanced off my shoulder and disappeared through the open window. Luckily I'd been slowing for a crossroads, or we may have driven into the nearby storm ditch. What a pain in the ass *that* would have been.

Huddled in her seat with arms folded, Diane's face was set in a frown. 'Aw come on,' I relented. 'Don't go off on one. Just nip out and find the damned map, then maybe you can work out where we are.'

'*Don't go off on one?* Hah! If you hadn't jumped out of the way like some wimp, the map wouldn't be out there, now would it?'

I sighed, thinking I couldn't fault her logic – twisted though it might be. 'No, I suppose not. But let's face it; if I hadn't, you could've put my eye out,' I volleyed back in my defence.

'That's right. It's all about you as usual.'

'Oh God I give up.' Leaning forwards I rested my forehead on the steering wheel.

Then in a mercurial mood switch, she said, 'Look, why don't we just calm down. It's been a long day, we're both shattered, and this is getting us nowhere. I'll get out and find the stupid map. But then we'll *both* look at it. I mean it's not rocket science is it? We must be nearly there by now.'

Climbing out of the car she arched her back, stretching with a groan. Eyes stinging, I watched as she strode off determinedly, her backside oscillating wildly in my rear view mirror. In the mirage created by melting asphalt, she'd taken on the form of a shimmering belly-dancer. 'That's my girl,' I sighed.

Switching back to reality, I picked up the thermos, my damp shirt clinging to my back. Pouring out a chilled drink, my parched lips almost whimpered in anticipation. Holding the cool cup to my brow first, I slumped down in my seat. With the throbbing engine shut down the silence was exquisite – until the ticking of the cooling radiator broke into it. As the temperature stabilized even that noise ceased. Then the only sounds punctuating that aching silence were cicadas chirruping nearby, accompanied by water trickling along the storm ditch. In that arid landscape, the only signs of life were a few scrawny sheep way off in the distance.

Eyes closed I lay back, pole-axed by the oppressive heat, the smell of hot tar wafting in through the open window. However, my hard won peace was about to be rudely shattered.

'Hey Schumacher; start her up and let's get going. I think I know where we are.'

It was Saturday the eighth of September 2001, when our ferry docked in the port of St Malo. The six hour overnight voyage from Portsmouth had been tortuous, but in those days that was the cheapest way to reach mid-France. However, with cabins seeming pricey considering the little time spent in them, hardcore travellers besieged the information desk when boarding. Sometimes a discounted cabin would become available due to cancellation. If so, they were snapped up quickly. For everyone else though, it was the economy deal including recliner seats. With all the comfort of dentist's chairs, they should've displayed a government health warning; as in my opinion, only contortionists, or those of a vertically challenged disposition could sleep in them.

When boarding it'd been survival of the fittest. Competing in a manic version of musical chairs, passengers fought for a seat or settee. Those who missed out – like us, were reduced to finding a space on the floor. First come first served was the way it worked.

With loading completed, the ramp was raised and bow doors sealed. As the marine diesels shuddered into life, hawsers were cast off bollards and hauled aboard. Set free at last, the huge craft edged away from the dock. With exhaust smoke issuing from its funnels and its propellers churning an oily froth, we headed downriver.

Leaning on the stern rail we savoured the novelty of departure; filling our lungs with briny air, and braving the chilly breeze until we'd cleared the estuary. By then, the majority of passengers had vanished below decks, swallowed up in the brightly lit interior. Watching the port recede from view, we waved to anglers on the harbour walls, as with a deepening engine note the vessel increased speed. Then, changing course slightly to starboard, it entered the choppier waters of the Channel itself.

As dusk fell, just a few lights were visible on the shoreline. And with nothing more to see, we descended to the lower decks where crowds were slowly dispersing. Already the restaurant was full and queues were forming at the bar. Within minutes, a tannoy announced that we'd reached the three mile limit, causing an indecent rush for the duty free shop. Under harsh lighting, eyelashes could be seen fluttering coyly at the perfume counters, promising untold delights to weary husbands. Past caring by then, they reached for their wallets with a sigh.

With darkness engulfing our little community by then the ship ploughed steadily onward. In the dimmed lighting set for night-time running, all that was visible in the salon windows were ghostly reflections of the interior. Overtaken by tiredness travellers sprawled everywhere, strewn like wind-blown chaff in a wheat-field. Joining them, we found ourselves a space on the floor. Then using rolled-up coats as pillows, and with our valuables hidden from view, we stretched out. Young, old, rich or poor, we were as one family, trying to block out the creaking and groaning as the ship breasted the swells.

And so the night unfolded. Absorbing the gentle vibrations coming through the floor, we ignored the occasional cough or fart, as we tried to grab some sleep. Like the aftermath of a Roman orgy, the mix of cultures settled down together. Uneasy bed-fellows we may have been – but like some tired old music hall act, it was for one night only.

*Bing Bong*! The scratchy P.A system announced our imminent arrival. Like extras from a zombie movie, passengers lurched upright; some late night revellers managing to look even

9

rougher than the rest of us. Following a quick wash and wipe in the toilets, we joined a disorderly rabble heading for the car decks. As for queuing, forget it. Brits used to do it, but not now.

Slowly nudging into the dock, reversing screws brought us shuddering to a halt. The anchor chain rattled, hawsers were cast and tied to bollards, then foot passengers were allowed to disembark. Shouldering his way through the crowd, a steward unclipped the rope barrier, whereupon vehicle drivers shuffled forward like automatons, descending crab-like down narrow service stairs. Reaching deck five we located our car. Safely inside it with seat – belts fastened, we assembled paperwork for French customs. Then we waited.

Within minutes, a metallic booming noise signalled the opening of the bow doors. As a shaft of daylight speared the cavernous interior, crew members in hi-vis jackets directed vehicles to the unloading ramp. With the strains of *La Marseillaise* trumpeting in my brain, we followed traffic out of the hold, noting signs urging us to keep to *le droit.*

After a cursory passport check by customs, we snaked along in convoy through the dockyard, dodging service vehicles while seeking signs for the *Centre Ville.*

Exiting the town in a cavalcade, we peeled off onto an Elf garage forecourt, where we filled up with very cheap fuel and extremely expensive coffee. While paying at the counter, the grinning attendant sold us the aforementioned roadmap. Then, with both the car and ourselves tanked up, we headed for the Autoroute and the city of Rennes.

Being newcomers to the area, we cruised carefully along the motorway, becoming accustomed to the different conditions. But we soon found ourselves overtaken by other Brits, who seemed more familiar with the road. And of course French drivers, whose cars seemed to be propelled by rocket fuel, hogged the outside lane with complete disdain.

Almost sixty kilometres later, we burst out of a tunnel lights blazing, to be met with a breathtaking view of Renne's twin cathedral spires. Wending our way down the hillside, we avoided the traffic jam inching slowly into its heart. Joining the ring road instead, we headed south, reaching Le Mans one hundred and forty kilometres later.

Sucked into the city's rush hour maelstrom, we jostled with other traffic; competing for pole position as we snaked through the outskirts. But alarmingly we couldn't find the Tours exit. With it being poorly marked we almost missed it, and just managed to take it at an insane speed. Then noting a sign for Saumur, we followed it and joined the dual carriageway.

On the last stretch, we took the slip-road when the majestic château appeared on the cliff-face ahead. Swinging onto the city's imposing bridge we crossed the shimmering River Loire, headed towards our final destination Montreuil-Bellay.

What inspired Diane and I to make that journey, was a unique combination of circumstances. Like many others, we'd grown weary of harsh British winters and depressingly wet summers. And having moved up to Northumberland, we'd endured our first winter huddled over a log-fire in a rented shepherd's cottage. With wind and rain pebble-dashing the windows, one bright spot in our bleak existence was watching *A place in the sun*. This TV programme showed alternative lifestyles in sunnier climes, which could be ours for the asking. As we'd already developed an affinity for France after a touring holiday in Brittany, we thought maybe we should check it out as a lifestyle choice on our next holiday.

We were finally spurred into action by a game-changing fortnight in August 2000. Both of us were middle-aged divorcees, with five teenage children between us. Diane had three girls, Nadine, Helen and Kay; and I had two boys, Michael and Chris. With us firmly settled in our new relationship, we rashly suggested taking them all to France for a bonding experience. Nadine declined, as she was leading a busy life in Essex with her partner, but the others agreed to go. Yes, I know, it had disaster written all over it! It could have been a

'Perfect Storm.' But with blind optimism, we thought we knew better and continued planning.

Needing a roomier vehicle for the trip, I bought an old Peugeot 505 eight-seater estate car; intending to sell it when we returned. After treating it to a full service and fitting a roof rack, I slapped on a GB sticker. It was time to go.

With the rack full, I shoe-horned everyone aboard; including Helen's boyfriend Stewy who simply couldn't be left behind. Hopelessly overloaded, I drove off, white knuckles gripping the steering wheel, and my heartbeat attuned to that 22 year old engine. Praying fervently to the Gods of motoring, and with sphincter muscle gently twitching, I prepared to challenge the highways and byways of France.

What seemed like a lifetime later, we trundled into the hamlet of Chiné. After nursing the old Peugot along we arrived very late at our cottage, where a terse note pinned to the door said the key was under a nearby stone. Bone-weary we let ourselves in, dumped our luggage then filled the kettle. Everything else we left in the car. After a cuppa, we crashed out exhausted after allocating rooms.

Waking to a gorgeous morning, Diane soon had bacon sizzling in the pan. Hearing a knock at the door, I opened it – to find Pat and Steve, caretakers for Brittany Ferries. Pat apologized for not meeting us; but with other clients to attend to and us being so late, they couldn't hang about, she said. Sensing a frosty atmosphere, I apologized and offered them a cuppa. The climate then thawed appreciably; and with the ice broken we found out more about our custodians.

They'd moved across from the midlands eight years before, after snapping up a derelict farmhouse with outbuildings. Working day and night they'd renovated it, turning two units into holiday gites. Now this was intriguing!

Plying them with questions we picked their brains; gathering information which could prove valuable, if we ever decided to find our own place in the sun.

The holiday itself proved a huge success; the kids becoming great friends. However, after exploring the cottage and grounds they'd become restless, and set their sights on the nearby village. They planned to visit the local bar; unfortunately, Kay and Chris were below legal drinking age. It wasn't a problem on-site as Diane and I weren't naïve. After all, we've all been teenagers. So we let them have a few bottles of beer. But flying solo was the boys preferred option; a chance to play bar games and meet the locals. The girls were happy lounging in the garden, but sensing a mutiny from the boys, we agreed. However, being older, I asked Stewy to look after my lads.

It worked just fine, until the night they all rolled in three sheets to the wind. Well, actually Michael limped in, his beige chinos trending a new look for the Paris season – one leg black and smelling like crap. He'd fallen into a storm ditch on the unlit track from the village. 'One minute we were walking along chatting – and he just vanished,' Stewy said. 'Suddenly we heard this weird voice coming from below us.' Sniggering, he weaved unsteadily across the kitchen.

When I asked why they were all obviously bladdered, he replied, 'We had a drinking contest with some French kids.' (France v England, say no more.) Apparently *Entente cordiale* was stretched somewhat, but no real harm was done. The lads had gotten along just fine with the French youths, ribbing each other about football. But for some reason, an older guy began having a go at Michael. Now Michael at six feet three is no shrimp, but they said the other guy was a huge blockhouse of a man. Behind 'The Hulk's' back, the barman was frantically signalling that he was crazy. And since Stewie had chosen that moment to flake out across a table, Chris and Michael were persuaded that a strategic withdrawal might be wise.

Supporting Stewie (the guardian) between them they left. However, as they stumbled back along the road, the street-lights suddenly fizzled out; and seeing a tree looming out of the darkness Michael stepped aside to avoid it. Splash! Into the ditch he went.

Mind you, as a supposedly responsible adult I was no better; losing the plot with a French boy-racer who cut me up the next day. I chased him for miles, but he was toying with me. Let's face it; our old car with its seven whooping occupants just wasn't going to hack it against his tricked out BMW.

Inevitably, as incomers to a tight- knit community there was a feeling of isolation. With double gates thrown open on the humid Saturday evening, we sat listening to a house party on the outskirts of the village. At first all went well – but then the noise level spiralled dramatically. A drunken argument flared, a fight broke out, and a resounding 'smack' was followed by screams. In a moment of alcohol-fuelled madness all hell broke loose; the disturbance spilling out into the road.

Moving swiftly, I locked the compound's double gates. Then turning off the lights we adjourned to the upstairs front bedroom, where we watched the action from a safe vantage point. At one stage, with his blood stirring and caught up in the moment, Chris suggested 'inserting' a metal *boule* into a sock and joining in. 'This isn't a game on your X box son,' I said. 'This is for real. Besides, it's not our business. Let the *gendarmes* handle it. We can't even speak the language.'

As is often the case though, it was soon over. No gendarmes materialized, and most of the party-goers drifted off peacefully. Soon afterwards, much to Chris's disgust there was silence.

The highlight of the holiday was *Futuroscope*, a virtual reality theme park. The special effects were incredible. Strapped into a mocked up Apollo spaceship, its seats vibrating and tilting, it was easy to believe we were travelling through space – though common sense insisted we were on 'terra firma.'

Unfortunately the heavens opened later, but cloaked in free ponchos it couldn't dampen our spirits. And as a finale, a laser show projected onto water-fountains made for a spectacular end to a great evening.

To no-one's surprise, we got lost while trying to leave the gigantic car park. With the volume of traffic it seemed inevitable. With everyone suggesting different ways out of the snarl-up we took a vote. Michael won, so we followed his advice – and ended up back where we'd started. Chris commented dryly, 'Well done Mick, the directional guru.'

Once we'd escaped though, the drive back was a hoot – until we ran over something lying on the unlit road. Though worried at what we might find, I turned back, but there was nothing. Mightily relieved, we began throwing out wild suggestions as to what it might have been. With our imaginations running riot, the ideas became all the more absurd, making us laugh until our sides ached. Daft – yes, but it helped pass the time.

Our last night was spent at a Thai restaurant, where the waitress, dubbed Susie Wong by Stewy (yes, I know) served the boys Tiger beer in special glasses. To their testosterone fuelled delight, each emptied glass showed an image of a naked girl on its inner base. Subtle it wasn't; but what a devilish sales ploy for my young crew to resist. So it came as no surprise to Diane and I when the bar ran out of Tiger beer!

Side-stepping Michael's request to 'have a go' at driving when we left, I somehow got them all aboard. As we drove off, the bar owner was waving fondly by the kerb. No doubt he was thinking of the world cruise on his bucket list, which thanks to us he could now afford. Meanwhile, a shattered Suzie Wong quickly closed up the bar; her fixed smile evaporating like snow off a dyke.

The drive back was raucous; with the girls rolling their eyes as the boys treated us to a glassy-eyed karaoke. A fitting end to a great holiday, I thought. But what next, I wondered?

# Chapter 2

## Should we – or shouldn't we?

It was only ever meant to be a holiday. But with the kids dropped off, we returned to the bleak Northumbrian moors and a reality check. In a thank you letter to Pat and Steve, we enquired about returning early the next year. But this time it would be just Diane and I, and we'd be looking at properties to buy. They replied, saying we could book a gite at mate's rates, and they'd be happy to help if needed.

Our next step was advertising our venerable old estate car in the Autotrader. We were reluctant to let it go; but it found a new home with a nice local lady, which was only fair after the service it gave us. It was a close call though, as the first enquiry was from a London based Nigerian guy who wanted to take it down South – until he worked out all the costs involved.

Once again we were plunged into autumn; commuting to work in the dark through gales, fog and rain. By then Diane drove a Citroën Xantia, while I'd traded in my Daihatsu Fourtrak for a more economical Peugeot 405 TDI. Though we worked for different companies on either side of the river Tyne, we travelled together when shift patterns permitted to save fuel.

With a worsening weather forecast we prepared for a savage winter; stockpiling coal, logs and non-perishable food. And oh boy, it certainly proved to be savage.

Setting off one fateful morning, we were blissfully unaware, that by mid afternoon we'd be cut off by snow-drifts in our cottage three miles from the main road. We'd travelled in separately that day, and after hearing a forecast for heavy snow on our car radio's we asked to leave early. We were both refused. When I was finally allowed to leave, I rang Diane, who said she was just setting off. She was picking up some supplies on the way, but would see me back at the cottage.

The 26 mile journey home was horrendous; slithering and sliding along untreated roads, in what had become a howling blizzard. After an hour I reached my turn-off; almost missing it, before cornering carefully and driving on blindly in a white-out. Ploughing through snowdrifts, I reached the hairpin bend leading up the hill to our cottage. Through the frosted windscreen, I glimpsed the flaring brake-lights of a car ahead. I'd found Diane.

She'd tried running the gauntlet, and had 'sledged' back down the hill. Before long we were both hopelessly bogged down; the shrieking wind piling drifts over our cars. Huddled together in Diane's Xantia, we set the heater on full blast. However, we needed to act fast or we'd become entombed. Once the exhaust pipe was covered, the engine would cut out due to back pressure, and we'd be in a life threatening situation.

Forcing the door open I went for help; but returned unsuccessful wearing a skullcap of frozen snow. Diane said I resembled a huge crow as I loomed out of the blizzard, my black coat flapping wildly behind me like wings.

Miraculously, we were discovered none too soon by a passing farmer. With ghostly headlights piercing the snow, he materialized on a tractor pushing a dozer blade. He'd come across us as he cleared the road to his sheep enclosure, otherwise God knows what might have happened.

Dragging both cars out of the drifts on a chain, he towed us one by one to the Knowsgate Inn hotel. With the manager informed, we abandoned the vehicles in the car park. Then, climbing into the tractor carrying our emergency shopping, we were given a lift home by our Good Samaritan; the three of us squeezed into his small heated cab, with him on the only seat.

Getting underway we lurched from side to side, windscreen wipers slapping furiously. On one relatively straight stretch, he turned to us where we clung precariously, and in a rich Northumbrian burr, he said with a wry grin, 'You must be the newcomers then.'

'No, we've lived here for over a year,' I replied.

'Yup, the newcomers,' he said.

He dropped us off at the field-gate leading up to our cottage; and thanking him profusely, we set off wading up the track thigh deep in powdery snow. Shopping bags held to our chests, we battled the blizzard, arriving cold and wet almost ten minutes later. And from that moment on, we were without power for more than a week. Lightning had struck an electricity pylon on the moors, we discovered later; so miles away from the nearest village we were snowed in. With an open fire as our only means of heating and cooking, and with candles providing a feeble light, we made keeping the path clear to the woodshed our priority.

The alarm clock woke me at three thirty the next morning. Diane wasn't due into work, but sadly I was. Not only that, but I had a very early start. Trying not to wake her, I dressed, had a quick cuppa, a slice of toast then crept out. Free-wheeling the Peugeot down the rutted track, I jump-started it near the bottom. I made it onto the road okay, but almost immediately I became bogged down in wind-blown drifts. Abandoning the car, I slogged back home and woke Diane up. With snow falling heavily by then, we trudged back with shovels, dug out the vehicle; then sweating and cursing we struggled to get it back up the track.

As the phone was still working I rang my manager, giving him time to re-arrange his work rota. But rather than thanking me, he suggested I should walk to work. What? He knew I lived over twenty six miles away. That's a marathon by anyone's reckoning; and even more ludicrous in those conditions. Was he for real? When I protested, his next line was another classic.

'Well it isn't snowing here,'

'Maybe it isn't – but I'm not there, I'm here,' I snarled.

His final brainwave was, I should walk the three miles through knee high snow to the main road, where someone could pick me up. Knowing that the main route to Newcastle was blocked, and even the snowplough had been abandoned on it, I said, 'Fine; there's a call-box at Ponteland. Get him to ring me from there – then I'll set off walking.'

The MENSA reject rang back later, saying, 'The driver couldn't get through. You'll have to take a day's holiday, or it'll go down as unauthorized absence.'

Such a caring guy! And did he thank me for getting up at stupid o' clock to try to get into work? Or for ringing him so he could arrange cover? Well, what do *you* think?

When I finally managed to get in ten days later, I stormed into his office and slapped a Polaroid photo onto his desk. It showed me waist-deep in snow, holding a homemade placard stating the date and time. I advised him very firmly, 'Never imply that I'm lying again.'

One 'kiss-ass,' living less than a mile from the office didn't attempt to turn up or even ring in, but nothing was said to *him*. Diane had much the same treatment from her boss. Managers – I've seen more intelligence in a zoo.

But that sort of treatment just made us even more determined to change our lives. Then researching into buying French property, we found a book titled, *Living and working in France*. Though it proved invaluable, it made us seriously question our decision to live abroad. For instance, it said that in France, the buyer paid all the costs for both parties, which added roughly twenty percent to the asking price. And if they backed out, they were legally obliged to pay the seller ten percent of the full asking price as a penalty. Undaunted though we pressed ahead, our minds firmly made up.

Inevitably the long hard winter passed, replaced by the warmth and colours of spring. It was 2001, time to come out of hibernation and make plans. But as so often happens, life got in the way; and it was mid-summer before we could book our *gite*.

With the possibility of a mortgage in the offing we met with our financial manager; and following a discussion, we knew our options before setting off. We'd booked the gite for September, the die was cast, but we had no idea what we were getting into. If we had, I'm not sure we'd have gone ahead. But hindsight is a wonderful thing, isn't it?

After a now familiar journey, we arrived in Montreuil-Bellay to an Indian summer. Driving on to St Jean, we were met by Pat and Steve, who'd rented us an en-suite in their farmhouse. Unpacked and showered, we met to discuss tactics over a bottle of wine. (Well, okay then, three.) At first they seemed a little cagey; then later they explained why. Guests were often seduced into buying French property whilst in holiday mode. But after enlisting the couples help they usually backed out. Sensing a little reluctance on their part, we thought it best to go it alone.

Adopting 'Franglais' and a little mime, we made some appointments to view with *Immobiliers. S*ome of them tried to offload 'fixer uppers' onto us; most of them in appalling condition. One of them was merely a shell of a cow byre, with solidified cow-pats for floors.

'But Monsieur, they have great potential,' I was told. Indeed, we were lucky to be given such opportunities. Maybe the French also watched *A place in the sun.*

With our hosts to fall back on if required we continued our legwork; visiting three *Immobiliers* the next day. Then, with information copied from their window ads, we drove off after breakfast the following morning; with a map, a thermos and a packed lunch.

However, looking for properties wasn't easy, as some were way off grid, which meant asking locals for directions. This could be fun, we thought. Anyway we stuck at it; finding one after another, though none of them were suitable.

In the late afternoon, we arrived at a small hamlet, which at first seemed deserted. Our brochure showed a farmhouse nearby which looked really promising – if only we could find it! As we sweltered over our map in the car, a young couple left a nearby house carrying a ladder. Propping it against the gable end, the guy climbed it while the girl 'footed' it for him.

Jumping out of the car, I hustled across to ask directions, and fortunately the young man spoke some English. Climbing down, he listened politely, before asking me to follow him up the outside staircase of another house. There he introduced me to an older man, sat at a table in the upstairs kitchen. Attired in a grubby vest, and with red braces framing his ample paunch, he looked fresh in from the fields. Still wearing his cap, he was devouring his midday meal with relish, his stubby fingers tearing apart a baguette. My new friend turned to me, saying, 'He is the Mayor of our *commune*, and must know this farm.'

Knife and fork then clattered onto the table, as 'the Mayor' began speaking, arms waving and shoulders shrugging. With a look of weary resignation; his wife, who was working at the kitchen sink, wiped her hands on her pinafore. Then gesticulating wildly, *she* launched herself into the discussion. Eventually the young man said, 'He knows an Englishman living outside the village. Perhaps he could help you. The Mayor, he will direct you, yes?'

'Please thank him for me, I'd appreciate his help. And thank you also,' I replied.

After wiping his moustache, then his hands, on his wife's tea towel, *Monsieur le Maire* accompanied us out to the car. Bemused by the arrival of my grinning new acquaintance, Diane climbed into the back seat while I explained 'the plan.' With a lecherous, '*Bonjour Madame*,' the Mayor made to climb into the car – appearing startled to find his ample posterior descending into the driver's seat. However, once I'd directed him to the *correct* passenger seat, we were ready to go.

21

Waving goodbye to the helpful young guy we left the hamlet, the Mayor grinning inanely whilst directing us. After half a mile or so, I pulled up with a screech – the brakes, not me. The unscheduled emergency stop was caused by the Mayor, who'd grabbed my arm and shouted, '*Arrêtez.*'

We'd arrived at a glaringly white troglodytic dwelling. Eager to please, my volunteer navigator knocked on the heavy oak door. When a tall rangy guy appeared, they exchanged a few words in rapid French; then the stranger turned to me saying, 'Hi I'm Archie, how can I help?'

At that the Mayor mumbled, '*Au revoir monsieur et dame,*' and shaking my hand, he doffed his cap to Diane before setting off back along the road.

'Hang on, doesn't he want a lift?' I asked.

'Nah he'll be fine. He's a nice old guy who likes to help. And being a Frenchman, he's got an eye for the ladies of course. Now what can I do for you?'

We never did find that farm. Archie didn't know where it was, so we'd need the *Immobilier's* help after all. By then we'd had enough anyway, and were more intrigued by *his* home, which was little more than a cave. The front structure was fieldstone slabs, buttressed onto rooms gouged from the limestone cliff-face. It was chaotic and in a state of genteel dilapidation, but it suited *him,* he said. Besides, he had no choice. His marriage was 'down the crapper,' as he succinctly put it, and the marital home in the Dordogne was up for sale. Over coffee we learned a great deal about the area; passing a pleasant hour with yet another eccentric character we'd met on our travels.

Having helped Steve finish building his *boules* court when we returned, he invited us for an inaugural floodlit match. Broaching a couple of bottles of Merlot the tournament got underway – becoming rather erratic quite quickly, as the red wine affected our accuracy. Hurling expletives after one particularly wild shot Steve suddenly changed tack, asking if we were still keen on buying. If so, a friend of theirs was selling *his* house. Like Archie's it was part of a divorce settlement. Steve thought it could be a bargain, as Graham the owner desperately needed money. It was on the outskirts of the village, he said. We could nip over in the morning and give it the once over. Graham was arriving on Sunday to check on the property. We could speak to him about it then if we liked. What did we think?

However, the next morning, with heads thumping and eyes squinting, the plan was rapidly losing its appeal. But after a greasy full English breakfast we rallied. We decided that we'd go for it – though Steve should never have driven. At the end of our *boules* evening he'd barely been able to stand. Trying to be tactful, I suggested we put it off until later. Outraged by this slur on his abilities, he assured me that the French had a more liberal attitude than the UK towards drinking. Everything would be fine, he insisted. After all, the gendarmes were hardly a shining example, parking their patrol-car outside the bar every lunch-time while they washed down *croq monsieurs* with beer and *pastis*. Feeling justified after this outburst – but looking deathly pale, our tarnished hero drove off shakily.

Fortunately for us all though, it was a short journey on quiet back roads. We pulled up intact at a run-down looking farmhouse, its outbuildings surrounding a courtyard. We were met by the elderly Blondine, Graham's neighbour and caretaker. Fussy and effusive, she first gave us a tour of her garden, before ushering us into Graham's farmhouse. With rose tinted spectacles set firmly in place, we made light of the shabby interior. Then outside again; ignoring broken stable-doors and flaking paintwork we strode around the courtyard mesmerized. Imagining a genteel life as landowners, we gazed fondly at the rundown outbuildings, blithely dismissing pan-tiles sliding wearily off the sagging roof. We were hell bent on making that classic mistake – buying the first half decent house we'd seen. 'It just needs a bit of work,' I whispered.

'Yeah, just think what we could do with it,' Diane replied.

Oh yes, we were hooked alright.

Meeting Graham on the Sunday he seemed keen to sell. However, his face fell when I made him an offer below his asking price. Thinking it was best not to lean on him, I left him to sleep on it. And before he left for the ferry the next morning I rang him. Reluctantly accepting our offer, he said he'd be in touch later before putting down the phone. 'Yesss,' I said, fist-pumping the air. Where would we get anything like that in the UK, and at such a ridiculously low price? Where indeed, I thought later, with the benefit of hindsight.

Buoyed up we showered and changed, but were then interrupted by a rapid knocking on our door. Opening it I found an agitated Pat, who asked us to quickly follow her to their living room. There we found Steve, grave-faced and eyes riveted to the television screen.

It was Tuesday September 11th and a news-flash showed a huge skyscraper ablaze. The shaky amateur footage then panned across to a second skyscraper, just as it was struck by an airliner. Smoke billowed out of the damaged building; the vortex scattering debris along city streets. Then without warning, the first building collapsed like a stack of cards. What the hell was going on here? People were screaming 'Oh my Gard' while fleeing the scene. It was pandemonium, as arriving fire-appliances bullied their way through reporters and rubberneckers; klaxons blaring as they fought to get closer to the scene. It was a day that became infamous in history, remembered globally as 9 /11.

We sat there hushed, as New York correspondents reviewed the carnage. Terrorists were being blamed and retaliation promised. With the world's governments on red alert regarding repeat attacks, we thought maybe it was time to go home.

Unfortunately, our ferry was booked for the Friday night. To cancel and re-book – if that were even possible, would be expensive. Besides, there could be people directly affected by the disaster who were desperate to get home. Until we knew more, It wouldn't change a damned thing for us; though looking at houses seemed trivial and pointless.

Nevertheless, we felt we should go through the motions. After all, remember Millennium-Eve? Forecasts of global disaster, computer meltdown, and planes falling from the skies, all came to nothing. Maybe this would be the same. One thing was for sure though. It's said everyone remembers where they were when J.F.K was assassinated, I know I do. And now we'd remember this day for the rest of our lives.

Though our hearts weren't in it we carried on house hunting, whilst keeping up with breaking news daily.

On Friday afternoon we said our goodbyes, setting off for our ferry with mixed feelings. Who could say when or *if* we'd return? As we know now, all hell broke loose after that, and the rest as they say is history. Let's just say we got home safely.

With the Twin Towers relegated from the front pages, I tried catching up with Graham; and thus began the most frustrating period of our lives together for Diane and I. After accepting our 'offer in principle,' he changed his mind and the deal was off. Then he raised the asking price; suggesting the dubious practise of an ex- gratia under the table payment. This erratic to and fro went on for months, by which time even Pat and Steve were sick of him. I eventually pinned him down on a phone-call, and pushed him for a decision. His latest excuse was, he and his wife were thinking of getting back together, so perhaps he should hang onto the house.

'Stick your house up your arse,' I snarled, and slammed the phone down. All that precious time wasted. Here we were heading towards 2002 with nothing sorted. Angry and frustrated we put everything on hold; throwing our energies into work, and grabbing as much overtime as possible. We reasoned we'd need lots more capital if we wanted to start looking again next spring. Then surprisingly, things took a turn for the better.

# Chapter 3

## Madame says yes

Here we were in April 2002, older, and a lot wiser. Adopting a new approach, we took out a subscription to 'French Property News.' We needed to find an agency with an English speaker; someone who'd do the legwork for us and arrange viewings. Though we hadn't a specific area in mind, we chanced upon the ideal *Immobiliere* in Noyant, a market town in the Maine-et-Loire region. Paula, an English agent answered the phone. She said she could spare us a week in May to blitz the area. She'd sort out hopefuls from her listings, and after driving down, we'd sift through them and formulate a shortlist.

When Diane informed her eldest daughter Nadine of our plan, she said she'd like to come with us. Being heavily pregnant, and with her partner Nick snowed under at work, she needed a break before the birth. In return, she'd keep us grounded, and provide a balanced no-nonsense opinion.

With the ferry and accommodation booked, the time came for us to travel down to Maldon Essex. Picking Nadine up, (figuratively speaking of course) we headed to Portsmouth, where we caught the overnight P & O ferry to Caen. Luckily we snared a cabin, due to Nadine's obvious condition. Dumping our luggage inside we wandered around the ship; ending up on the foredeck where we watched final boarding.

As the huge craft slipped her moorings we stood at the bow, the wind whipping our faces. While we enjoyed reprising the famous scene from the film Titanic, we decided we'd rather miss out the bit involving the iceberg.

After reversing out of the dock, the props changed direction, and the craft thrust ahead into the shipping lane. Ablaze with lights she surged downriver, towering over Nelson's flagship Victory. Marooned in her dry dock as a tourist attraction, she seemed forlorn and lost.

Leaving the Spinnaker tower behind us, we entered the wider estuary, skirting Royal Navy warships at anchor. Then with a shudder the speed increased, as we left the Solent for the swells of the English Channel.

Windswept and ruddy-faced we went below decks, relaxing in the bar sharing a bottle of wine. Taking turns we sampled the cabin's bunk beds, Nadine going first. However sleep was out of the question, as we were situated next to the disco- bar which stayed open until one am.

Nonetheless, four hours later we left our cabin yawning infectiously. Setting off for coffee, we picked our way through a maze of recumbent bodies. And when the ship docked at six am local time, we stood bleary-eyed and dishevelled near the head of the crowd.

Once the ramp was lowered, we drove down and crossed the docks to *Douane,* or customs, where a sleepy officer gave our passports the merest glance. Within minutes, we'd left the *Centre Ville* and after crossing '*the Pont de Normandie'* we followed signs to the *Autoroute*. We were off and running.

A gruelling seven hours later we arrived at our destination, a Napoleonic manor house near Noyant. Converted to a *Chambre d'Hôte* it stood resplendent in the afternoon sun, its sandstone walls and grey slate roof providing an oasis for weary travellers. After booking in, we unpacked then rang the agency. But it seemed we'd arrived on a public holiday, and Paula was enjoying a day off, though her boss confirmed our meeting the following morning.

27

Refreshed after a shower, we drove to Saumur for the afternoon. Parked up near the *bateaux* jetty, we crossed the road and meandered around town, wending our way up to the Château. The views from the gardens were fantastic, overlooking the town and river way below us. Descending later we negotiated narrow old cobbled streets; steeped in shadow on one side and bathed in sunlight on the other. Ingredients in a human cocktail we flowed along with the crowd, exploring uniquely French boutiques, café/bars and patisseries.

As Nadine was flagging by then, we stopped at a café. Seated outside with coffee and croissants, we soaked up the sunshine, while enjoying the age-old pastime of people watching.

With our vitamin D and caffeine levels boosted we strolled along the cobbles; absorbing the sights, sounds, and smells of the bustling old market. As a plethora of animals and birds called out raucously, we stopped transfixed by it all. With the potpourri of colourful stalls, displaying fish, meat, cheeses and olive oil, the North of England seemed light years away.

Obscenely early the next morning, we woke to the crowing of a cockerel with a death wish. Determined not to let our feathered friend spoil our morning, we headed downstairs, where we found a continental breakfast set out on our dining table. As there was no-one around to ask, we dived in. Then bloated with croissants, preserves and bowls of Kellogg's finest, we drove off to the agency.

Entering at nine am a buzzer sounded, and a ruddy-faced young woman appeared from an office. 'Hi, I'm Paula – be with you in a minute.'

Returning, she mangled my fingers with a wrestler's handshake. (Mental note; don't mess with Paula.) Leading us to her office, which had all the space and comfort of a broom-closet, she produced a huge tome resembling a wallpaper pattern book. From this property bible we winnowed out twenty to visit – four per day unless we hit pay dirt quickly. Opening my mouth I formulated a question ...

'Right, let's get going,' said Paula, leaping to her sturdily booted feet. 'Follow me guys,' she commanded, striding off briskly.

Taken aback we galloped (or in Nadine's case waddled) along behind her. Gasping for breath after our unscripted 100 metre jog, we arrived at a battered old Renault saloon. World weary and a bilious shade of green, its patina was liberally enhanced with rust.

'Pile in,' said our leader, sweeping a waxed jacket, compost bags, and assorted rubbish off the back seat.

'Hold on tight,' she advised, turning the ignition key. With a consumptive cough, the diesel clattered noisily into life. Crunching into first gear we rumbled off.

'It could probably do with a service, but it gets me around,' she shouted, turning her head towards us. As the car had wandered into the opposite lane by then, I sucked in a breath, hanging firmly onto a safety strap. With a fixed grin, I wished fervently that I was driving.

At the intersection we lurched across the main road – just ahead of an approaching truck. Then having made it out of town alive, we headed off on the first of our visits.

The week passed in a pleasant haze, being whisked from one property to another. Our first viewing was a dilapidated old restaurant, set next to a crossroads in a quiet little hamlet. 'It's a damned good business opportunity,' said Paula. *Only if the new owners shipped in punters by the bus-load*, I thought.

Next we were shown a *Maison de Ville,* or town house; its huge rooms crammed with a lifetime's junk. The eccentric widowed owner was including racks of keys, as her late husband had been a locksmith. It could be a going concern, we were told. Possibly; but *my* only concern was how quickly *we* could get out of there.

The next property was an abandoned house on a hillside. When Paula eventually forced open its warped door, we were totally unprepared for what followed. We'd stepped into a land-locked version of the *Marie Celeste*. The owners had vanished, leaving plates of mouldy food draped in spider's webs. Alternately, for a lover of Charles Dickens, it could have been Great Expectations brought to life. All it lacked was Miss Haversham's wedding cake set centre stage on the dining table.

Ah the French; self proclaimed exponents of style and finesse. Why on earth would they present a house for sale in such a condition?

Driving back along country lanes we mulled over our visit. Then turning a bend we were amazed to witness an old woman wearing a horse-collar, pulling a plough in a field; her husband holding reins attached to the harness. It's heartening to see those E.U farming subsidies making a difference, now isn't it?

Grinding up a long drive on the Thursday, we approached the last house on the list. Lolling in our seats half asleep, we were feeling the effects of a hot drive following a heavy lunch. As the Renault shuddered to a halt, Paula yanked on the handbrake. 'Right, we're here guys,' she proclaimed, pointing to a modest looking old farmhouse. 'It's called La Ferronnerie.'

Bleary-eyed, I gave it a cursory glance. 'Nah it's too small, let's go.'

Shrugging her shoulders she turned the ignition key. And just then the house door opened. 'Ah shit, she's seen us,' said Paula eloquently. 'I suppose we'll have to go in now.'

Turning off the ignition she climbed out. Cursing heartily I went to help Nadine, who said, 'I'll just stay here. There's no point in me getting out really, is there?' Hurrying off, I caught up with Diane. Meanwhile, Paula was babbling away in French to a woman stood in the doorway; the conversation rattling to and fro like machine gun fire. As Paula nodded towards us, the house-owner turned. Holding out a claw-like hand, she grinned gruesomely through yellowed teeth. We just stood there smiling inanely. Well wasn't this fun?

Invited in by Madame, we decided to go through the motions then find an excuse to leave. Once inside though, we were surprised to see that the interior was Tardis-like. Though it's often a misused expression nowadays, it wasn't in this case. At the front a full length extension had been added, which was unnoticeable when we'd driven up. It'd created a huge downstairs bedroom, and a baronial dining room.

If you ignored the hunting themed wallpaper, and avoided eye-contact with the profusion of deer heads lining the walls, it actually showed a lot of promise. Though, a shotgun in the umbrella stand gave me food for thought, and a desire to locate another exit – just in case.

'So whaddya reckon?' I whispered like some 'B' movie gangster.

'I'm not sure yet. Let's see what Nadine thinks.'

Sidling out to the car, Diane returned with a frazzled Nadine, who had a, 'This'd better be worth it,' look on her face. I left them to their inspection, with Madame hovering over them like the Angel of Death. Wandering through the cool, dark, kitchen, I stepped out over the threshold, into a blinding wall of heat. Unperturbed however, Paula was striding around outside like the Terminator on steroids. Clipboard in hand and impervious to the withering temperature, she was scribbling notes.

Leaving her to it I circled the house, taking in sweeping lawns at the front, overlooking a field stretching down to the road. Moving around to the rear, more fields swept up to woods on the horizon. 'So what's this place called again?' I asked.

'La Ferronnerie. I think it was originally a blacksmith's or metal-works.'

'And how much land comes with the house?'

Pre-occupied with her paperwork, she waved vaguely, saying, 'That there.'

'What where?' I asked gazing around me.

'That *there'*, she said described a 360 degree circle.

'What – all of *that?*'

'Oh yes,' she mocked. 'You've been saying all week that you wanted land. Well now you've got it – that is if you really want it. There's the house and gardens, a double barn, a wine *cave*, a wood-shed, a tool-shed, sheep-shed and other outbuildings. Plus, there's three point five hectares of land including an orchard, and part of that wood. Oh, I nearly forgot; there's also a well.'

I just stood there my mind blank; mouth gaping like a stunned mullet. Gazing up the fields to the horizon, I found it all too hard to absorb.

'Now I know this is going to sound dumb,' I said, 'but what's three point five hectares in acres?'

'Just under nine, 'she said. 'Now is *that* enough land for you?' Eyes twinkling devilishly, she grinned, as I stood there gob-smacked.

We left soon after; shocked into silence until we reached the road. Then all of our questions tumbled out at once. When asked about surveyors reports, Paula said, 'In France they don't bother on old properties like those. They've got no foundations, but they're built on solid bedrock. It's assumed, that if they haven't moved before now, they aren't likely to in the future. The rest you take as seen. You could commission a survey if you wanted to of course, but very few do. It's very expensive and takes forever to get the report.'

She answered this and other questions while trying to concentrate on driving. However, it was far too much to take in right then, so she suggested we sleep on it. She'd arrange return visits to any property we were interested in.

Well no-one slept much that night I can tell you. We talked into the early hours; and as soon as the office opened, I rang, asking if we could re-visit three properties. Maybe then we could make sense of it all.

'No problem, I'll see you at the office,' was Paula's reply.

We arrived half an hour later, and were taken to review the short-listed three. Dropping us back at lunch-time, she arranged to meet up with us before we set off home. After packing, a last minute discussion was convened in our room. With all the paperwork laid out on the bed, we analysed the three candidates in depth. But it was a foregone conclusion. Whether we thought with our hearts or our heads, there was only one real contender. We'd arrived at a decision.

After settling our bill we loaded the car. But before we headed off for the ferry, I rang Paula, saying sorry we couldn't meet up as planned, we were running late. Thanking her for her help, I added, 'Can you make Madame Renard an offer on her house?'

Well there was no turning back now. If all went well, we'd soon own a small farm in France; and all for the price of a two bedroom terraced house in Northern England.

On the motorway half an hour later Diane's mobile rang. Scrambling to get it out of her bag, she said, 'Hello?'

'Hi Diane, it's Paula. Madame says yes.'

# Chapter 4

## It could have been worse – I think

Due to our last minute viewings, the drive up to Caen became a high speed race to catch the ferry. However, events conspired against us as we became trapped in traffic jams and road works; seeming to catch every red light en-route. With a smell of burning rubber we finally screeched into the docks; only to witness the ferry leaving the harbour. 'I don't believe it,' I groaned, slumping back into my seat.

'It can't be helped. Let's try the ticket office and see what's available,' Diane suggested. Leaving Nadine in the car we entered the busy foyer. At the counter we were met with supreme indifference by a bored looking receptionist, who announced snootily, 'I regret Monsieur, there are no more ferries tonight. The next one arrives in the morning at six am.'

Damn, seven hours to kill. Worse still, we then found the cost of a ticket on Brittany Ferries had spiralled to a staggering one hundred and sixty euros. As the assistant was busy elsewhere by then we couldn't ask why. 'That's highway robbery,' I said, 'they're not holding *us* to ransom.'

This was a tad hypocritical, as *we'd* been exploiting a loophole in *their* booking system. A well known national newspaper was issuing vouchers, offering return trips to France for a pound. By buying *two* newspapers, it was possible to use one voucher for travelling out, and the other whenever you liked for your return. Of course they weren't intended to be used like that. They were for day return trips. But a seasoned traveller had given us the heads up, saying they weren't dated, and were never checked at the ticket booths. 'Only idiots pay the full price,' he laughed. 'If you only have one voucher, hand over a few euros for the return trip at the ticket office. It's simple. Everyone's doing it.'

Back then, the ferry companies were in fierce competition for business, however this offer had backfired. But it seemed the loophole had been closed. We learned later that transactions had changed to bank-card only, and were checked against personal details online.

However, high on misplaced testosterone, I decided to 'dash' up to Le Havre further up the coast. Driving red-eyed through the night, I arrived to find the same price as at Caen. We'd gambled on finding a far cheaper carrier there because it was much further north. Blithely unaware that this change was industry-wide and affected all ports, I drove on to Calais determined not to be ripped off.

In retrospect, considering the extra fuel used to gain a marginally cheaper ticket later, we reckoned our misplaced outrage saved us a mere six euros. And that was only because it was a much shorter crossing. Ah well, *C'est la vie*!

Our marathon drive ended around one thirty am. Pulling into the dockyard, we found the ticket office closed until nine am. At *that* point we almost lost the will to live. Totally shattered, I drove to an unlit corner of the empty car park, where we could rest up until morning. With Nadine sprawled across the back seat out of necessity, Diane and I tilted our seats as far back as possible over her. And in the cramped space available to us we all tried to sleep.

An hour later the ticket office light came on. And with Diane and I still awake, I suggested we lock the sleeping Nadine in the car and stroll over to the building. Maybe we could negotiate a cheap ticket. Heading off with stiff joints protesting, we'd crossed maybe a third of the car park when a furtive movement caught my eye. Behind glaring security lights a shadowy mass erupted, morphing into a group of ghostly shapes which began moving toward us. We stopped dead in our tracks; as dishevelled figures, some of them masked broke into a run. 'Quick, get back to the car,' I hissed.

We turned and ran. Fumbling to open the car doors, we threw ourselves in, I fired up the engine, and looking up, I saw a crowd of men and youths closing in on us. In seconds I'd pressed the central locking button, slammed into reverse gear, and shot back across the car park. Spinning the car around, I then tore across the asphalt to the embarkation area. With all of the lurching around, Nadine surfaced rubbing bleary eyes. 'What's happening?' she yawned.

'Don't ask. You'll not believe it when we tell you. I'm not even sure I do yet.'

Passing deserted ticket booths, I sped across the docks and parked behind cars in the 'ticket only' queue. At least there was safety in numbers there. To hell with tickets, they'd have to wait until later.

Over coffee in the waiting room, a trucker told us the group were illegal immigrants, desperate to cross the Channel. They'd broke out of a holding camp at Sangatte near Boulogne, and due to the scale of the problem, French police had lost control of the situation. Both there and at Calais, gangs were openly roaming the docks, seeking a way into Britain. It was becoming a massive problem, he said, as their trucks were often searched and cleared by French police, only to have stowaways found by UK customs. Fines of £2,000 per stowaway were imposed on drivers when this unwanted human cargo was discovered. He knew one owner-driver who'd been forced into bankruptcy, after repeat offences beyond his control, he asserted.

'How did they get on board?' I asked.

'We've all got our suspicions,' he growled. 'Let's just say money talks.'

He hinted at bribery and collusion; and where there's money involved, who's to say?

As dawn broke his point was proven, when police vans wheeled into the docks. Men and dogs leapt out, and began a sweep of the area checking all vehicles. As dogs barked, police shouted and blew whistles. It was unnerving to see figures emerge from under trucks, mobile homes and trailer tarpaulins; desperate souls who scuttled off into the shadows – only to return again the next night.

With the police still patrolling the area we boarded; and an hour later with watches re-set we docked. Home at last, we left Dover's Eastern Docks after a comforting check of our passports, the car and its occupants by UK customs officers. Wending our way up the spiralling dual carriageway, we filtered into the A2 lane leading to Canterbury and the M25. Three hours later we delivered Nadine safely home, none the worse for her 'restful' holiday.

Following a comfort break, we joined the A1 for the long drive home. We could hardly believe it. We'd bought a farm in France! We were on a total high. But then reality kicked in. What in God's name were we going to do with all that land? Our long term plan would be to live in France running a holiday let business; however, with limited funds it might prove tricky. It was an exciting pipe-dream, but like countless others we were on the daily treadmill of working; even more so with this new millstone around our necks. But at least we had a foot in the door. We'd just bought our very own home in the sun.

# Chapter 5

## Sign here, here – and here

July 2002 found us heading for France again, with my son Chris and Diane's daughter Kay in tow. We were on a bargain break, staying in a mobile home near the beach at La Rochelle. The area was remote and stunningly beautiful; and once we'd settled in we began exploring. We began with Rochefort, then Dompirre-sur-Mer; both of them breathtaking. We then crossed the causeway to Ile de Rè, with its white sands, crashing surf and huge open skies. To use an overworked American adjective, it was awesome. But even in *this* remote beauty spot we managed to cause an incident. Whilst innocently inspecting some oyster beds, a group of fishermen erupted from a nearby shed shouting angrily at us. 'Come on lads, we weren't trying to take any. I mean, do we look like the oyster-gang?

Overall though we had a great time, despite an outbreak of athlete's foot which threatened to ruin it for Chris. That is until Diane produced the medical kit. 'We'll have no jessies on *our* team,' she said, dealing swiftly with the problem.

It was our last day and we'd swung inland, intending to show the kids the house while touching base with Paula. But arriving at the agency, we found there'd been a new development. Madame Renard suddenly wanted the process speeded up. She'd bought a house, and wanted to move in A.S.A.P.

This was infuriating; as after our offer had been accepted, Paula had posted the *Compromis du vent,* or sales contract to us in England, which we'd signed and returned immediately.

We'd then arranged a mortgage with Abbey France, opened a bank account with *Casse d'Espargne* and paid our deposit. With everything sorted at our end, we'd waited for Madame to get her act together. Only then could the joint signing and official hand-over take place in the *Notaire's* office.

At no point had anyone proceeded with any urgency in France. But now Madame wanted to move. So here we were; just across the street from the *Notaire's* office – and all our relevant documents were back in the UK!

Before leaving home we'd asked, 'Should we bring any paperwork with us? Is Madame anywhere near ready yet?'

'Nah you're fine; it'll be ages before she gets her act together,' Paula had assured us.

We left the office feeling furious. However, driving out of town we meandered through fields of golden sunflowers, which calmed us down and lifted our spirits. But our natural good humour really kicked in when we passed a house festooned in Christmas lights, reindeers and plastic Santa's. We found out later, that the Romany family who lived there left decorations up all year round. Set in a landscape of rusting trucks, caravans and other exotic detritus, this Dali-esque home remains seared onto my eyeballs forever.

Pulling up the drive to La Ferronnerie soon after the kids seemed suitably impressed, saying 'Ooh' and 'Aah' in all the right places as we drew up to the house. Thankfully no one was home; but the downside to that was, we couldn't show them the interior layout. Though we gave them a quick tour around, and looked through the windows (as you do) before leaving.

All things considered we'd enjoyed a great break; and okay that *was* the original plan. But with a little thought and communication, we could have signed for the house while we were there.

Headed back to England, I once again assumed the mantle of my alter ego Michael Schumacher. My mission (should I choose to accept it,) was to get Chris back in time to watch

Newcastle play their historic rivals Sunderland in a vital derby match. It was a clash not to be missed by a devoted 'Toon Army' fan. But, however hard I drove, the Xantia was no F1 racing car. Screeching to a halt outside St James Park it was fifteen minutes into the game. Not bad after an 850 mile trip, *and* being held up by an accident on the A1. But as he ran up the stairs to the stands, a roar from the crowd told him he'd just missed a goal. Still, Newcastle won two – nil which was some consolation.

Our next excursion across the channel was planned for 28th October; our only chance to take leave. We were finally attending the *Act de vente,* or signing ceremony. However, at the 11th hour, and with Brittany Ferries on speed-dial, Madame pulled out. Apparently she wasn't quite ready yet.

Once again everything was put on hold. Then three weeks later she decided she was ready. But there was a slight problem. She needed to leave her furniture in the house after we'd taken possession. For some reason she couldn't put it in her new home. *Well tough tittie,* I thought. *Now you're really taking the piss lady.*

Heartily sick of Madame by then we declined her request, arranging a later date for the signing with the *Notaire.* We stressed that the house had better be empty when we arrived. If not, we'd bill Madame storage-fees on anything left behind. Either that or we'd throw it into a rubbish skip.

After squandering our holidays due to her selfishness, we had to take unpaid 'sickies,' book a ferry, then drive almost 900 miles to Noyant – then return the following day. Hey, no problem Madame, I'm a driving machine, and made of money.

On the day of the journey we set off fuming inwardly; and after a long hard slog we boarded the late ferry completely strung out. We hadn't eaten since breakfast; and though we knew better, we opened a bottle of duty-free vodka as a nightcap.

It was a really bad idea, as having swigged the whole bottle between us, I threw up. Luckily, this put me on the road to recovery. However Diane slept on.

When it came time to disembark though, I definitely shouldn't have driven – especially off a packed ferry onto the wrong side of the road at night. And driving through the *centre ville* wasn't much fun either; as my navigator was comatose; held upright (well sort of) by her seat belt. God only knows how I got her below decks and into the car. But after inserting her, she couldn't be coerced into consciousness at any price.

Concentrating ferociously I managed to overcome these minor problems, picking my way carefully through passport control, (she's sleeping Monsieur,) the docks, and *centre ville.* Then finding a deserted country road, I pulled into a lay-by where we slept it off.

We agreed later that it was a valuable lesson learned, and we were exceedingly lucky to have gotten away with it.

Having survived an epic journey made worse by torrential rainfall, we met Paula at the agency. Grabbing paperwork we dashed over to the *Notaire's* office with minutes to spare. Soaked to the skin we opened the door – to find Madame, her son and daughter sat waiting patiently, fortitude written across their faces. Their nine km journey from Le Lude must have been so exhausting.

All present, we began three hours of signing and counter-signing. With Paula translating for us, we waded through the quagmire of French bureaucracy. Mentally drained at the end of the experience, we finally emerged clutching the keys and the deeds, which in France are received at the time of signing.

After buying provisions and kitchen utensils at *Intermarché,* we drove to the house in a storm. Leaving Diane to get settled in, I ran out to the woodshed, where I found some pitiful scraps of wood left by our generous benefactor. Dashing back in I lit a meagre fire. Then *'sans èlectricitè,'* we cooked food and brewed coffee on the glowing embers.

With our meal finished and our wet clothes strung up to dry, we snuggled down on the tiled floor swathed in a duvet. Nodding sleepily, we watched shadows cast by the dying embers dance around the walls. Even empty the house felt warm and friendly, standing rock-solid against the howling gale as it battered the shutters. With wood-smoke permeating the rooms, our handful of candles helped the fire in its struggle to pierce the darkness. And though we admitted finding the bathroom might prove difficult, the disconnected electricity wasn't really a problem. Madame had taken all the lamp fittings and fixtures with her.

As the area recovered from the storm the next morning, we drove into town through the brutalized landscape. After topping up with fuel and basic provisions at *Intermarché,* we loaded luggage back at the farm. Then with a flask of coffee and sandwiches prepared, we set off for the late ferry.

In the storm's aftermath driving was dangerous; and making it to the Autoroute, heavy winds and rain scoured the open highway. To make matters worse, Diane had developed raging toothache. Being a stalwart map-reader however, she soldiered on; and we eventually arrived at the ferry terminal completely shattered – only to find a bulletin on a notice board saying, 'The crossing on The Pride of Portsmouth is delayed due to worsening weather.'

Two hours later, a decision was made to board all traffic. We had to leave whatever the conditions. Though setting off in a force eight gale was a horrible experience for those with a weak stomach. Thankfully our digestive systems were fine; but for those of a more delicate nature it was a hellish trip, as they staggered back and forth across undulating decks to the overflowing toilets.

Approaching Portsmouth after a nightmarish crossing, we hove to outside the harbour, while two tugs attached themselves to our vessel by hawsers. They then struggled to keep us clear of the massive walls on entering. Sadly, as the ship battled huge swells they were forced to cast off, abandoning us to our fate. 'Whoa,' I said, as the wind caught us broadside on.

'Oops,' sniggered Diane, as we crashed into a Royal navy destroyer sheltering in the harbour.

We learned later, that it had just returned from sea trials after being commissioned. This was unfortunate to say the least. But how's that for making an entrance?

Calling into Nadine's on the way home, we rested up for a while, re-living the crash vicariously on local TV news. But to those who asked us about it later, we professed ignorance of the event. I mean, how could we know anything? We were in the North-East tucked up in our sick beds – weren't we?

# Chapter 6

'Is there a doctor on board?'

With the house signed for and mortgage payments locked in, we began planning for 2003. But with a hard winter to endure first, we began wiring money to our new bank *Credit Agricole,* a much bigger institution. Setting up standing orders to cover utilities, we transferred funds when the exchange rate was favourable. Considering mortgage payments, our UK rent and other living expenses, it's easy to understand why our lives revolved around work– and grabbing any overtime available. As they say, needs must when the Devil drives.

February was inked in for our next trip to France. Chris had volunteered his services; and Kay, home from boarding school was hitching a lift to Nadine's. Hiring a large –and mercifully unused horse-box from a friend, we crammed it with furniture and set off to pick up Chris in our latest car, a Peugeot 405. The Xantia had been written off in an insurance scam. Another story for another time.

Heading down the A1 the car sprang a leak. If the engine was switched off it stopped. Fired up again, the fan blew water everywhere. Unable to locate the source and running late, we bought a pack of bottled water at a garage, and stopped regularly to top up the radiator.

Detouring to Diane's sister Nicola's home near Hull, we left after our visit with a three piece suite, tools and other 'house warming' items. Husband Rob was clearing out his garage; but with lots of rooms to fill, it was a win-win situation for us.

After limping into Nadine's later she called out the AA, who replaced a split hose hidden down under the engine. Then after loading a spare bed-settee we prepared to leave. Kay then asked if she could come along with us. Apparently she'd brought her passport with her. A coincidence do you think?

Following a laugh a minute journey we arrived at La Ferronnerie. But the laughter died when we swung around the hedge into the drive. We were confronted by a prairie of chest high weeds blanketing the fields and garden. They'd even broken through the asphalt drive. Right then, the enormity of what we'd taken on hit home. Switching on the power, we unpacked in a sombre mood. However, it wasn't long before the sunny blue sky lifted our spirits, reminding us why we'd opted for this new lifestyle in the first place.

While filling the cupboards, Diane noticed a gas-pipe running behind the kitchen units. But when I traced it there was no gas bottle of course. To rectify the situation quickly we drove to town, passing a mushroom factory and extensive apple orchards en-route. While stocking up on provisions at *Intermarché*, we bought a gas-bottle from their garage forecourt. It cost fifty six euros for a start-up bottle. We knew then why Madame hadn't left one. But let's face it, a Brit must have his cuppa whatever the cost, *n'est-ce- pas*? I also refuelled the car while we were there, which back then was outrageously cheap compared to the UK.

Returning to the farm I connected the gas bottle; and while Diane and Kay rustled up a snack, Chris and I explored the barns and outbuildings. We quickly realised however, that anything left behind by Madame was either broken or useless; though I kept an old horse collar and harness to display somewhere later. Yes, I know – sad isn't it?

Up with the larks the next morning, I cleared an area for al fresco dining, using a piece of steel bar I'd found and sharpened. I'd unearthed a rickety old table and two benches at the back of the woodshed. Though riddled with woodworm and destined for firewood, they were clean, and would serve until we could buy replacements.

The next few days were a whirlwind of activity, clearing out rubbish left by Madame. It seems *her* vision of the rural French idyll, included stuffing empty crisp packets behind the bidet, which incidentally had the tap fitted upside down. Go figure as our U.S friends might say! And the separate toilet, well that was a real hoot. The floor, walls and *ceiling* were all coated in matching brown linoleum. I'd be stretching it to say it was decorated. It was just glued on. These and other subtle touches must have escaped our notice on earlier visits. Rose tinted spectacles again I presume.

Feeling claustrophobic after using this affront to porcelain, Chris and I decided the lino had to go. Of course, when we tried removing it, half the plaster came along with it, leaving the walls and ceiling resembling a relief map of the world. Informing Diane of our toilet's contemporary new look, Chris and I hastily moved on.

We decided to tackle the upstairs *grenier* ceiling, which had been panelled over while making box-bedrooms for Madame's kids. We removed all the plywood sheeting, which completely opened up the top floor, exposing massive oak beams. In a bid to gain even more space, we also ripped out the end wall of the larger room. As the dust settled, I found we'd uncovered a large chimney breast with a grain store behind it. The late Monsieur Renard had covered up some of the best features of the house. Emerging from the resulting debris looking like ghosts, we grinned sheepishly at Diane; ridiculously pleased with our afternoon's work.

One slightly off-putting problem was re-filling the log-basket after dark. I'd filled it earlier in the afternoon with dried branches and old off-cuts, but the fire was insatiable; and when darkness fell it was totally black out there.

As I'd been unable to locate any light switches anywhere I ventured out the first night, it was only fair, I thought. It was unnerving, as the outbuildings were barely visible against the night sky. Unable to find the torch anywhere, I stepped out jauntily in the pool of light spilling from the kitchen doorway. Passing the tool-shed though, everything was thrown into pitch-black shadow, and I groped my way blindly along the wall. I should have looked harder for the torch, but it was a man thing I suppose. I managed to get the job done, but it was quite an experience after what I saw in there, believe me.

The following night Chris returned from *his* stint – again torch-less, saying the huge shed was the creepiest place he'd ever been in. The lightest breeze rattled corrugated metal panels, and moonlight flickering through gaps in the planking caused eerie effects. It was also unsettling that rats could be heard – and sometimes seen scuttling about.

Time to send Kay out we thought!

'No problem,' she said, setting off, while Chris and I just sat there grinning, waiting for the inevitable screams. Strolling back in as cool as you like five minutes later, she plonked down the basket then began casually reading a magazine. Glancing at Chris, who also looked puzzled, I just had to ask. 'Didn't you find it scary?'

'Nah, I just switched the light on.'

She'd found the torch; and using it she'd found a switch hidden behind a beam.

By the time we packed to go home, the house resembled a war zone. But beaten by the workload, we'd just run out of time. Following a massive tidy up, we switched everything off, locked up and headed for Caen, physically and mentally drained. Some holiday eh? Well actually it was. Okay we'd worked hard, but we'd also had lots of laughs, sunshine, good food and wine. So what's not to like?

The docks were deserted when we arrived. Being early, we parked in line then strolled into town to find a well advertised duty free shop. Then Sod's Law struck! As we hurried back running late, Diane slipped off a high kerb and wrenched her ankle. With Chris and I supporting her, we struggled back to the docks. Unfortunately, I had to remove her shoe as her ankle had ballooned. This was fine as temporary relief; but come boarding time, she had to struggle up three flights of stairs from the car deck. With impatient passengers pushing from behind, not an ounce of humanity was shown in the rush for seats, the bar and restaurant.

Once settled on the upper deck though, I asked at reception if a doctor was available. I was told the ship didn't carry one. The purser doubled as medical officer, and would be with us as soon as her duties allowed. Roughly ten minutes later, a uniformed French lady arrived and began attending to Diane's ankle. She then asked how it'd happened. Deciding that in this situation honesty definitely wasn't the best policy, I launched into a fabricated account of Diane tripping over a car deck mooring ring. Being unmarked as they were, they could be dangerous in the gloom below decks,□ didn't she agree? I'd hoped this story might gain Diane some sympathetic treatment, but not what happened next.

The situation changed rapidly, as Diane was given pain killers and fussed over, while we were all given hot drinks. We were then ushered to a cabin. 'No charge Monsieur,' I was told. Well, I certainly didn't expect that.

When the ship docked, Diane was ceremoniously whisked away in a wheelchair by a personal steward, with Chris, Kay and I striding behind toting the hand luggage – looking suitably concerned of course! We arrived at a service elevator, the envy of other pushing, sweating passengers. Then like royalty, we descended to the car deck at the head of the queue.

Though disembarking carefully, it was still a jolting experience for Diane. And the journey to Nadine's was spent by our invalid on the car's rear seat, her leg draped across Kay's lap. Following a pain-filled night, Nadine drove her to Chelmsford Hospital's A & E department, where she hobbled into the waiting room using Nick's golf putter for support. After a three hour wait, she was diagnosed with a broken ankle and torn ligaments. As a plaster cast couldn't be fitted until the swelling subsided, she was told to visit our local A & E when we got home. Unfortunately, much to Nick's annoyance, his club was forgotten in the confusion. OOPS! Ah well, maybe surgeons could use it to sharpen their game when relaxing off duty. (Sorry Nick.)

As for Diane; she spent the next eight weeks off work. More wages lost. Now surely nothing else could happen – could it?

# Chapter 7

## Least said – soonest mended

August 2003 found Diane and I heading off to the farm for a working holiday. We were headed for Nadine's, but just before joining the M25, 'Bang,' the driver's side rear tyre blew. And being overloaded as usual, it took us some time to stop.

'Here we go again,' I sighed, climbing out to assess the damage. The wheel-rim was settled on the tarmac, the tyre completely shredded. And to really make my day, the spare wheel was in a cradle underneath the car. A modification designed to allow maximum luggage space, it was normally an asset. But being overloaded, the suspension was compressed *way* down. It was impossible to drop the cradle; therefore I needed the wheel-brace and jack to lift the car. Yep, you've guessed it! They were in the car boot under the luggage. Out came the carefully packed contents onto the hard shoulder – and that was when the Police arrived.

Blue lights strobing, two Range Rovers pulled up. I looked at Diane, whose expression must have mirrored mine. Damn, that's all we need. Apart from being grossly overloaded, what else might they find? I could get a ticket, maybe even points on my licence. These thoughts and others flashed through my mind in nano-seconds.

A door clunked shut, and a large officer in a high-vis jacket approached. Looming over me where I knelt, he blocked out the sun. 'Now then sir, what's the problem?' he asked; quite pleasantly, I thought, considering the situation. Fortunately I had a good jack, all the tools required, and a continental travel kit including two warning triangles. This seemed to impress him; and while the second officer cordoned off the inside lane, officer number one helped me change the wheel. Then with a cheery, 'Now don't forget to change that tyre as soon as you can sir,' he removed the cones. With the second officer slowing down the traffic, he waved us out into the inside lane.

Off we drove – very carefully.

Pulling up at Nadine's, we had a story to tell about our journey as usual. She was busy feeding Ben, Diane's first grandchild, who was by then ten months old. This was the first time we'd seen him in the flesh, so there was a lot to catch up on.

Some months earlier, Nadine had asked to visit La Ferronnerie. When Diane said we were having a working holiday, Nadine said she'd like to help. So Diane arranged a joint ferry booking. However, Nadine suggested we travel together in Nick's S.U.V, which would make sense as it had seven seats. I'd rather have driven down separately though, as Nick and I had an uneasy relationship. But taking two vehicles wasn't practical. However, the prospect of being on holiday with him left me cold.

It began badly, when after loading he refused to drive his own car, saying, he drove for a living and this was his holiday. Since he knew that I also drove in my job, and had just driven more than 300 miles down to Essex, I found that hard to take. Instead, a tight-lipped Nadine, pregnant again, climbed into the driver's seat. Diane and I weren't happy with that, but she insisted as the atmosphere was strained. Feeling sorry for her, I volunteered to drive through France. Well what a great start!

Climbing in behind the wheel in France, I had Nick sitting behind me, lecturing me on how to drive his car. I would normally have jumped out and told him to drive, but I controlled my temper for the sake of everyone's holiday. However, Diane could see that I was livid.

Arriving after what seemed like a lifetime of stilted conversation, we found the whole area overgrown with giant weeds. It was no surprise to Diane and I, but it didn't go down well with Nick, who stated huffily, that he was used to five star accommodation on *his* holidays.

Most of what happened after that is best left unsaid; but to avoid conflict, Nadine took Nick and Ben out every day. The highlight of their week was a visit to La Flèche zoo, reputedly one of the best in Europe. Apart from trips out, the girls all worked together and I worked alone. Where was Nick? Well here's a clue. It has four legs and a mattress.

Working alone was especially annoying when the temperature soared to forty two deg C one day. Hacking back undergrowth on my own for hours using my homemade machete didn't help my mood either, I can tell you.

Anyway, one day when Nadine had driven off, I returned from the barn and found a concerned Diane. 'Thank God you've returned,' she said. 'We've just had a visitor. He stuck his head through the window when I was cleaning. It gave me a hell of a shock.'

'So, what happened?'

'Well nothing really, he just said *Au revoir* and walked off.'

We realised then how little we knew of our neighbours, or how to communicate with them. This was reinforced later, when a Peugeot 306 rattled up the drive pulling a trailer. Out climbed a little old guy, wearing bib and brace overalls, a battered cap, and with a pair of specs perched on his bulbous nose. 'It's him from this morning,' Diane whispered.

Stepping forward he held out his hand. He spoke in a gravelly voice, like a catarrh sufferer clearing his throat. I managed to pick out the words Henri and Plombière, but the rest was unintelligible. Leaning into his trailer, he pulled out a strimmer. Pulling the cord he fired it up, laid it down and pointed to it. I stood there bar in hand. '*Pour moi?*' I asked.

'*Beh oui,*' he replied.

Touched by the generosity of this stranger, I asked him carefully how long I could use it for.

'*Un heure, un jour.*' An hour, a day – he shrugged as if it weren't important. After then unloading spare fuel, he doffed his cap, then wishing us '*Bonne chance,*' he drove off in a cloud of dust. As the air cleared I looked down. The strimmer lay ticking over expectedly at my feet.

Waving Nadine set off the following morning, Diane, Kay and I set off to explore the garden. Hacking through chest-high weeds, we reached the greenhouse; and in full Indiana Jones mode by then, I went to force open the warped door. Spotting a large hornet's nest on the frame though, Diane pulled me back. 'Whoah,' she cautioned. 'We can't get past that.'

'You reckon?' Striding off, I returned with a twist of newspaper and a box of matches. 'Right – stand back and be ready to run.'

Stepping forward I touched the flaming torch to the nest. Whoosh! Up it went, out flew the hornets, and off I shot; passing Diane and Kay on the way back to the house. 'Some hero *you* turned out to be,' Diane gasped, fighting for breath.

Though the holiday had been tense at times, I tried ending our last day on a high. Firing up the BBQ, I began cooking the last of the meat. However Nick decided he should take over, having been trained as a chef. But after burning the sausages he lost interest, so I ended up doing it anyway.

The final straw was his insistence on tying down the load, saying he did it for a living. As the rest of us had packed it all, we agreed. But first, he needed a nap, he said. Unfortunately it rained while he was in bed, so everything got soaked.

The journey back home was less tense, due I think to our relief that it was almost over. When we arrived Nadine invited us to stay for a while, but when Nick began complaining about something, we decided we'd had enough. Saying our goodbyes we left Kay to continue her visit. And after having a new tyre fitted nearby we headed for the A1 North.

# Chapter 8

## A moonlight flit – well sort of

In 2004 we realized our dream. As part of a restructuring process, my firm was offering a limited range of enhanced redundancy packages. Crunching the numbers, we found that taking one would enable us to move to France. As we were renting in the UK *and* paying a French mortgage it made sense. I was fifty seven years old at the time, Diane forty nine; and with our grown-up kids living with our ex's or partners, it was now or never. Gathering them all together we discussed our idea. They agreed we should go for it, while planning visits to help us with renovations.

With my redundancy package secured, we terminated our respective jobs, ended our lease, and began pricing our move. Unfortunately, when enquiring about removal costs, we were quoted over four thousand pounds. This seemed ridiculously high; too high for our tight budget anyway.

So born out of desperation, Stewy and I hatched a plan. Stripping a donated old family caravan to its chassis, we freed off the brakes and fitted a new wiring loom. I then towed it up to Northumberland, where with the enthusiasm born of ignorance I began constructing a trailer. Delivering our mail later, the postie said, 'It's gotta be the first trailer visible from outer space.'

And when Diane came in fresh from shopping, she gasped, 'Hell, it's nearly as big as the Twin Towers.'

Not the best analogy post 9/11, I thought. And when she suggested I should halve its height, I protested indignantly; though I conceded it might be a just a tad high. 'I admire your enthusiasm,' she said. 'But do you honestly think our poor car could pull *that* thing loaded with furniture?'

Ah well, back to the drawing board!

Modifications were made, the job signed off by Diane, and on March 27th I finished work. Accepting a cash whip-round, I said goodbye to colleagues, some of them envious. Then with a final wave, I left the building forever.

Thus began our move, which seemed easy at first but turned into a five day operation. At times I drove Diane dangerously close to throttling me. You see, I'm a hoarder by nature: brought up in tougher times after WW2, when make do and mend was the motto. Over my lifetime I'd amassed a wealth of 'stuff,' which *I* considered priceless, but to Diane was patently rubbish. Therefore, most of her time was spent trying to prise me loose from this 'treasure.'

In an attempt to preserve her sanity, and with time running short, we donated to a craft group, local charities, and finally the municipal dump.

Throughout that week, a pall of smoke hung over the house, as decades of my history was reduced to ash. Diane shrewdly pointed out that it included my first payslip issued in the early 60's. In my defence, I suggested that a future episode of 'Time Team' might have found my hoard illuminating. Countering this obvious ploy to hang onto 'stuff,' Diane quipped, 'If it was all buried with you, you'd need your own landfill-site.

Embarking on our three-stage saga, we dropped off the first load with Stewy and Helen 'temporarily.' Then returning to Northumberland we loaded up again, leaving the residue stored at our cottage until the lease ran out. We planned to make the first run to France, offload, then after a break return to Stewy and Helen's. What could possibly go wrong?

Well now, let's start with the trailer. Including the tow-bar, it was way longer than the car and eight feet wide. Worse still; when loaded it could be almost twice the car's height. Coated in brown shed stain, and covered with a virulent green tarpaulin when travelling, it was tied down with luminous orange safety netting I'd found in a ditch. Even empty, it was massive and kind of different. And viewed from the rear, it bore an uncanny resemblance to the face of a hippo.

When we eventually set off, spectators privileged to witness our departure seemed emotionally drained by the experience. Indeed the huge squat trailer became the stuff of local legend; assuming the mantle 'Hippo in a hairnet' on its inaugural run.

Rolling up to at La Ferronnerie after our first trip, we unloaded then spent two days chilling, before setting off back to the ferry. After a weekend's rest at Stewy and Helen's, our next trip began after a going away party the night before.

Exceedingly early the next morning, criminally overloaded, we left under cover of darkness. I was driving, Diane was navigating. Accompanying us were Helen – pregnant, Stewy – anxious, and Chris – laid back and cool. Diane and I were committed, (some said we should have been) but the kids had rashly decided to come along for a break.

Due to the early hour we tried to sneak away quietly. Yeah, like that was going to happen!

At first I thought the brakes had seized; as despite revving lustily (and loudly) the car refused to budge. 'This is bloody ridiculous,' Diane shouted over the noise. 'The damned car can't move, and we've got eight hundred and fifty miles to go. We'll just have to unpack most of it.'

'Nah, we'll be okay,' I said, with a confidence I certainly didn't feel.

Finally, with most of my team out pushing, we managed to get underway. Clutch juddering we inched forward. With everyone piling back in, we headed for the first of four speed bumps in the street. As the car rose over the first one, there was a hideous screech behind us and we ground to a halt. I applied more power – and with a nerve jangling 'bang' we were over it. Getting out I looked underneath; then straightening up quickly, I got back in and drove off. 'Watch out for the jockey wheel,' someone shouted as we approached the second bump.

'Forget the jockey wheel,' I replied, 'It was ripped off back there.'

'What? That's it then, we can't carry on. This is flaming madness,' said Diane.

'We have to,' I said. 'Our *life's* on this trailer and the ferry's booked. We'll just have to go for it.'

Agonisingly slowly we crept along the street, lurching over each of the consecutive speed bumps with a bang. But ahead of us lay our scariest problem. As we left the village, we came to the infamously steep hill with its hairpin bends, leading down to the main road. With the car shuddering, and the smell of burning brake linings, the overloaded trailer pushed our poor car down that hill.

Safe at the bottom, I let the brakes cool down before heading for the A1M south. Luckily for us it was still dark; and thank God we didn't see a police car.

'You see, we made it,' I said, unclenching my fists.

'Yeh, wonderful – now we've only got eight hundred and forty eight miles to go,' came Diane's withering reply.

As if cursed, it then began to rain; and it rained solidly the whole way there. Often the wind blew the tarpaulin loose, and we wrestled with it on the hard shoulder with traffic roaring past us. By then we were all soaked; along with everything in the trailer, including our mattresses and bedding. But somehow we made it, arriving *eons* later at Portsmouth ferry-dock, where we parked up and altered the headlights for continental driving.

When it came time to board though, we were waved to one side and told to park up. All other traffic was then loaded, until there we stood alone. No-one bothered to inform us why. And our only contact throughout, was with some dockworkers, who sauntered over at one point, looked at the trailer, and walked off grinning.

At last, conspicuous as the only vehicle on the dockside we were waved forward. By then curious passengers were lining the deck rails, straining to see what was happening. No pressure then. Trying to ignore the audience, I asked my fellow travellers to jump out. I was hoping the car's suspension would lift a little; giving me enough height to clear the ramp. Praying silently, I floored the accelerator. Engine bellowing, the car lurched forward. As it hit the ramp, a screeching noise and a shower of sparks came from the jockey housing. Shooting into the hold, I slid to a halt in front of my loyal team. Cheering hysterically, they whisked me off to the bar after I parked up. I couldn't drink of course, but I didn't need to. I was high on adrenalin.

Though anything but elegant, our departure from the hold was much easier, and soon we were off. It was still dark, but this time we had French rain lashing down on us.

Now, the French must be able to see in the dark, as they don't use road lighting or cat's eyes – a British invention. So there we were, building up speed nicely and rain cascading down the windscreen. With the wipers slapping furiously and my face almost pressed to the windscreen, my eyes strained to pierce the darkness. Suddenly I heard a shout, 'Look out, roundabout.'

I too had just spotted faint chevrons, on a sign almost hidden in the dark. Cursing, I slammed on the brakes. Immediately the car began aquaplaning; the overloaded trailer pushing us towards the roundabout at frightening speed. As the unit began to jack-knife, I instinctively took my feet off the pedals. Then as we slewed sideways into the roundabout, I stamped hard on the accelerator, pulling the car and trailer back into line. Snaking through the turn we made it safely to the other side.

Back in line I carried on driving. Strangely calm, I asked, 'Okay everybody?'

I was met with stony silence. Glancing into the rear view mirror I saw Stewy staring fixedly ahead, a living manifestation of Munch's painting *The Scream*. Then I remembered. He'd been involved in a near-fatal car crash some years before. Spotting an *Aire-de-service* ahead, I pulled in, and exhausted, we collapsed in a heap of bodies.

The rain had eased when I woke an hour later, so I decided to press on while conditions were favourable. On previous trips Diane had taken over driving if I was exhausted; but having a knee injury on this trip she couldn't. Others in the group held driving licences, but they were useless in France due to age or insurance restrictions. Therefore I carried on driving; taking rest breaks if needed, and drinking lots of coffee from a flask.

The rest of that trip was a nightmare, as torrential rain and gale force winds continued to batter us. Come daybreak however, conditions improved slightly; and eventually we limped up to the farm, looking like the Beverly Hillbillies.

It was around two pm when we tumbled out of the car. Grinning in relief we had a group hug, reserving a special one for the poor car. It was short-lived though, as both car and trailer were ruthlessly abandoned when the duty free booze was unloaded. After celebrating our safe arrival (a few times,) we crashed out for a couple of hours virtually comatose.

The evening was spent eating and drinking, while conducting a post-mortem of that awful journey. Often we found ourselves laughing – while privately thanking God that we'd made it intact. Though a saying of Diane's made us all go quiet for a while. 'Well at least nobody died,' she said, with a wry smile. A quaint little idiom, but so nearly proved wrong on this occasion.

# Chapter 9

## Well – we've made a start

Back to our usual perky selves the next morning – albeit a little hung-over, we shook off the cobwebs by walking the perimeters of the property. Hiking up to the tree line thighs aching, we gained a view across the valley. Then with lungs full of fresh air we returned to H.Q, where we began tackling years of flagrant rubbish tipping.

After a good workout collecting and sorting it, we ended up with a satisfying pile in the trailer, before the boys began dismantling huge net-covered enclosures attached to the rickety old chicken- coops. I'd also invested in my own *coup bordeur,* or strimmer by then, and with other tools I'd brought down with me we cracked on.

We had a high old time working out in the sun; gaining a tan while being served with beers by the girls. At one point, Diane took a group photo of us in our oddball work-wear, posed in a pastiche of TV's Auf Wiedersehen Pet. A new series just waiting to be written called Au revoir Pet perhaps? Well Englishmen grafting hard in France whatever it was named.

It wasn't all work and no play though. If the heat became unbearable, we'd often break off and head for Le Lude's camp-site for a dip. At least we were made welcome there, unlike the municipal pool, where the boys were ejected for wearing shorts. They were told that wearing budgie smugglers (Speedos) was mandatory. Really?

In that oppressive heat, even a shopping trip to Saumur could include a swim, in a small pool fed by the river. Though murky and weedy, it was sited near the yacht club and shaded by a bridge, making it popular with both locals and holiday makers alike. And often during that glorious weather, I'd fire up the stone-built BBQ; cooking over pine cones gathered from the woods. *Boules* marathons staged during those languorous outdoor meals were often alcohol-fuelled affairs, where the 'clacking' of metal orbs echoed across the valley to shouts of encouragement. Oh yes; who couldn't get to like *that* lifestyle?

Knocking at the door early on the Monday, Henri invited us to his house La Minoterie for aperitifs. Diane and I had met his wife Annette on our last visit, and knowing how she'd like to meet the family, we thought we'd do our bit for *'Entente Cordiale.'*

Matriarch to a large family, Annette was delighted to meet the pregnant Helen, and duly made a fuss of her. Poor Helen was embarrassed, but it took the heat off the rest of us, who were getting to grips with Henri's aperitifs. Poured out generously by our host, those bombshell shots were the fiery spirit *'eau de vie,'* or water of life. They certainly made the *boy's* eyes water, I can tell you. Distilled from pears it was 80% proof moonshine. As designated driver however, I took just a token sip out of politeness. Winking and tapping his nose, Henri informed me that many locals possessed their own 'still.' He implied that my next-door neighbour had one in his *cave,.* though he wouldn't admit to having one himself.

When we eventually met our neighbour, he said Customs and Excise allow a personal distillation of sixteen litres a year duty free. But with the French hatred of tax in any form, this law was flouted outrageously. Excess production should be hidden under the house-holder's bed he said, as some archaic law states that a Frenchman's bedroom is sacrosanct, and authorities can't enter it without his permission. It's probably just urban myth, but that's the premise they worked on.

We too had a *cave,* (pronounced carve) a cool, dark tunnel, hewn into the bank-side facing the kitchen. We'd been shown it when buying the property, and hadn't given it much thought back then. But in light of our new knowledge, a myriad of possibilities spooled through my mind.

All too soon the holiday was over, and after Henri offered to be my ' *sentinal'* in our absence, we returned to the UK towing the empty Hippo. Following a break at Burnhope, Diane and I loaded the last of our Northumbrian hoard; setting off with mixed feelings on the last of our three trips.

By then the trailer's leaf-springs were sagging due to overwork. However, the journey went amazingly well, and provided entertainment for curious motorists on the A1M. Showing generosity of spirit though, we decided they must be jealous and waved. Plodding on sedately, we arrived at Diane's parents, where we broke our journey overnight.

Suitably refreshed, we left the next day with even more 'stuff,' and succeeded in making good time for a while. But of course things were going *far* too well.

Shortly after joining the M25 we became snarled up in a huge traffic jam. After an hour, we realised our planned visit to Nadine had gone up in smoke – literally. The car's oil warning light was flashing, and the temperature gauge red-lining. Then with a loud hiss, steam began belching from under the bonnet.

Diane was driving at the time, and as our map seemed useless, I rang Nadine on our cell-phone asking, could she find us an alternative route off the M25 to Portsmouth on her computer? She replied, saying her truck driver neighbour advised taking the M40. With that turn-off almost upon us, Diane made a command decision. While I frantically waved down other traffic, she took our lives in her hands. Jaw jutting determinedly, she scythed across two lanes of traffic, the Hippo swaying wildly behind us.

Coming as no surprise to me, this manoeuvre caused mayhem, as until then, no-one had been prepared to give an inch. But flat out of options and with our exit looming, we bullied everyone out of our way; reasoning (correctly) that they wouldn't want to tangle with the Hippo. Tongue in cheek we waved our thanks, and with smoke then billowing from under the bonnet we limped off the motorway.

Parked up on the hard shoulder, both we and the car cooled down. Topping up the radiator with bottles of fruit flavoured water which was all we had, I checked the electrics, engine oil etc. before cautiously setting off again. Following our alternate route we arrived shattered, just in time to make the ferry.

Grossly overloaded yet again, it was a swine getting on and off the ferry. And what followed was another white knuckle ride down the French motorways, kept awake by numerous cups of coffee, poured from two flasks this time.

Arriving in the early afternoon, we ditched the car and trailer then staggered wearily into the cool, dark house. Closing the shutters against the glaring sunlight, we crashed out exhausted. Waking an hour later we unloaded the trailer, before driving to Le Lude for bread, milk, and the real essentials for the harassed long distance traveller – wine and snacks.

Gradually unwinding over the next three days, our first order of business was visiting *La Poste;* to send postcards to family, assuring them of our safe arrival.

After queuing for ages, all the locals had been chatted to and served. Then *we* stepped forward. The postmistress, who'd been watching our progress in the queue for some time, then chose to ignore us as if invisible. When she finally lifted her head and deigned to acknowledge us, I asked, '*Excusez-moi Madame, parlez vous Anglais*?'

'*Non,*' was her tight-lipped reply.

We then struggled to obtain two stamps and two postcards. I asked in many variants of French – only to be met at each attempt with a bored look and nothing else. After making me sweat for almost ten minutes, she then asked me *in perfect English,* 'Are you asking me for two postcards and stamps, for posting to England?'

With gritted teeth, I replied, 'Yes.'

Then, with a queue stretching into the street by then, she proceeded to lecture me on my pronunciation of the word *timbre*, or stamp; wagging her finger at me from behind the safety of a glass screen. It was lucky for her that the screen was there, the arrogant old witch.

However, with mayhem avoided and postcards sent, we returned to the farm, where we soon fell into a routine. Diane unpacked and set things out, while I tackled the garden.

During one of my weed-killing forays, a shout from Diane interrupted me. Not knowing what to expect, I hurried quickly to the house, where I found her peeping through the kitchen window. 'What's up?'I asked.

'Maybe nothing, but Henri just arrived muttering, "*Madame Renard*", and staggered off up to the woods.'

While we wondered what this could mean, he returned empty handed. Still puzzled, we watched him disappear down the drive, waving casually as he went.


A couple of days later while enjoying a beer on the terrace, I spotted a lone figure approaching. It was Henri again. He'd seen us and was waving cheerfully, so it was too late to hide. But why *should* we hide? This was our house. The problem was, his guttural accent was hard to master, and we felt embarrassed by our ignorance. Feeling we should make more of an effort, I plastered a sickly grin on my face. Preparing myself for yet another verbal onslaught, I invited him into the kitchen. '*Un bière Henri?* I asked.

'*Aaah, merci* Stewaard,' he croaked, obviously parched.

I passed him a 'cold one,' which he quickly gulped down. Smacking his lips he then began speaking – and do you know what? Suddenly we experienced an epiphany. Maybe it was the beer he'd drunk, or possibly the beer *I'd* drunk. Who knows? But for the briefest of moments the fog lifted. And for the very first time we totally understood each other. But only for a little while mind you!

Feeling benevolent, I invited him to sit at the table with another beer. He looked at the table, pursed his lips, and said '*Poof,*' signifying that it was too small. Finishing his beer, he left, shaking his head sadly.

Surprisingly, he drove back soon afterwards, Annette sat beside him. Balanced precariously on the trailer behind them, was a large white plastic garden table. Pulling up, he beckoned me to help unload it. Not knowing why he'd even brought it, but wary of offending him, I lifted my end, wondering why we were setting out garden furniture. That is, until he headed towards the house with his end. Apparently our new kitchen table had just arrived.

While Henri and I sited it 'temporarily' on our terrace, Diane was making coffee. Awestruck, Annette watched Diane pour the steaming brew into huge coffee cups, before she said tactfully that the French mostly drink it from *tiny* cups – cool, and often black. With that particular social gaffe sorted, and modified coffee poured, we sat looking at each other; a language barrier separating us like a yawning chasm.

Fortunately; just as the silence was becoming painful Annette waved her hand vaguely, encompassing the whole room. Nodding her approval she glanced longingly towards the staircase. Quick on the uptake, Diane offered her a tour of the house. Squirming with curiosity, Annette couldn't wait to see what the mad '*Anglais*' were up to *now,* and shuffled off behind Diane towards the stairs.

Leaving them to it I stepped outside, where I found an elusive Henri eying up the fields of overgrown grass. Turning towards me he pointed, uttering something completely incomprehensible. Nodding sagely, I said, '*Ah oui,* while not understanding a damned word. We then adjourned inside as the ladies returned from their tour.

After finishing their coffee, and to the relief of us all I suspect, they departed with a cheerful toot of the car horn.

Bright and early the next morning, Henri turned up with a tall lugubrious guy; a local farmer who would cut our grass *'gratuit'* in exchange for the resulting hay. However, after a closer inspection and much head shaking, I was informed that my fields contained *beaucoup de mauvais herbes,* or many weeds, so the crop would be unsuitable for the delicate stomachs of his fine cattle.

A more radical solution presented itself the day after, when a massive tractor roared up the drive. Perched high on the footplate, a grinning Henri introduced Emile the driver, who would cut our grass for *un bon prix.* Stepping forward I shook his proffered forearm (normal practice if hands are dirty.) However, Emile first needed to 'walk the land,' as it had been neglected for two years, and could prove difficult even for *his* mighty machine.

Following a closer inspection of the terrain, which involved muttering, sighing, and shaking of heads, we arrived at the kitchen, just as Diane with perfect timing reached into the fridge. *'Une bière Messieurs?'* she suggested, and two weather-beaten faces lit up.

Seizing the moment, I asked, *'Combien pour le travail,* 'or how much for the work?

With Diane waggling the bottles tantalisingly, a deal was quickly struck. Then with a parting shake of two forearms, they jumped aboard the tractor and roared off.

'So when's he coming back then?' Diane asked.

'Soon, he said.'

'Yeh, that'll be a fortnight then.'

At five fifteen the next morning, the windows rattled as a huge machine advanced up the field, engine roaring and huge spotlights piercing the shutters. 'Guess who?' I smirked, as Emile's Komatsu thundered towards our bedroom window.

It took ten hours spread over three days to tame that land. There were many stoppages, due to tangled undergrowth and having to break off for pre-booked jobs. But at long last it was finished and Emile knocked on the kitchen door. Henri, who was there to inspect the job hovered behind him. The deal was for two hundred and fifteen euros, based on a 'guess-timate' of six hours work. Expensive enough for having the grass cut, I thought. However, when I laid out the cash Emile scowled, turning to Henri his voice raised in complaint.

Taking a pencil from behind his ear and licking the point, Henri carefully wrote the figure 325 on a note-pad. Passing it to me, he indicated with both hands that the work had taken ten hours. '*Non,*' I said, the price was fixed, and offered Emile the money again. Turning away, he stormed out angrily, Henri chasing after him.

Following a few heated words by the tractor they returned together, Emile scowling darkly. Eventually though, after swigging a couple of beers he calmed down; and after some more haggling he settled for two hundred and fifty euros. We then all shook hands and he drove off.

After another beer and some strained small talk, I thanked Henri warmly for his help. And off he went, happy in his new role as 'Henri' Kissinger. With the tricky situation resolved, we were touched by his desire to help, and decided not to judge our new neighbours so quickly in the future. But would our new-found belief in our fellow man be justified? I wondered.

# Chapter 10

## Meeting 'them next door'

While painting the kitchen shutters a few days later, I heard the 'clip clop' of hooves on the drive. Two fine horses hove into view, their teenage riders glancing at me in a curious, but friendly manner. Reining in his horse, the leading rider wished me, *'Bonjour Monsieur;'* then went on to bombard me with rapid French. Oh-oh!

*'Bonjour. Pardon, je suis Anglais. Je ne parle pas Francais,'* I replied hesitantly.

'Ah – you are Eenglish. Ow arr you? I learn Eenglish for my school, you understand?'

He was our neighbour's son from Le Lavendu, the farm next door. He said his mother had spotted us when we first viewed the house in Paula's green Renault. Then again when we brought Chris and Kay in the red Peugeot *quatre cents cinq*. Not much gets missed around here then, I thought.

Introducing himself as François, and the other rider as his cousin Philippe, he said they'd heard new neighbours were arriving. But not that we were English. After a pleasant chat, we shook hands before they rode off together along the track.

'He seems like a nice young lad,' said Diane.

'Yes he does, but this is getting a bit complicated.'

'How do you mean?'

'Well, when we first met Henri, he mentioned the word *plombière* right? Now I know it means plumber; but is that his surname, or was he a plumber before he retired? And this kid François didn't give *his* surname, but if I remember rightly, Henri mentioned the words *charpentier* and *voisin*. Well I know *voisin* means neighbour, and *charpentier* carpenter. So is that his surname, or is his dad a carpenter? If he is, he must run his own business. Have you seen the size of their farmhouse?'

It was all too much; and as the sun had apparently addled my brains, we went off for a *'petit somme'* to re-charge the little grey cells.

An hour later, I woke feeling even more washed out than before, due to the pole-axing humidity. Staggering out of the bedroom to grab a cold drink, I'd just reached the fridge when there was a knock at the door. Wondering who the hell this was, I peered through the kitchen window. It was the kid from next door. What was his name again? Oh yes, François. What did *he* want? Opening the door, I strove to look both awake and welcoming. I wasn't finding it easy to be either.

'*Bon après midi* Stewaard; my fazzaire, he say to ask, would you have aperitifs with heem and my muzzaire soon?'

Oh shit. 'Er, *oui* of course. When?' I croaked.

'Tonight at seven hours. Is okay?'

'Er, *oui* is okay. Tell your fazzaire, er father thank you. We'll see you then. *A'bientôt.*'

Hearing Diane enter the kitchen, I turned, hardly daring to meet her eyes. 'Who was that then?' she asked pleasantly.

'We're doing *what?* You've agreed to go next door for drinks at seven o'clock? Are you mad? I've got loads to do; plus now I'll have to shower and dry my hair. And another thing; what are we supposed to wear eh? I bet you never thought about that did you? Well thanks a bunch.'

Disappearing into the bedroom, she closed the door forcefully behind her. (Slamming, I think some people call it.) Maybe it would be best if I ironed my own shirt then.

At six- fifty-five precisely we walked along the track leading next door, both of us perspiring in the balmy evening air. I was carrying two bottles of wine; one white, the other a local *rosé*. Diane followed, tottering carefully on low-heeled shoes. We'd

70

eventually decided to dress smart but casual, gaining the impression from Henri, that our neighbours were 'well heeled' and aloof.

With a feeling of trepidation, I opened the garden gate leading to their house. As it creaked open there was a frantic scuffling noise behind a patio wall. In a blur of movement two dogs hurtled around it, scrabbling towards us barking frantically. One was a large hound, the other a yapping long-haired terrier. Stepping back swiftly, I put the gate between them and us. Appearing from behind the wall, François shouted at them; and as they slunk away he motioned us to enter – which we did, carefully. Guard duty done, the dogs fell in line, loping happily beside us as we entered a courtyard.

Our next shock was seeing our neighbours. Not the overdressed stuck-up people we'd been dreading, but a smiling middle- aged couple, attired in shorts, tee- shirts and flip flops. They eyed us in a bemused manner as François introduced us; then a work calloused hand shook mine very firmly.

It transpired that Bertrand and Véronique were ordinary working people. He was a truck driver, hauling to and from the mushroom *cave* where Véronique worked as a picker. They weren't at all arrogant or stuffy. In fact Bertrand reminded me of Inspector Clouseau from the Pink Panther films; whereas Véronique was petite, blonde and quite attractive. While François resembled neither of them; being dark-haired and blue-eyed. The family surname was Charpentier. Problem solved.

When I explained about Henri's misinformation they laughed, as it explained why we'd arrived as if dressed for the Queen's garden party. François said some people – Henri included, thought his parents had received an inheritance; when actually they'd bought a ruined building with a tract of scrub-land when they first married, and by working day and night, they'd transformed it into a small arable farm. It'd taken twenty years of long hours and seven day weeks worked around their day jobs. But of course some people envy others their success; attributing it to luck rather than hard graft.

We'd just had our first introduction to French village life, its gossip and rumour; which from now on of course would include '*les Anglais.*'

Once seated, we were served dishes of *petits saucissons*, *radis*, *fromages* and olives. Accompanying them were slabs of baguette lathered with *beurre,* washed down with a chilled *rosé*. With François interpreting, his father and I tested each other for common ground, while slowly forming a friendship.

However, after an hour of pleasant conversation, we politely made our excuses, stood up and prepared to leave. A puzzled François said, '*Non Stewaard,* my muzzair she has prepared us a meal.'

We sat down again hastily, as Véronique re-appeared carrying more platters. The evening then unfolded as we relaxed over the feast. Popular misconceptions of each other's cultures and idiosyncrasies were aired and laughed at, revealing a cross cultural sense of humour. With wine flowing freely, a full five courses were enjoyed over three and a half hours.

As dusk settled patio lighting was activated, attracting any insect equipped with wings to the party. In turn, bats homed in on the fluttering invertebrates. Though enjoying the evening, we remembered our hosts had an early start in the morning, so we made our excuses, getting up to leave yet again. Bertrand then jumped up, insisting he guide us back by torchlight past the crumbling storm drain. Though it was dry as a bone, it was deep, full of nettles, and who knows what animal life?

We'd learned a lot of fascinating stuff throughout the evening; about our house and its previous owner Monsieur Renard. A heavy drinker, he'd suffered a heart attack while hunting with his mates. Carried back to the house *morte*, he was laid out in the downstairs room we were sleeping in, which coincidentally, was the coldest room in the house by far.

That could explain a lot; especially if you believed in the occult like Nadine. When she'd visited we gave up our room, as with Ben and a large cot she needed extra space. The next morning she entered the kitchen saying, 'Bloody hell it's freezing in there.'

She insisted she'd woken during the night, and seen a tall figure dressed in blue overalls leaning over the cot. Oh-oh! Now whether you believe in 'spirit 'or not, Nadine says she can sense, or see things. Could this have been the ghost of the infamous Monsieur Renard – or was her mind playing tricks? Hey, I wasn't about to give her an argument either way.

What we *did* find out over dinner was, the Renard's had been bad neighbours. When Bertrand and Véronique first moved in, they'd often return from work to find diesel, heating oil, cement or other items had 'disappeared.' And to add insult to injury, rubbish had been dumped on their property. On another occasion, a large field riddle vanished while they visited Bertrand's parents. The final straw was, when a whole pile of logs cut by Bertrand went missing while they were on holiday. François said his parents were looking forward to having *good* neighbours at last. Also, as '*étrangers*' living in France, they would help us in any way they could.

Mindful of the Emile fiasco, I asked François if he knew anyone who'd cut our vast expanse of grass for a reasonable price. In turn, *he* asked if his father could rent our bottom field to grow arable crops. Having ascertained from Paula that 'peppercorn' rents were all we'd achieve for spare land, we came to an understanding. Bertrand would take on grass-cutting and maintenance, help us sort out the mess left by their old neighbour, and handle security in our absence. In return he would have the use of the bottom field rent free. This way no money changed hands, and *Le Flic,* or the taxman wouldn't be involved – tax being a sore point with both French and English alike. I then drew up a written agreement for us both to sign. This at first puzzled François, who said, 'Why is a handshake not enough between neighbours?'

Reminding them of the problems with their previous neighbours, I said it would protect us both. Either side could cancel giving reasonable notice, which meant his crops would always be protected. François translated for his father, who saw that it made sense and signed. There we were then. We'd made friends with our neighbours and come to an agreement over the land. So everything would run smoothly now, wouldn't it?

# Chapter 11

## A rude awakening

The ringing phone shattered an idyllic morning; but though it was a welcome addition to our lives in some ways, we dreaded picking it up. Buying it had been a mixed blessing, as our knowledge of French often created misunderstandings. The most irksome problem though was the dialling tone, which was similar to the UK engaged signal. Until we managed to educate family and friends, they'd ring, then almost immediately put down their phone believing ours was in use. This was usually just before we reached ours, desperate to pick up in time.

On this occasion however, my gasped *'Bonjour!'* drew a request from François for a rendezvous. Not a romantic tryst I hasten to add, just a meeting next door. As Diane was busy doing womanly stuff in the bathroom, I shouted, 'I'm going out,' then set off along the track, not knowing what I was about to walk into.

As usual, I was greeted at the garden gate by Hermé and Lupé, who as always seemed intent on dismembering me.

'Arrêtez!' François yelled, aiming a kick at them while waving me to enter. Hearing the ruckus, Bertrand ambled out grinning hugely, offering a forearm as he wiped his hands on a rag. 'Steward, we must have a discussion of much seriousness,' François explained haltingly.

Leading me to an outbuilding, they showed me a large scientific looking apparatus spouting a bewildering array of dials and pipes. It was a water filtration system for our joint well, François explained; installed at a cost of three thousand euros eight years before. Back then, Véronique had contracted a debilitating illness which had dumbfounded the medical profession. After costly tests and treatment had failed, samples from the well were finally analysed at *Le Laboratoire*. Bertrand produced a report he'd commissioned at the time, and I was alarmed to see animal urine and faeces as major constituents of our water supply. 'Bloody hell,' I thought, 'What next?'

Well I was about to find out. After her husband died, Madame Renard had struggled financially, so she'd acquired six sheep as mobile lawnmowers. However vet's bills weren't on her agenda. During years spent crapping and urinating willy-nilly, the odd sheep had died; and their decomposing carcases, added to the mix had been left to leach down into the water table. When Bertrand had tried showing Madame his report, she'd poo-pooed it. (Sorry for the puns.) Although denying any responsibility, she switched to bottled water immediately. François advised me to submit a sample of our tap water for analysis at the pharmacy. A report costing fifteen euros would follow in two weeks. Until we had it, he explained solemnly, we should drink only bottled water. Oh great! Why hadn't he told me sooner? Ever since we'd arrived here, we'd been drinking well water by the gallon.

'And while his hands are dirty, can my fazzaire inspect your *fosse septique*,' he then asked.

From day one, a vile stench had permeated the bathroom. I'd fitted an extension pipe from the drain, which helped a little. However, Bertrand wanted to check something else. Though mystified, I agreed, and soon we were back at Le Ferronnerie. With a grim look François asked where the tank cover was. I didn't know, but it was virtually overgrown when we found it; and pulling out a screwdriver Bertrand levered it open. Grabbing an edge each we lifted together. Hell fire! The sight and smell that hit us was appalling. The tank was brim-full of stinking raw sewage; '*beaucoup de merde,*' or a lot of shit, as François graphically put it. It was obvious even to *my* untrained senses, that the tank had even been opened, never mind emptied as Madame stated haughtily at the contract signing. 'Whatever next,' I wondered?

François and Bertrand arrived early the next day, accompanied by brother-in law Maurice; a burly guy who owned sewage pumping equipment. He'd offered to empty our '*fosse*' as a favour to Bertrand, François said. Was I interested? Oh yes indeed. Maurice returned riding his beat-up old tractor, with François sat astride the collection tank. Soon the cover was off the tank, and as a thick hose was inserted, I tried not looking into that reeking pit. Almost gagging at the stench, my eyes streamed with tears from the acrid fumes.

For a while everything went just fine. Then the chugging, slurping noise changed to a screech, then a bang, as the pump ground to a halt. The drive coupling had sheared. Unable to do more until it was fixed, Maurice withdrew the hose, packed up everything and left, promising to return later. Taking a short cut across the barren lower field, he sprayed Madame's effluent as he went. Was this healthy? Was it even legal? God only knew. '*C'est normale,*' François said with a shrug.

As promised they returned after lunch, and with the coupling welded pumping resumed. However, just before completion it gave a loud 'bang,' and gave up the ghost completely. Maurice pointed out that the tank was virtually clean anyway, so I asked, '*Combien*?'

Shrugging, he grinned. '*Il est* gratuit.'

Free! Normally it was eighty to a hundred euros. François then suggested; maybe later in the year when grazing is scarce, Maurice could run a couple of horses on our land for a week. Hey, I had no problem with that!

With the tank empty, the stench disappeared. The brim-full tank had forced the fumes back up the drainage pipe into the bathroom. But that shouldn't happen even when the tank is full, François said frowning. So we obviously had *another* problem somewhere. And that's not all. We then had a young lady from the *Mairie's* office arrive. She was conducting a survey; and after measuring, she found that the tank was now sited too close to the house since Monsieur Renard had added the bathroom. Apparently, new laws were coming into force, and we might have to have it moved at a cost of ten to fifteen thousand euros. Now why didn't any of this surprise me?

With the tank problem on hold, it was time to catch up with other issues. The aforementioned bathroom was a joke. Nothing worked properly, so completely frustrated we ripped it all out. The weird bidet we left in place. It was useful as a foot-bath after barefooted excursions outside. Just as well it wasn't required for its original purpose though!

After plastering, I added fittings and tiles, before applying a new paint scheme. In the midst of this chaos, Bertrand and Véronique turned up escorting a stately old lady, who they introduced as Anna. She was Véronique's aunt, and had been François' nursemaid as a child. Now in her eighties she was venerated by the family. François said her visit was a seal of approval, and signified that we'd finally 'arrived' in the valley. After formal introductions she was led around by François, and was soon scowling. With curled lip, she called Madame Renard *sal*, or dirty – and though she sympathised with us, she implied we'd been naïve at the very least. Then to rub salt into the wounds, François asked, 'Did you *see* this house before you bought it?'

What could I say to *that*? However, the sting was taken out of his remark when Anna produced a house warming present, a bottle of her home-made liqueur. With a magician's flourish, Bertrand whipped out a gnarled olive-wood corkscrew, and with glasses hastily assembled, a toast was made to our new home whatever its problems. The unique brew contained coffee, orange juice, sugar and *eau de vie*. Fermented for forty-four days it was appropriately named *quatre-quatre,* (cat-cat) and was rich and smooth with an explosive kick. Unfortunately it was gone all too soon. But with snacks hastily assembled and wine produced, we had ourselves a party, where it soon became apparent that Diane had caught Anna's eye. Before we became too light-headed though, Bertrand pointed out other faults we'd been blissfully unaware of. Unwilling to go into greater detail right then, it was agreed that a full inspection should be made '*instamment.*'

The family left soon after amid much cheek kissing; three kisses being '*de-rigueur*' in this region. Then rather unsteadily we began clearing away; though thoughts of the mounting work and hidden pitfalls had a somewhat sobering effect.

As we lethargically chewed breakfast the following morning, François appeared at the open kitchen door. He apologized for interrupting our '*petit dejeuner,*' but he had urgent news. While we slept downstairs the previous night, a car showing no lights had idled up our drive and parked some distance away. While pursuing his *études* on the computer, he'd spotted it from his room. Grabbing his mountain-bike he'd ridden over, and interrupted two men peering into our window. The noise of his bike on the gravel had disturbed them, and they'd quickly ran off then driven away. He described the car as a white Renault 14, and its occupants as *gros hommes,* or big men. He thought they could be gypsies 'casing the joint,' or hunters who'd shot illegally on the land while the house stood empty. Whoever they were, thoughts of future confrontations were worrying; even if, with teenage bravado, he'd exaggerated their size.

Yet again, we realised how vulnerable we were, isolated in a virtually non- English speaking community. Thanking him for his intervention at some risk to himself, I said we'd be on our guard in future. And while it didn't put us off our breakfast, it definitely gave us food for thought.

Mulling it over later though, we decided it could be a one off, and putting it aside we listed jobs to tackle the next day.

First, without central heating, we relied solely on the log-fire. And those two hundred year old houses with metre thick walls could be chilly, even in late spring. On our deeds it said the chimney had been swept as required by law. Madame R had even given us a receipt, supposedly issued by *Le Ramonuer,* or the sweep; but remembering the septic tank, I lit the fire dubiously. And wouldn't you know it, almost immediately smoke gushed into the room. Even with the fire door closed, it seeped into the kitchen and upstairs rooms through wall vents.

'Right, that's it,' I shouted, driving off to *Bricomarché* to buy a set of sweeps brushes. However, when I returned and assembled them, I found the broken fire damper jammed in the stove-pipe. I pulled it out, and *'Voilà'* the chimney was unblocked. But now we had no damper control. Who needs one I thought? At least we'll be warm. And with that I returned the unused brushes for credit. Wronnng!

When winter arrived, much of our heat vanished straight up the chimney. Therefore; as well as decimating our meagre wood supplies, we contributed vastly to global warming.

Worried by our heating problems in general, we decided to tackle the upstairs insulation. After Chris and I had ripped out the ceilings it'd opened up the area, displaying impressive oak beams. Unfortunately, one of the side effects was significant temperature changes. When the summer sun beat down on the un-insulated roof, the upstairs turned into an oven. Of course, in the evening the effect was reversed as the heat escaped. But we'd made plans to fix it.

In the meantime, even with Velux windows open and fans blowing, it was often too hot to work up there. François said Loire winters could be extremely cold, with temperatures often plummeting to minus 16C; so houses were heavily insulated. Conversely, in summer, sleeping upstairs could be unbearably hot. The locals dealt with the problem by sleeping downstairs until autumn returned. Ah well, when in Rome …

Meanwhile, leaving the upstairs until the weather cooled, I made the toilet my next mission. This eyesore was *long* overdue for redecoration, but it wasn't giving up without a fight. And what should have been an easy job, turned into a full morning's work chiselling off the remaining lino. Monsieur

Renard must have been revolving at high speed in his grave, as I cursed him for his stupidity and meanness. Every job was taking twice as long as it should, and costing twice as much as it needed to.

Now I don't mind admitting that I like saving money. But Monsieur R was the 'Master of Mean.' Because of his unique wallpaper paste, (flooring adhesive at a guess) chunks of plaster had parted company with the wall and ceiling. Ergo, a simple job became a full scale renovation, as it seemed sensible to replace the toilet suite at the same time. Clearing up the mess afterwards we though *that* was bad! Oh boy – we hadn't a clue what was still in store for us.

# Chapter 12

## A little 'R and R' perhaps?

Two weeks into June, and the house was looking much more presentable; eclectic maybe, but fully furnished. François had popped over with plants from his mother, saying the family were going away for the bank holiday weekend. That was it then, we couldn't put off gardening any longer. Along with our own purchases from Noyant's market, we now had Véronique's home grown varieties to deal with. We had the tools so we had no excuse. If we wanted vegetables we must plant immediately, François said. After their break they'd return to inspect a thriving new garden. Apparently, failure wasn't an option.

Wishing him '*bonne* vacance,' we promised miracles on their return. And as the family drove past later, we were 'heads down arses up,' as the saying goes.

Having raked the newly-dug patch, we staked it out; breaking off as the sun hit its zenith. Returning in the cool of late afternoon, we planted out leafy greens, potatoes, swedes and tomato plants; watering them in well afterwards.

Waking early the next day I strode eagerly down to the garden … and found most of the plants decimated. Dammit! Kicking a stone in frustration, I went back inside to plan my next move.

We first heard the strange clanking noises after lunch. Forming a background to the throaty beat of powerful engines, the metallic clattering grew gradually louder; until a thunderous roar reverberated throughout the valley. Striding to the dining room window, I said, 'Whoa, look at this.'

From the kitchen, Diane shouted, 'What's up?'

'It's only a line of *tanks* coming up the road. We've got half the French army out here.'

With a screech, the leading machine ground to a halt opposite our driveway. 'Clang,' the turret hatch opened, and an officer's upper body emerged. After scanning the area through binoculars, he turned to the following units and pointed ahead. Then with a fist-pump he disappeared, the hatch banged shut, and with a roar and a puff of black smoke the vehicle clanked off up the road. To the sound of squealing tracks it was followed by the others. As they rounded the bend the echoes grew fainter; until finally, quiet was restored to the valley.

Turning to Diane, I was met with, 'Don't even go there.

Over the next few days we occasionally glimpsed the tanks through the trees; but mostly it was the revving engines, and crashing tracks that we noticed. When our neighbours returned from their *vacance,* we asked about this military intrusion.

'Where *are* these tanks?' asked François anxiously.

'Don't worry, they're not after you. But why are they here?'

'I think they, how you say, practice war.'

'Ah, manoeuvres,' I said. He looked puzzled, so I explained.

'Ah, *j'ai compris,'* he replied.

But suddenly it ceased to be of any importance to him.

'*Mon Dieu*, what has occurred with your *legumes*?' he asked, as he and Bertrand stared aghast at rows of mangled veggies. Cringing inwardly, I explained my planting methods and watering schedule in great detail. Following a translation from François, Bertrand waggled his finger; which was normally a sure sign of a lecture. But not *this* time. The phase of the moon was correct, François relayed. Also, I'd planted on the correct day, at the correct time, and in the correct manner. Therefore everything should be in order. It must be the fault of *les lapins* (rabbits,) or *cers* (deer.)

With the property standing empty for so long, our garden had become a wildlife corridor leading up to the woods.

Pointing to cloven tracks, he said, 'You also have other problems, I think. These are the marks of the sanglier.'

'Sanglier?' I queried.

'Yes; I think you say, the wild pig.'

On the 13th of June the Charpentiers arrived *en famille*, catching me watering our bourgeoning garden; a miracle of survival against enormous odds. '*Bonjours'* were exchanged and my forearm shaken, which still seemed odd to me. I then received three kisses from Véronique, which I endured manfully, while Diane dealt with her quota stoically.

With pleasantries over with advice was then dispensed. As work had stopped by then, we adjourned from the sweltering heat into the cool dark kitchen, where Bertrand produced a bottle of *rosé* for us to sample. It was made by his father, he said proudly. No *Appellation Contrôlée* with *this* vintage then.

Carrying his glass, François strolled into the kitchen and casually asked if I intended watching the match later. Without a TV or newspapers to enlighten me, I asked, 'Which match?'

'*Which match?'* he asked incredulously? 'Why, it is *La belle* France playing *L'Angleterre* in the European cup. It is essential that you watch it.'

Concerned at my supposed predicament, he explained our lack of reception to Bertrand, who asked to examine our TV. After a rigorous inspection and much tutting, he excused himself, and disappeared through the French doors. He returned ten minutes later carrying a huge, boxy old TV, which he'd lugged over from Le Lavendu. Setting it down on our coffee table he connected it up, our three pin plug and adaptor causing much amusement. Suddenly we were watching a cycle race.

All too soon though, both the race and wine were finished; and mellowing nicely by then, I mimed opening another bottle. Declining politely François stood up to leave; my heart plummeting as I saw Bertrand unplug the TV and carry it to the door. Sensing my pain, François said, 'No Steward, you do not understand. We would like you to visit our house later to watch the match, yes?'

That game is etched into my brain forever. With England playing much better– as even my partisan neighbours had to admit, the game was deadlocked. At nil–nil it went to extra time. Then suddenly, against the run of play the French snatched two quick goals. I was stunned. It was over. However, Bertrand and François, who'd been looking suicidal until then, leapt up cheering. It was party time. Oh yes – again.

France two – England nil … *C'est la vie – C'est normale.*

Throughout the following week, we really got stuck into the garden. Our two major jobs were (A) strimming a large tract of brush, and (B) climbing Monsieur Renard's rickety old ladder to paint the barn. Not a lover of heights, Diane quickly grabbed the strimmer. Let's see now, what did that leave? Shouldering the ladder I set off.

It was a fiercely hot day with a cobalt blue sky. And Diane, stylishly attired for the occasion was insect bait, as she advanced remorselessly wielding the strimmer. Decorated with plant clippings, and dust from the parched earth, she cut a fine figure in a little off the shoulder number. Accessorised with a baseball cap and wellingtons, she strode resolutely onwards. Why the wellingtons? I hear you ask. Come on now – let's not forget the vipers and scorpions.

I spent *my* morning balanced precariously against the barn. The walls of the vaulted building were roughly six metres high, the ladder about three. Imagine me then, on the highest rung possible, gripping a telescopic mop-handle with a paintbrush tied to it and you get the picture. It promised to be messy, so I didn't ask to borrow Bertrand's shiny extendable ladder.

Sweating and stretching I painted the hot zinc sheeting; my skin burning from the reflected heat of the sun. While beneath me, a carpet of nettles eagerly awaited my fall.

We persevered over the next two days; with both of us exhausted at the end. By then Diane was covered in large

itching bites, I was sunburned and sore, and we both ached
from head to toe. But finally, after raking up Diane's brash
we'd finished. In the autumn we planned having a bonfire, as
burning during the summer was banned due to the risk of forest
fires. If you caused the *Secours de Pompiers,* or fire and rescue
to be called out, a large fine issued by the '*Mairie's*' office
would be the *least* of your worries.

At last we could relax for a while. It was June 19th Diane's
birthday; and we'd decided to celebrate by attending Saumur's
*Fête de Géants,* or Festival of Giants. Wall posters around town
depicted revellers on stilts, wearing bizarre costumes and
enormous papier-mâché heads. A carnival atmosphere was
promised involving floats and bands. And with food and drink
stalls expected to be lining the streets, I was almost salivating
with excitement. We arrived for this promised extravaganza
and what did we see? Nothing!
We enquired at the *Bureau de Informations*. The event had
been cancelled, said the flustered receptionist. It'd been
postponed for a week. Temporarily deflated, we sat by the river
and took stock. Okay then, we'll go for a meal. '*Pardon
Monsieur we've stopped serving lunch,*' was the response
everywhere. Eventually we settled for filled baguettes from a
sandwich van; eating them as we browsed the market stalls.
After buying Diane perfume as a consolation present, we
decided on a drive into the country.
It was an Elysian afternoon. And after a pleasant drive we
ended up in Montreuil-Bellay. Strolling past the ruined castle
we spotted a secluded restaurant, but it too was closed, so we
cut our losses and headed back home.
Arriving de-hydrated by the oppressive heat, we drank water
like a pair of camels, before going into the shuttered bedroom
for 'a wee nap.' We woke at ten pm stupefied; but unable to
sleep, we sat doing crosswords in bed until three am.
I opened the card and laughed. It was Fathers' Day, and both
cards were outrageous as usual. Coffee in hand, I eagerly

awaited the usual phone calls. There was only one, which stopped after a couple of rings. As Helen had rung earlier, we knew *our* phone was working, so we waited to see if it rang again.

We'd breakfasted when the Charpentiers arrived; the redoubtable Anna leading the way bearing gifts. A home-made strawberry gateau was graciously presented for Diane's birthday, and a bottle handed to me, as I was wished, '*Joyeuse Fête des Pères.*' Birthday kisses were then bestowed on Diane, and out came our *chilled* bottle of *rosé* with a '*Joyeus Fête des Pères*' from us to the beaming Bertrand.

By then we kept a rack of wines, and at least one bottle ready at all times. Oh yes, we knew the score by then.

During their visit we laughed a lot, as I flirted outrageously with Anna, while she in turn tried to keep a straight face. And as usual the time just flew by, until the howling of the abandoned dogs told our guests it was time to leave.

On the way back they detoured to inspect our re-planted garden. We followed, aghast as we were confronted by lacerated lettuces, savaged sprouts, and trampled tomato plants. It was apparent that *cerfs*, *lapins* and *sangliers* had joined forces to hold their *own* party overnight; leaving a confusion of tracks in their wake. A case for the French C.S.I, perhaps?

'*Catastrophe,*' was Bertrand's outraged comment.

Passing the phone at seven pm it rang. Scooping it up quickly, I heard a frustrated Chris. He'd been ringing throughout the day to wish me Happy Father's Day, and he'd presumed the phone was either engaged or broken. Of course he'd forgotten the dialling tone, which I'd mentioned often. For teenager read airhead.


E.D.F turned up unannounced the next morning, to inspect the pylon below the woods. This inspection involved trampling over our land, decimating undergrowth and saplings. If during this inspection any branches were considered a danger to the overhead cables, they'd cut them arbitrarily then charge us for the privilege, I'd been told. The cavalcade consisted of two vans, an excavator sporting a lethal looking hedge cutter, and half a dozen workmen. Given the circumstances we thought it best to go out for the day. It seemed a good time to visit the coast; checking route and distance for future visitors whilst enjoying a day at '*la plage.*'

In the event it was a fair old distance. Negotiating Baugé, Angers and Nante, we finally ended up near St Nazaire's WW2 German submarine pens. Using 'B' roads, it was two hundred and forty kilometres and took over three hours. Sadly, when we arrived, we found St Nazaire to be sprawling and urbanized. However, a leaflet we'd picked up showed the resort of La Baule to be much more appealing, so we drove there instead.

On our arrival though, we became enshrouded in a ghostly sea fret. Making the most of it we enjoyed our meal at a seafront restaurant, whilst imagining the view across the beach.

As the weather looked set for the day, we headed for the Pont de Nazaire; the huge suspension bridge which soars majestically over the Loire basin. Once safely across, we were disgorged onto a remote peninsula of windswept sand-dunes and coarse marram grasses. Dazzling white beaches graced both flanks – one calm and lagoon-like, the other a shrine to surfers riding tumbling waves. Breaking through low cloud, the sun highlighted the finger of land ahead.

Traversing the causeway we drove through St Michael, a town called Chef, then on to Poric, before returning to Nante.

We arrived home three hours later, tired, red-faced and weather-beaten. Pulling up the drive, I espied a monstrous gap in the tree-line. Like the hollow left by an extracted tooth, it stood out against the skyline. E.D.F, a law unto themselves had completed their inspection. Ripping into the woodland with their excavator, they'd left a devastated area of broken timber for me to deal with. Thanks guys!

We didn't know it then, but that was the least of our worries.

# Chapter 13

## Now where should I begin?

Though the summer solstice had arrived, savage storms swept the area the following week, damaging power lines and uprooting trees. With outside work almost impossible, we concentrated our efforts on the lounge and dining room instead.

On the first calm day Diane went shopping alone. On her return, she asked me to take both her and the trailer back to La Flèche. Oh-oh! Off we went along the *Route de Sable* to pick up a bargain carpet. Damn, I knew I should have gone with her.

Feeling rather delicate the next day after an outrageous Billy Connolly night, we eased slowly into Saturday. The previous night's drink-athon had involved wine sampling on a biblical scale – but strictly for research purposes you understand.

On the cards that day was a trip to Saumur, for the re-scheduled *Fête-de- Géants*. But right then, even breakfast was a mountain too large to climb. So sipping carefully at our coffee we came to terms with the day.

In need of fresh air we picked blackcurrants from our bushes; ingredients for Diane's jam making enterprise. After this gentle pursuit we felt much better, and devoured brunch with a vengeance. Invigorated by then, we set off for Saumur, where we found a re-vamped *Emmaus* with lots more stock on display. On the downside though, prices had increased. With no bargains to be found, we left empty handed; driving on to *Gifi* where I bought a tripod-mounted telescope with Chris's Father's day cash.

Leaving *Gifi*, we cruised the tree-lined boulevard; passing the grandiose military equestrian academy, before parking up next to the *Bateaux* jetty. Crossing the busy road we made for the town centre; stopping off first at a toilet near the *Bureau de Tourismes*. Diane had expressed a need – but returned rather quickly. She'd discovered that the toilets were the infamous Turkish variety, where you squat over a hole with your feet on two blocks. Opening the door was as far as she got, saying they were foul beyond belief, with blood and excrement everywhere.

After sneaking into the *Mairie's* office to use *their* facilities, we returned, mounted a tiered platform, and settled down in our seats. At last, we were about to witness the spectacle of the giant's parade.

The carnival was electrifying; wending its way through the streets, infusing both locals and tourists alike with its energy. And what started out as a small event, evolved into a joyful street party without a hint of discord. The '*Géants,*' mostly on stilts, sported monstrous *papiere-maché* heads adorned with a range of expressions. Even more outlandish, were others balancing giraffe-like necks with heads perched on high. A viewing slot was provided at the base of the neck – essential for steering I'd imagine. As for music; drums were banging, trumpets blaring, and people singing. It was riotous and uplifting.

Oh, it was a far cry from the 'Mardi Gras' maybe, but everyone was enjoying themselves immensely, dancing joyfully to the marching bands. Those spirited musicians represented local villages, competing with friendly rivalry for best band of the day. And though discordant, the outpouring was exuberant, and a welcome change to the usual market day.

Swept along the streets by the throng we passed under packed balconies, while above us, Newton's Law was severely tested, as people leaned out to get a better view. Carried along in the swaying crowd we ascended to the chateau.

As the crowds milled together on the cliff top, we enjoyed the spectacle for a while, then worked our way back through the side streets. We'd enjoyed it for what it was, Diane's belated birthday treat.

With the festive weekend over we returned to work mode, where Bertrand on an 'inspection' visit advised me on the French way to restore our house walls. Cobbled together from a variety of dubious materials, they were a total miss-match. He advised chiselling off the crude render and starting again.

So respecting his knowledge, Diane and I chipped it off; raking out old mortar from the stone-work and providing a key for new cement. After two brutal days of chiselling, our hands and wrists were swollen.

On the positive side, we uncovered a limestone block set into the wall, with the date 1810 carved into it. Did it mark the building of the original house? Or was it the birth of the ironworks? It merited investigation whatever it was.

On the third day *'Maitre'* Bertrand arrived early, his apprentice François in tow. As I assembled tools and materials, François warned me that cement doesn't bond to *tuffa,* or limestone. The French way, (oh please, not the French way again,) was to drive small nails into the limestone at intervals. Then stringing wire mesh over them, it provided something for the cement to bind to. I said it seemed plausible, so they left me to continue, saying they'd return later for the inevitable inspection.

In their absence I checked under the eaves. At some time a new roof had been fitted onto the fieldstone walls, and crude gaps had been left. Whilst they allowed air to circulate, it also gave entry to 'critters.' Heeding another piece of François' advice I checked for evidence of bats before continuing.

'You must remember,' he'd warned, *'Chauve-souris,* or bald mice are protected in France.'

I told him the same protections apply in the UK; so once I'd checked for bats, any gaps were sealed. Then by inserting metal grills the house could still breathe. To paraphrase a popular saying – no bald mice were harmed during our alterations.

The guys returned after an obligatory two hour lunch break, with some clamps and a ball of twine. Attaching a clamp to one end of the house wall, they then stretched the twine to a second clamp on the other. At intervals, wooden wedges were driven into the mortar and the twine attached. Taking a sighting along the line, I'd have a level to work to. Brilliant!

We did the stringing then stood back to inspect it. Nodding his head in satisfaction, François then asked, 'Where is your cement mixer?'

I had to confess that I was hand-batching, as they say in the trade. 'What! Mixing by hand? This is not good,' he cried, informing Bertrand.

Shooting off on the tractor, he returned towing a battered cement-mixer. After thanking him profusely, he replied, 'It is not a problem.'

Next my tools were inspected; and though normal in England, were deemed incorrect by them. 'Luckily, my fazzaire has brought *his* tools,' François said proudly.

'Great,' I said sarcastically – which seemed to escape his notice. Anyway, after managing to mix a batch of cement lecture free, I doused the bone-dry wall with water. Then with mortar board loaded, I began applying the first layer. From behind me I heard a tutting sound. Teeth gritted, I turned around, to be met by Bertrand, finger wagging furiously.'Non-non,' he said, producing his trowel and stepping forward.

I thought it was too good to last. His trowel seemed gigantic; much larger and broader than mine. Carefully loading it with cement, (then discarding half of it) he shuffled quickly forward. And with a theatrical flourish, and an upward flick from the hip, he splattered the wall with the mix. Presumably this elaborate routine was 'the French way.' Sensing that I was just a little peeved by then however, François explained hastily, that applying it this way keyed it into the gaps. Understanding the logic behind it, I began again – this time in the 'correct' way. Satisfied, they left me to it, and returned home to feed their poultry.

Over the next couple of days I hurled cement at those walls like a demented lacrosse player, copying the style and panache displayed by Bertrand. And do you know what? It seemed to work. Finishing the last section, I surgically cleaned Bertrand's tools, then called over to drop them off.

With no dogs to be seen, I warily entered the courtyard; where I found Bertrand repairing a section of crumbling wall. Nearby François looked on. Studying the Maestro at work, I realised he hadn't chiselled out the old mortar; nor was he applying the cement like he'd shown *me*.

'Why is your father not doing it the French way?' I asked François.

'Because it is not necessary,' he grinned.


The garden swallowed up all our energy throughout the next week. And despite local wildlife's attempts to destroy it, fledgling veggies had finally raised their heads above the parapets. Our idea of stringing silver foil at intervals helped scare off birds, but with the house to prioritize, the huge plot was simply too ambitious. No matter. As we'd finally managed to grow *something;* the least we could do was nurture it. While we hoed around these precious shoots, I heard, *'Bonjour Stewaard et Deanne.'*

It was Véronique and Bertrand. They'd called around to say they'd spotted hoof-prints near our orchard. Perhaps we should inspect them together. Thankful to leave our backbreaking labour – and avoid a lecture, we followed them. Arriving at the orchard we found deer prints. He'd been worried he might find *sanglier* tracks, or ruts scored by tusks unearthing roots and grubs. Thankfully there were neither, as those huge porkers were prone to attacking people if disturbed. Not the most endearing visitor to have in your back garden.

Whilst walking between the trees he said, '*Regardez, tous avez pêche, cerise, et poire.*'

Cherries and pears we'd identified – but not the peaches. Yum! He explained how to get the best crops as we strolled up the garden together; lizards darting out of our path, and grasshoppers leaping ahead of us through the undergrowth. Hellfire, this place was *heaving* with life. The air was thrumming with the drone of insects. And you could almost hear the grass growing.

Back in the kitchen again, we nursed cold drinks while discussing materials for an upstairs en-suite. But first, Bertrand said, I must return our unopened bags of sand and cement for credit. He knew much cheaper sources.

Mid-conversation, we were interrupted when a car drew up. François bounded in flashing a dazzling smile. He'd passed his driving test three days earlier, and his proud parents had bought him a second-hand car. After polishing the life out of the gleaming Peugeot 205, he'd proudly driven it over to show us. As he'd no doubt hoped, we made a fuss of it, while praising him for passing his test. Perfectly satisfied, they all left around an hour later. Ah well, to hell with the weeds; there's always tomorrow, we agreed.

# Chapter 14

## Discovering the quarry

Taking Bertrand's advice, I returned the sand and cement to *Bricomarché*. After asking repeatedly for a credit, only to be met with blank looks and shrugging shoulders, I finally sorted it at the *Accuiel,* or office. Then, driving to *Agriloire* I bought the same cement far cheaper. When I got back, Diane said François had called. Could I rendezvous with his father? After unloading, I walked over, meeting Bertrand at the gate. By then I could understand most of what he said and fill in the gaps. He was off to the *carriere pour sable,* or the quarry for sand. Would I like to go with him? '*Beh oui,*' I replied; so he set off to collect the tractor and trailer.

With the units coupled up, we bumped away down his drive, the dogs running alongside us barking insanely. Leaving them in our wake we joined the main road, with me perched precariously on the mudguard clinging to an upright bar. Halfway past the mushroom *cave,* he hissed, '*Merde,*' then fished out an orange light from under his seat. Clamping it to the bar he switched it on. It began revolving; and with the flashing filament flickering over his fiendishly fiery features (try getting the kids to say *that* quickly) he tapped the side of his nose, saying, '*pour les gendarmes.*'

Careering along the road, he beeped at acquaintances as we entered a hamlet. Weaving through a chicane of flower planters we left the houses behind us, eventually reaching the main road to Tours. Crossing it we entered a work-site, where we bounced along a track towards the quarry.

After pulling over occasionally to let trucks pass, we drew up on a weighbridge. Jumping down we entered a small office, where with a cheery, '*Bonjour*,' a young girl read off the unladen weight of our unit. Writing it down, she instructed us to drive into the quarry; and once inside I just sat there transfixed.

The quarry floor was a moonscape of sand and gravel mounds; and as I watched, a huge excavator gouged material from the walls then loaded it into a large hopper. An Archimedes screw then drew it up into a crusher, where after processing it spewed onto a conveyor belt, which then fed a mound below. Other crushers around the site produced different sized aggregates; the smallest of them being ground down to coarse or fine sand.

Negotiating our way across the quarry floor, we were mindful of tipper trucks rushing back and forth servicing nearby construction projects. Finding a sand-pile marked with the correct grade we waited. After filling a truck, a monstrous excavator loader roared over, bouncing on enormous cleated tyres. The driver pulled up next to us, and climbing up an integrated ladder to the footplate, Bertrand shook his hand and they spoke for a while. Then climbing down, he stood aside as two huge buckets of sand were dumped into the trailer. The guy then switched off his engine and climbed down, whereupon Bertrand introduced me and we shook hands. After some chatting and shrugging, hands were shaken again then we left.

Wending our way back to the weighbridge, we drove onto the ramp and dismounted again. This time the girl read off the laden weight, deducted the previous reading, and presented Bertrand with a copy invoice for the difference. At the month's end he'd be billed by post, he said. I was then introduced to our weighbridge operator, who said coyly in schoolgirl English, that I could buy materials on Bertrand's account until I opened my own.

Arriving back at Le Lavandu after a fascinating excursion, I jumped down prepared for a spot of hard shovelling. But as usual Bertrand had a surprise up his sleeve. Dropping the tailgate he pressed a hidden button, and the load began inching jerkily to the rear, where it cascaded off and began forming a pile. Examining the trailer bed, I saw that it was actually a broad canvas conveyer belt stretched over rollers. Wicked!

I calculated afterwards that Bertrand's sand had cost him twelve euros a tonne. I'd paid fifteen euros for a hundred kilos at *Bricomarché*. Yet another lesson learned.

Returning to the house, I had a cold drink then began removing render from a wall. A phone call from François soon put a stop to *that* though. His parents had decided to celebrate him passing his exams and driving test. Perhaps we'd like to join them? Just for aperitifs of course.

Here we go again, I thought. But how could we refuse? They were justifiably proud of their only child, and rewarded his achievements. He worked hard around the farm and was always polite and friendly. What more could parents want?

After freshening up, we once again ran the doggie gauntlet. Though they still barked, they were getting to know us by then and were less threatening. By eight pm we were sat on the patio, glasses of blush pink *rosé* in hand. In the lingering warmth of the setting sun we toasted François' success, before discussing news and local gossip. And *that* was when we found out about the Renard's.

Our ex house-owners were apparently a local legend. After topping up our glasses, we were regaled with tales of eccentricity, stupidity, cupidity and a flagrant disregard for authority. Enthusiastically translated by François, it was both funny and worrying at the same time.

It transpired Monsieur Renard was very tall; and when plastering his extension, he'd persuaded a diminutive friend to balance a board of mortar on his head. Walking behind him, he flicked the mixture onto the wall as they moved along. Now that's inventive! He'd also moved the washing machine outside, then rigged up an air compressor in the kitchen where he sandblasted items on the tiled floor. Then as an avid hunter, he'd once caught a fox in a trap; then kept it caged in his car for a week whilst driving to and from work. His car had also played host to a poisonous viper in a sack for a while – his version of intruder deterrents possibly?

We knew by then, that some of the land contained buried *saloperie;* and the ramshackle enclosures we'd inherited had housed rabbits, ferrets, quail and chickens. We then learned that a large concrete enclosure had housed hunting dogs, which was quite normal in the area. But what really worried me was, he'd dragged a scrap car up the field and hidden it in the wood, rather than taking it to a scrap yard. I was to find out, that this was just the tip of one very large iceberg.

In contrast to the late Monsieur Renard, Bertrand was hard working and seemed fair and honest. Le Lavendu was also well kept and constantly being improved. Now I knew why he was glad we'd moved in.

Whilst discussing our house, I mentioned the date 1810 carved into the stone lintel. Was that when the ironworks was built, or when it was converted to a farmhouse? He didn't know, but they'd obtained documents dated 1854 for Le Lavendu from the records office at Baugé. We should ask there, he suggested.

By then it was ten pm, and Véronique sideswiped us again. Appearing on the patio François said, 'My muzzaire, she say, could you please sit for dinner.'

We couldn't believe it. A veritable banquet was served to us; consisting of *champignon-de-Paris*, guinea fowl with *haricot verts* and rice, alpine cheeses, ice cream cake, coffee, *eau de vie* and wine. Yet somehow it seemed perfectly natural in these surroundings, beginning this impressive meal at such an hour and ending around midnight.

The sky was a black velvet blanket studded with stars, the air perfectly still; and in a temperature of twenty degrees C we watched bats swooping on insects attracted to the table candles.

We could have happily sat there for hours; especially when François stated ingenuously, that an ingredient in one of their liquor's was *vernis*, or varnish. Diane and I laughed out loud, while they all looked bewildered. He then went on to tell us perfectly seriously, that the reason our first lettuce plants were eaten by rabbits was, we hadn't planted them on a Saturday. Local folklore states it is essential, he insisted. Nothing had eaten *their* lettuce, and they always planted on a Saturday, he said, so that proved it. Faced with such irrefutable logic what could I say? Well how about; you have two dogs that sleep outside, and bark when they sense something. Could that have anything to do with it? Maybe it was time to call it a night.

Yawning contentedly, I wandered out the next morning to check on our new lettuce plants. I met François walking towards me. He'd forgotten to tell me, he was driving to his new apartment near Marseilles the next day. His parents had rented it to help his transition to college. Would we like to accompany them when they next visited him? I was proud to accept; even though a four hour journey with only a French/English dictionary to help us communicate would be a strain. His parents must also have been apprehensive. Nonetheless, warm hearted and generous they'd still offered to take us. We'd certainly come a long way since first arriving in the valley. Everything was going just fine now – wasn't it?

# Chapter 15

## A grand celebration

The heat-wave in July signalled a rampant growth spurt in the garden; the air literally zinging with insect life. With it being so freakishly hot though, it was often hard to get motivated. Sitting on the terrace with a cold beer seemed to make much more sense.

The upcoming 14th was a big date on our calendar. Yes, it was Bastille Day in France, and a time when many French headed off on '*vacance*.' But more importantly for us, it was Jill and Dale's joint 70th birthday celebration. A huge party was planned in the UK; and with family and friends arriving from far and wide, it was an occasion not to be missed. Eagerly, Diane set about booking the ferry.

Unfortunately, after the long hot spell a storm was brewing. The forecast was ominous, with severe gales being threatened. Not the best conditions for a channel crossing. Beaten down by extreme humidity, we broke off working and drove to Noyant.

Sorting out things for the upcoming journey, we began by visiting the bank. But arriving home we couldn't find Diane's credit card. Panicking we searched everywhere; almost stripping out the car before doing what we should have done first. We rang the bank, and were told it'd been found and put behind the counter.

We didn't need that second run to Noyant. We'd planned to visit La Flèche instead, where *Gifi's* sale promised 70% discounts; perfect for grand children's birthday presents. We also needed to find a large *brouette* somewhere at a bargain price. Luckily, after collecting our card we found one in

*Agriloire's* sale. After the UK trip, I really needed to begin landscaping, and a barrow was essential.

Nadine rang early on the morning of the journey. She'd heard gales were sweeping the UK, especially the south coast. We decided to ring Brittany Ferries before setting off, but they couldn't guarantee anything running. Just turn up and we'll see what happens, we were told. *Excuse* me!

But we had no choice, we had to go. Also, we weren't the only ones who storms would affect. The Tour-de-France had organized a stage to pass through Le Lude. Plus, after consulting 'The Oracles,' Bertrand had taken holidays to harvest his crops. He was facing a mini-disaster if the storm hit.

After a day of packing and sorting out travel issues, we didn't need a promised visit by Henri and Annette. As Diane was busy packing, I tried ringing to head them off. Their phone rang for ages before it was picked up; only for no-one to answer. 'Hello, Henri?' I enquired. There was a hollow silence, followed by some muttering and background noise. Then I heard a click as the receiver was gently replaced. I rang again. This time it wasn't even picked up. Ah well, at least I'd tried.

Five minutes later Henri's car pulled up, containing him, Annette, and their two small granddaughters. They'd driven up to find out why I'd phoned!

Over the obligatory coffee, my laboured explanation failed to get through to my blank-faced neighbours. Frustrated, I gave up. Then stepping forward daintily, one of the little girls said patiently – in English, 'You should have rung us to cancel the visit.' Oh My God!

They left soon after … but not until Henri had inspected the garden. Thankfully, after packing and shutting down the electricity and water, we managed to grab a few hours sleep.

The alarm jangled at three am. Forcing down coffee and toast, I filled a flask before we set off at three thirty. Bleary-eyed, we battled through the increasingly wet and windy countryside, the trailer wallowing along behind us. Despite the extreme weather warnings however, we arrived safely, and the sailing went ahead on schedule. All things considered the trip turned out to be a breeze – not the gale predicted.

As we were making good time we detoured to Nadine's, where after lunch and a chat, we loaded some wardrobes which Nadine had promised Helen. We left around five -thirty, just as Nick arrived home from work. Oh dear, what a shame.

Fighting our way up the A1 was appalling. Whipped up to gale force eight, shrieking crosswinds shook us like a demented terrier worrying a bone. When we arrived at Grantham worn out and weary. the trailer cover and our nerves were in tatters. So what's new eh?

The next day's weather was much better, so we all walked into town. I replaced my tarpaulin at Halfords on a walkabout with Dale, while Diane and Jill headed off to the hairdressers. Then, suitably coiffured it was party time.

The affair was a huge success; crowned by a surprise visit from Diane's ex-pat sister Joanne, who'd flown in from Canada. It was enjoyable playing catch-up with all the family, and gratifying that everyone had managed to make it from 'Up North.'

Back at Jill's and Dale's later, I received a long awaited phone call. My first grandson Dylan had entered the world; and the family had just gotten back from hospital.

Following lunch the next day, we set off eagerly for the North East. We were staying with Stewy and Helen who'd returned earlier, and on our arrival we walked in on a family party. Unfortunately it was dark by then, and unhitching the heavy trailer without a jockey-wheel would be too dangerous. Ringing Darlington, I put back our visit until the next morning. Besides, with another forty miles to drive, we'd have arrived after the children's bed-time anyway.

Meanwhile, presents and duty free items were handed around, including a huge garden gnome unearthed at a *brocante;* a present for Pauline, who immediately christened it Pièrre. But after attempting to stay awake we crashed out early. Our journey had finally caught up with us.

Swinging by Durham the next morning, we collected Kay from her Dad's. She was dying to see the baby, so bundling her aboard, we drove to Darlington. On arrival, we were met with a hesitant smile from my two year old granddaughter Lydia, and a hug from the grinning proud dad Michael. A tired looking Miranda led us over to see baby Dylan tucked up in his cot; his shock of thick black hair catching us by surprise.

Over the week we caught up with family, my sister Janis especially. I also had a long overdue hospital appointment to attend. The time just seemed to fly by. All too soon, after *another* going away party it was time to leave. With Stewy and Chris, casualties of the party, helping me pack the trailer, we prepared for our return trip. Saying our goodbyes we set off for Grantham. Busy, busy, busy.

Rested after a sound sleep, we headed off the next morning for Nadine's to attend Ben and Lewis' joint christening. Of course it was raining when we arrived, which was one thing we *didn't* miss in France. Parked up, we were roped in to help erect a gazebo before changing for the event. Then suited and booted, we all set off on foot to the church; the walk necessitated by parking restrictions.

It was a strange old day, as first Nick and the godfather got lost on the way while chatting. Then we found that the service was being conducted at short notice by a female lay preacher. Apparently, the usual priest, reputedly an alcoholic was 'indisposed' in London. With hyper-active kids running around, and strangers wandering in during the service, it took on a surreal quality.

However, back at the house the weather picked up – and suddenly we had ourselves a street party! Lucky old me … I got stuck with a well-served Nick, who acting like my 'bezzy mate,' rambled on for ages about nothing before 'reclining' on the lawn. With a long drive ahead I couldn't drink – and feeling like spectres at the feast, we said our goodbyes while people were still capable of hearing them. Putting my foot down I set off for Portsmouth. We had a late ferry to catch.

As usual the journey was entertaining. First a headlight failed; then the tarpaulin came loose – and just kept on coming loose. Arriving late, we were just in time to check in. But our bad luck continued as we were waved aside for a customs search. Thanks to Her Majesty's finest, all the cabins and seating had been taken when we boarded; so once again we assumed the foetal position on the floor.

By three am I was prowling around the ship. Unable to sleep, I stepped over those lucky people who could; one of them being Diane who was stretched out comatose.

Disembarking at seven fifteen local time, we took a different route, and once on the motorway Diane dozed fitfully, waking as the dawn light flooded the windscreen. Arriving safely around eleven am we opened the shutters, letting in the first sunshine we'd seen in more than a week.

While the washing machine whirred away, I inspected the garden. It'd grown outrageously in such a short time, but I suppose that's the price you pay for all that sunshine. Right, where's the lawnmower?

After we'd set off the previous week, Bertrand had begun harvesting; but he still found time to mow the fields bless his cotton socks. The sweet smell of newly mown grass was intoxicating, and under the fierce sun, it'd turned into buttery yellow windrows. They'd soon become *roules*; some going to Maurice's pony club in return for cleaning out our *fosse septique*.

In our absence, François had recorded the Tour de France, which *did* pass through Le Lude after all, and he'd begun work experience with S.A.U.R the water authority. Driving a little white van, he tootled around all day doing meter inspections, but he still helped on the farm in the evenings. However hard I worked, I always felt humbled by their huge work ethic.

As further proof of this, Bertrand proudly announced his latest project. In our *commune*, the *Mairie* allowed the construction of a twenty square metre extension to a property each year, with no planning permission required. Catch that happening in the UK! Bertrand had already built two. One housed a caravan, their cars, a motorbike and a ride on mower. The other was a fully equipped workshop; useful for repairing farm equipment which was mostly inherited and ancient. He said he was planning another. My head spun at his accomplishments and his plans for the future. Could we ever hope to compete? Moreover – at our time of life did we really want to?

# Chapter 16

## Back with a vengeance

It was a balmy Tuesday 20$^{th}$ of July when we arrived back at the farm. For a while it'd been hard to get used to, but this small part of France was now our home. And though it was nice to visit everyone in the UK, it wasn't long before the sunshine and relaxed lifestyle had us itching to return.

In our *new* lives, we opened the shutters most mornings to dazzling sunlight. We'd see buzzards spiralling high above the tree-line on rising thermals, their mournful cries carrying to us down below. And breakfast on the terrace was often an absorbing affair. We'd sit for ages fascinated: watching lines of ants carry off fallen crumbs with military precision, only for lizards to dash out of the shadows and grab both crumbs *and* ants. Nature's comedians, they'd dance from one foot to the other on the hot pathway, or run up the walls of the house chasing flies.

But delightful though it all was, it wasn't a holiday; it was a lifestyle choice and there was work to be done. First on the agenda was the bulging post-box. If it overflowed while we were away at anytime, Jorge the postman left the extra next door. I'd nip over later to check, but right then we waded through the first batch. Junk mail was binned, except the non-glossy variety which we used for fire lighting. Brown envelopes were treated with respect, as they usually enclosed something important – even more so after any absence.

Leaving the rest until later, we dealt with the car tax reminder first. We spent most of the morning sorting mail; the downside of our quasi-nomadic lifestyle.

Having just returned, and with much to catch up on, you'd think the last thing on our minds would be job hunting. But money had been haemorrhaging from our bank account due to mounting renovation costs. Our trips to the UK had made matters worse; and our three year budget was beginning to unravel. In short, we needed to plug the drain on our finances.

Enter Jane, Paula's replacement at the agency. Bumping into her at Noyant we discussed the bleak job market. She and her boyfriend had arrived the previous August, and had found work apple picking. It was readily available, she said, and *Cartes de Séjour,* or work permits weren't needed anymore due to relaxed E.U rules.

Discussing the job situation with Bertrand later, he said our limited French vocabulary was a disadvantage, though apple picking shouldn't present a problem. But it was hard, gruelling work; often in extreme weather conditions and for minimum wage. Talking it over, we naively decided it was only for a few weeks. And let's face it, how hard could it be?

Hearing that workers were employed from within the E.U, and as far off as Morocco, we drove to the nearby *verger de pommes,* or apple orchard to register for employment.

At the office, *Madame La* Secrétaire took our details and inspected our passports, before adding us to a list. Maybe we'd be sent for when the main harvest began in August, she said. The regulars had previously culled the crop in June, allowing the best fruit more space to grow. Until then, we'd no idea that apples begin life growing in bunches like grapes. We also learned that apples are cold-stored, and released onto the market throughout the year, ensuring regular supplies and steady prices. In fact the apples we eat are often a year old. We left feeling bemused, dodging busy forklifts as they loaded delivery trucks.

A knock at the window later proved to be Bertrand, who said he'd heard of something that might suit *me* better. Véronique worked in the nearby *cave de champignons,* or mushroom cave, and a guy nearing retirement was on long term sick leave. They needed someone to cover for him. Was I interested? With blind enthusiasm, I replied, '*Beh oui.*'

An interview was arranged with the owner Armand, who said at the outset that he'd only employed French people before to avoid communication issues. However, the French he'd interviewed so far didn't want work. I told him I was keen, and prepared to slot in anywhere; to which he asked, could I drive tractors and forklifts. I answered yes, but confessed it'd been a while since I'd driven either. In reality I'd only ever driven fork-lifts, and that had been thirty years before. But I was desperate. As he still seemed reluctant, I offered to come in for a day *gratuit* to hone my driving skills. He said he admired my enthusiasm, but said that wouldn't be necessary.

'Let me think it over. Give me your phone number and I'll get back to you.'

I left feeling less than confident, but I'd given it my best shot. Returning home I changed clothes and began strimming; which on our huge plot was never ending □– like painting the old Forth Bridge used to be. The farm had stood untouched for two years before we moved in, so we had a monumental task ahead of us.

My epic stint was interrupted by François, who after admiring my progress, went on to advise me on the *correct* way to do it. He was heading off to Le Lude to meet his cousin.

'First, will you come up into the woods with me?' he said, 'I would like to show you something.'

Now back in the UK, saying *that* could get you arrested. However, allowing for his naïve translation I kept a straight face. But to my amusement, before we set off, he insisted that we wear wellingtons. It was a scorching twenty-eight C, but I suppose in certain *haute-couture* salons, shorts, tee-shirts and rubber boots could be the latest look for the country set. However, noting my quizzical look, he said, 'Poisonous vipers, they live up in the trees.'

I'm sure he meant up in the woods – but you get the drift. Swatting midges while I watched out for *ground* based vipers, we entered the wood. After walking for a while, François indicated a tumbledown fence, and said, 'This is the end of your trees.'

Apparently the wood had been divided between three families generations ago, and had passed down through the children. The section ahead of us had recently been bequeathed to a son in Le Mans when his father died, he told me. I said it wasn't much use to him up there, (meaning the son in Le Mans, not the father in the after-life.) Pointing out fallen trees over the fence, I said what a waste it was, letting them rot like that.

'But those trees are not your trees,' he said solemnly. 'You would not like someone to take *your* wood, I think.' A fair point I suppose.

Striding back down the field, François beckoned me over to a copse. Pulling a bush aside dramatically, he revealed the rusting remains of a Renault 16 car. It'd belonged to Monsieur Renard, he said; and when it expired years before, he'd been too mean to have it towed to the scrap-yard; insisting instead, that Bertrand tow it up into the woods for him. I was angry at *Bertrand* then; but François said it wasn't wise to antagonize the late Monsieur, as he'd been bullying and vindictive.

He then pointed to the next field. Overgrown with bramble thickets, it was useless as it was. He said his father would like to cut it all back, treat it with herbicides, and re-seed it to pasture. This would benefit us all, he said. But what was preventing him doing it was this. Pulling back some brambles, he revealed in the sunlight the rear end of a Citroen 2cv. '*Voilà!*' he exclaimed.

I couldn't believe it, what was happening here? Apparently the farm had been treated as a huge dumping ground. Nothing had ever been taken to the *déchetterie,* said François. This fallow field held the carcases of sheep, dogs, ferrets and chickens. But it mainly contained scrapped motor vehicles, household appliances, wood and glass. Was it any wonder the water table had been contaminated?

We woke early, to the tolling of church bells across the valley. This Sunday was Le Lude's '*Grande Brocante*,' and we didn't want to miss any of it. The police had closed off the town to traffic, and a plethora of colourful stalls lined the main streets. The air was buzzing with excitement, as people promenaded in the hot summer sun. Stall holders, food vendors, café and bar owners were all taking advantage of the good weather and doing a roaring trade. It was only held on such a scale once a year at the end of July, giving friends a chance to play catch-up. The subsequent hand shaking, back-slapping and kissing provided street theatre for bemused tourists. Feeling that we were locals by then, we tried to look blasé; but the excitement of the day still got to us.

We spent a pleasant two hours rummaging; nabbing a chandelier for the house, a garden mattock, and other sundry items. We'd begun to really enjoy these events; honing our language skills by haggling with the *brocanteurs*.

But at noon a metamorphosis occurred, as all around us stall-holders began setting up small tables. Baguettes, wine and other delicacies were laid out, and the market virtually ceased trading. It was *Midi,* the sacred French lunch-time.

Recognizing a *fait accompli* we headed back home, our stomachs growling in agreement. After a meal we rang the kids; then with guests from the UK arriving the next day, I dragged myself out to tackle more strimming, while Diane disappeared upstairs to begin housework.

Bearing gifts from their *vacance* later, Bertrand and Véronique entered our kitchen. Not to be outdone, we surprised them with our own *petit cadeaux,* or little gifts – a huge slab of cheddar cheese, a tin of quality English biscuits; and two bottles of Newcastle Brown ale, a novelty which made Bertrand's eyes pop open. Their visit lasted two hours, with *le dictionnaire* helping as always. Inevitably, it ended with an inspection of our garden, which of course resulted in an invitation to see theirs. A lecture then followed, pointing out differences between the two. As usual, not a wilting leaf or weed could be spotted anywhere in their garden. And I swear the asparagus were standing to attention. Anyway; enough unto the day as they say. Who are 'they?' I often asked myself.

We strolled back home at eight pm, desperate for a cool shower and an ice-cold beer. Throwing open the French doors we tried to lure in a breeze, but only succeeded in attracting flies. Still without TV, I drank a beer watching Del Boy and Rodney Trotter on video, and we all had a 'bleedin good larf togevva.' Cheers guys!

# Chapter 17

## Blood, sweat, and fears

I leapt out of bed bright-eyed and bushy-tailed. We had lots to do. Eddie, an ex-work colleague was visiting with his wife and two children, before heading off to their camp-site on a touring holiday. With breakfast over, I made a start tidying the gardens and terracing. Then, after cleaning and arranging the patio furniture, I prepped the BBQ for action. Meanwhile, Diane continued house cleaning; re-making beds with fresh linen just in case. If it were possible, the house was looking even more welcoming than usual.

However, the weather wasn't brilliant; and while deciding whether to eat alfresco or not the phone rang. It was Eddie. After setting off in good time, they'd mistakenly taken the road to Nantes. Blissfully unaware, they'd driven on for a while before stopping at a 'great little restaurant' for a break. Whilst reading the map over coffee, they realised their error and rushed out. Unfortunately, fifty kilometres further on, his wife realised she'd lost her handbag holding passports, ferry tickets, credit cards and cash. Imagining the worst, they'd driven back to the restaurant in a blind panic. At the front desk no-one admitted to seeing the bag. Then a waitress coming off duty appeared at reception. She told the Manager she'd found the bag, put it under the bar for safe keeping then forgotten about it. Though suspicious of this tale, Eddie told me he was so relieved, that he just thanked her profusely. He even offered her a reward for her honesty. Declining his offer politely, she said she was just pleased to help. This put Eddie on the back foot, as he'd been ready to call the police.

Unfortunately their plans were now ruined. After comparing maps, we concluded they were much nearer their site than to us. While saying they were still welcome to visit, I advised that as the site was booked, it would be prudent to head there. Maybe they could call in on their return trip home – barring any more mishaps of course.

Ah well, back to strimming. Actually, with it being overcast by then it was much cooler for working. Diane, a little miffed at the cancellation, said she may as well 'modify' the bathroom tiles. Knowing better than to ask, I left her to it. Setting off down the drive, I pushed the barrow containing the strimmer, fuel and tools. It was a hefty load, but better than a long walk back for anything left behind.

Right, here we go then. Switching on, I primed the pump then pulled the cord. Nothing! After numerous pulls there was *still* nothing. 'Oh come on you worthless piece of crap,' I shouted, shaking the machine angrily.

And that was when a car and trailer pulled up. It was Bertrand on his way home. *'Vous avez un problème Stewaard?'*

*'Oui Bertrand, aidez moi s'il vous plait.'*

After a lot of tinkering, he managed to get the damned thing started, though it was running quite rough.

*'Oh lor lor,'* he muttered, and began stripping it down again. Half an hour later we'd fixed it – though neither of us knew how. Standing up, he scratched his head and shrugged.

*'C'est fini,'* he announced.

*'Merci mon ami,'* I replied; then asked him where he'd been.

*'Ah,'* he replied, *'Brico, pour un grand projet.'*

Grinning, he tapped the side of his nose, winked, and climbed into his car. He pulled away in a cloud of dust, a tarpaulin shrouding his trailer. And later, when he came over to drop off grease for my strimmer, I tried wheedling it out of him; but, his 'big project' remained a closely guarded secret.

By then, my friend and neighbour had assumed the role of Project Manager cum Quality Control Inspector in our daily lives. Nevertheless, concerned and caring though he was, he could often seem patronising. But better acquainted with the French mentality by then I'd begun asserting myself. By introducing the Charpentiers to British ideas and products, I was staging a fight-back; though even when something was blatantly better they wouldn't admit it. For example, the premiere French one coat gloss paint (name withheld) was as thin as milk; and no matter how it was shaken or stirred, it required two – even three coats.

'It's a bit of a bugger to use,' one of my ex-pat friends said, putting it mildly.

My sentiments exactly, as it ran down your arms if painting any higher than waist level. Of course my neighbours would have none of this. That is, until the day I introduced François to a tin of British non-drip one coat gloss, (name *also* withheld.) Prising the lid off, I dramatically turned the tin upside down – *over my head*. Not for long I hasten to add. Just long enough to prove my point. 'Tell your father, *that's* what we call one coat, non-drip paint in England.'

Of course I had to be careful not to upset their Gallic sensitivities. After all, we *were* living in their country. Besides, the difference between cultures was one reason we'd moved here in the first instance. It made life so much more interesting.

The shrilling phone woke me with a start. It was Stewy calling. He'd seen forest fires raging across Southern France on TV. Were we safe where *we* were? I thanked him for caring, but assured him we were three hundred kilometres away from *that* particular problem. After a chat, he said he had to head off to work, and it was raining as usual. Sighing, he asked wistfully what our weather was like. I almost hadn't the heart to tell him. But of course I did.

It then struck me forcibly, how ignorant we were of world events without TV. Of course we could have bought a French TV, or even newspapers – if we'd cared enough to drive into town to find one. As it was, without François to update us, we hadn't a clue what was happening out there. But let's face it, that's how we preferred it.

Of course, there were times when gaping holes were exposed in our reasoning. Like the day we drove into Saumur, and noticed a hoarding outside a *tabac* featuring the late President Reagan. We thought he looked a bit rough – even paler than usual. It was said he never dyed his hair. He just whitened his face. However his pallor was understandable on this occasion. It was a morgue photo. He'd been dead for two weeks! We supposed that keeping abreast of the news might prove beneficial sometimes; warning of a major catastrophe like an earthquake or a nuclear holocaust for instance. But what the hell could *we* do about it anyway? Ignorance was bliss we reckoned.

On our return Diane plundered our fruit store; her mission, making plum and vanilla jam in the bread maker. (Check it out – it's in the instruction manuals.) Meanwhile, I measured the death trap masquerading as our shower cubicle, planning to source a replacement at La Flèche the next day. However, in the event the search proved unsuccessful; so giving up on the idea, we bought a pole and shower curtain instead.

Arriving home, we assembled everything needed for the next day's jobs. Then, after a final hair-raising shower experience, reminiscent of Alfred Hitchcock's film *Psycho*, we sat down to our casserole. Simmered in red wine while we were out shopping, it was complimented by another cheeky bottle at the table.

Following a hearty breakfast the next day, I tackled small jobs first, saving the hellish shower cubicle for later. Ripping out that crappy old unit, would be the most satisfying thing I'd done in years.

By the day's end the shower was a bad memory. With 'fettling' done, a new tap and drain plug were fitted; and as the pièce de resistance, I installed a bathroom cabinet. As per usual though, the Renard curse struck halfway through the job. I swear to God, that man must have been haunting us. Why? Well due to the bathroom wall being so thin, most of the carefully fitted tiles fell off as I drilled holes for the shower pole. But taking a deep breath, I thought, calm down son.

After refitting the tiles I checked the time. I was on a roll, it was only five thirty. Cracking on, I installed an ornamental mirror and shelves in the *étoile* bedroom, and ended my shift by spraying the towel-rail with white enamel paint.

Returning from shopping Diane found me tidying up. Popping her head around the door, she asked, 'How about cheese, crackers and chutney?'

'But of course Madame,' I joked.'

Diane's 'River cottage' chutney was based on Hugh Fearnley Whittingstall's recipe. Something I told Hugh when we bumped into him and his son Oliver at Tours airport a while later – but that's another story.

'Would you like a beer with that?' Diane asked.

'Is the Pope a catholic?' I replied.

Appearing at the French windows soon after, François waved a video cassette at me. It was the Tour de France recording. He'd also returned some classic car magazines I'd loaned him. It helped him with his English lessons, he said, plus he loved classic British sports cars. A win win situation really. Thanking us for the cheddar cheese, he said his mother would use it in her cooking □– and the biscuits? Well they hadn't lasted long it seems thanks to Bertrand's sweet tooth. However, the bottles of 'Newcastle Broon' were being kept for a special occasion. Well how about when Newcastle win the F.A cup again? Now *that* would be special.

# Chapter 18

## Oh boy – it's getting hot

The temperature was in the 40's, and the humidity was stifling. This was often the prelude to a heavy storm. Those we'd experienced so far had been spectacular; elemental and alarming in their ferocity.

The most recent had occurred in the evening as the day cooled, beginning with lightning flickering above the tree-line. Eerily silent, it lit up the horizon like an artillery barrage. Rain-swollen clouds then rolled in overhead as the temperature plummeted. Then with the wind gusting sharply, 'BOOM,' a thunderous drum-roll echoed throughout the valley; followed by torrential rain which battered the corrugated roofs of barns and outbuildings. Totally helpless we could only wait it out, watching through rain lashed windows.

The bombardment lasted for half an hour, before ending abruptly in deathly silence. Minutes later the skies had cleared, the stars re-emerged, and the thunder was just a faint rumble in the next valley. And with the last of the rain gurgling down the drainpipe it was over.

Pulling up on his bike the next morning, François said Broc's temperature had rocketed to a brutal forty-four C the previous day. Then while I absorbed this information; completely out of left field, he asked, 'Were you disturbed on Thursday by my muzzaire killing a chicken?'

Taken aback, I laid down my strimmer, 'No, why?'

There followed another François classic. 'My muzzaire, she worries because of the noise; as the chicken's friends, they were not 'appy.'

Well, I don't suppose they were when you think about it.

By then it was noon, and I just had to stop working. Okay, mad dogs and Englishmen etcetera, but it was seriously hot out there. Even the lizards were applying sun-screen. Taking the hint I cleared everything away, before heading inside for a cold shower and *petit-somme*. Sadly my nap was rudely interrupted by Diane, who woke me insisting I'd promised to take her shopping in Saumur. I can only imagine that I must have been suffering from heat-stroke at the time.

It being Saturday, a visit to the new *Emmaus* was first on the agenda. Re-sited on a tree lined boulevard it'd been difficult to find at first; but once discovered we found the system remained unchanged. Serious buyers arrived well before two pm, and battled with dealers to grab the choicest items. Yellow numbered stickers were still attached by staff to purchases, with buyers claiming and paying for them later.

We'd always enjoyed going head to head with these veterans, occasionally beating them to a special item. Finding nothing interesting this time however, we left quickly, threading our way out through the incoming horde. It was hellish hot inside; and even with huge ceiling fans and wide open doors the humidity was oppressive. Mimicking John Wayne, I drawled, 'Let's get the hell outta here.' And out we got.

Driving across town, we checked out white goods at *Sésame,* an electrical dealer. We needed a washing machine, electric oven, gas hob and other smaller items. But this was no day to make important decisions; it was just too hot to concentrate. Buying snacks at a nearby sandwich bar we headed for the cooler riverbank. In the shadow cast by the bridge, we consumed baguettes and ice cold drinks, enjoying a cool breeze wafting off the river. Watching the shallow water trickle around exposed sand-banks, I realised how desperately we needed rain.

On the way home, we detoured through the pretty village of Thorée-les- Pins; something we'd often promised ourselves. As often happens though the reality disappointed, and did nothing to lighten our mood. A mood aggravated by hot air entering the car through air vents; not the cold air we so desperately needed. Mind you it was hardly surprising. I'd disconnected the car's A/C system to improve fuel economy. Arriving home at six fifteen the outside temperature was forty-two Celsius.

Therefore, I offer this advice to those contemplating life in a hot climate. It's not a fortnight's holiday with sun-beds and pina colada's, it's a radical lifestyle change. You'll be doing everything you'd do in the UK – plus a lot more if you take on a restoration project like we did. You could often be working sixteen hours a day, often in hot uncomfortable conditions. And with the many problems thrown at you, a working knowledge of the language is invaluable. It makes life easier and much more rewarding. Anyway, here endeth the lesson.

Sunday, we decided would be a day of rest, as the oppressive heat was making us both ratty. François said it's the reason rural French sleep downstairs during the summer. We decided to give it a try. But what we really needed was a change of routine. Firing up the car, we drove through Le Lude and headed out to the countryside. Passing the imposing château we crossed the river bridge, its handrails bedecked with flower baskets; something the French excel at I must admit. On a whim, we thought why not be tourists for the day?

Turning back we found a shaded parking spot; and after buying tickets, we were just in time to join a conducted tour. As chateux go it was impressive; its limestone walls and grey conical turrets dominating the town. But what made it special was, this was *our* château. We could visit it anytime; especially after the tourist season ended.

The change of pace was just what we'd needed; re-charging our batteries and stirring the blood. Invigorated, we returned home as the sun was waning. Following relaxing herbal baths and dinner, we settled down to a quiet evening. But who's to say how it happened? At some point a Status Quo video seemed like a good idea. Come three am we crawled into bed; voices hoarse and three sheets to the wind.

When we surfaced later that morning, The Boomtown Rats, 'I don't like Mondays' seemed *much* more appropriate. Inevitably the day was written off. But never mind; what doesn't kill you makes you stronger, they say.

When François drew up in his work van that morning it was freakishly hot. I'd been out early strimming, and was only too pleased to take a break – but not when he said why he'd called. Out of Diane's earshot, he said his father had spotted two men on our property the previous evening, while he was watering his garden. Months before, François disturbed two men peering into our windows during the night – while we slept a few feet away! He didn't know if it was the same two, but this was more serious as it'd happened in broad daylight. Bertrand said they'd driven off in a grey Renault 19; but the previous time, François had said they'd been driving a white Renault 14. He could have been mistaken I suppose, as it was dark back then; or maybe they'd changed cars. Was it the same two, or just coincidence? I asked if the police should be informed but he said no. They'd discussed it; but having little confidence in the local gendarmerie, he thought the dogs should be given freer rein at night. And instead of shouting at them for barking, maybe we should all take more notice of them in future.

'Okay Bertrand, I get the message'

As I rummaged around in the kitchen one afternoon, Henri and Annette drove up. Wiping my hands, I filled the kettle and shouted to Diane. Opening the door, I found our lecherous little friend stooped over our rose beds. *'Très beau,'* he said; admiring the roses, and Diane who'd appeared behind me. Rolling her eyes, the long suffering Annette pushed him through the doorway.

Seated with coffee, pleasantries were then laboured through. While enquiring about their sons who both worked at the mushroom *cave*, a pained look appeared on their faces. Jacques and Jean were burly lads, both married with kids and living nearby. Though not the sharpest tools in the box, they were nice guys; hard working but notoriously accident prone.

On *this* occasion, Jacques had reversed a forklift onto the loading ramp, and toppled backwards over the edge. Then, two days later Jean had somehow managed to slash his throat, Henri said. What! When my jaw dropped in surprise, he waved these statements off as insignificant. So, adopting solemn expressions we commiserated with them. Throughout this tale of woe however, he kept pointing at me and gesticulating. Hardly understanding a damned word he was saying, I just replied '*Ah oui*,' and nodded sagely.

When Bertrand and Véronique visited later, they said Henri had been asking me to ring the *cave*. They needed cover while the boys were off sick. Could this be my way into the French workplace? However, after he'd rung the office, my hopes were dashed when François said both 'casualties' were returning to work the next day. Apparently they thought it better to go back fit or not, as both accidents had been avoidable. They were scared of losing their jobs due to previous incidents; and jobs around here were as hard to find as rocking horse droppings.

He said they'd keep an eye on the situation though, as things could change; however, it was doubtful. Damn! We could have used the money.

To top off the day, Diane had heard about our unwanted visitors; and spotting a grey Renault 19 parked on our drive later, she stormed out to get a better look. At that it sped away; but not before she spotted its two hulking occupants. Talking it over later, we decided to leave a light on at night.

The next morning though; after waking at every little noise during the night we were exhausted. Deciding that we were over-reacting, we drove to Saumur seeking white goods again.

*This* time, we entered *Intermarché* with measurements at hand; and soon we'd bought a washing machine, freezer, oven and hob, at a seventy euro saving on *Leclerc's* prices. Diane, the ruthless haggler squeezed the poor sales assistant dry, and in a last ditch attempt to get rid of her, he threw in tap units and fittings *gratuit* – along with a free Friday delivery. Excellent, I couldn't wait to get started.

# Chapter 19

## Welcome to hell

That evening there was a knock at the door. Opening it I found a smiling Véronique. But when I invited her in she politely refused. She was delivering an invitation to the mushroom *cave*. Could I meet the supervisor Christine at nine am the next morning? She'd give me a tour of the operation, as Armand the owner was on vacation. As it seemed Véronique had spoken for me, I thanked her very much; assuring her I'd be there spot on nine. To have all my wits about me, I had a hot soak, a meal and a wine-free evening, before going to bed early.

Unfortunately, being keyed up I had a restless night. However I entered the *cave's* work-yard at eight fifty five; and lo and behold, Henri and his dog just happened to be passing by as I arrived. (A coincidence do you think?) Wishing me '*Bonne chance!*' he walked on.

Knocking on the office door bang on nine, I was welcomed by a petite young woman with a piercing stare and firm handshake. Introducing herself as Christine, she apologised for her poor English, whilst pouring coffee from a percolator. She then gave me a run-down of the business and their customer base. With our chat ended, we drained our coffee cups then clattered down the iron staircase; stopping to let a fork-lift pass.

Crossing the yard, we headed towards a gaping hole in the cliff face. Totally out of my comfort zone, I didn't know what to expect. Entering the *cave's* mouth we turned a bend, leaving the sunlight behind us. As the temperature dropped sharply in the gloom, I saw a tunnel strung with service lights stretching ahead into the distance. In places its walls were dripping with moisture. On the right about ten metres ahead was a small office hewn out of the tunnel wall. 'Before going further, you must sign the visitor's book,' said Christine, before giving me a brief safety talk. I was then issued with a blue denim cap, and a clip-on head-lamp powered by a belt-hung battery pack. (What, no hard hat?) Prior to moving off, I was told always check that the battery is fully charged before entering the tunnels.

She then set off; with me following closely, stooping in places to avoid hitting my head on the low ceiling. Being quite petite, she strode off confidently along the main tunnel. Following closely behind her, I was stunned when it opened out into a cathedral-like chamber with a vaulted ceiling. The main tunnel continued ahead like an artery, with secondary tunnels branching off it at intervals. To the left of us, two huge double doors were bolted into the rock, each daubed with large numbers. She pointed to the first of them. 'We work chamber fourteen this morning. Come, follow me, but be careful at all times. From now we must use our lamps.'

Entering the inky blackness, our lamp beams danced crazily along the walls. But apart from our hollow footfalls, the only sound was dripping water. After walking for ages and making numerous twists and turns, echoing voices and revving engines could be heard up ahead. As we approached the voices grew louder; the darkness pierced by the lamps of a team of workers. Nearing them, I saw two girls leaning over a large metal tray. Stacked two high along the walls like bunk beds, these trays, or beds contained a peat like mulch studded with gleaming mushrooms. As Christine introduced the female team, they broke off to offer a ragged '*Bonjour!*'

Nodding discreetly, I acknowledged Véronique waving hesitantly at the rear. Not stopping for a second the girls picked the trays clean, filling plastic baskets with button mushrooms. They then inserted a marker bearing their work number into them. Christine said they began at seven am after being designated a tunnel. Then walking to the far end, they'd work back through the galleries and side tunnels until the noon break. Returning at one thirty pm, they'd continue until they reached the main gallery. Apart from lunch, no other breaks were taken or expected.

Leaving the girls to it we returned to the main tunnel; the roar of engines and the smell of diesel fumes increasing as we drew nearer. The noise resonating throughout the tunnels came from small tractors, rushing pallets of mushrooms to the weigh-station for delivery to the end user.

Back at the surface we crossed the work-yard, where I was shown another arm of the business. In a large corrugated building, a production line was being serviced by a massive forklift, delivering a stack of six trays of mushrooms to the rear of a conveyor belt. Selected automatically, they were tipped one after another onto the belt. A worker then raked the upturned trays; and as the contents moved along, spores and mulch fell through 'riddles.' The remaining mushrooms passed under water jets, emerging ivory white and gleaming. While the belt agitated them, they swept around a bend. Here, two grim-faced guys waited in silent resignation as the mound bore down on them.

We arrived as the run started; and once underway the process was relentless; mushrooms pouring non-stop into baskets fed to the two guys by a young girl. Filled at breakneck speed by these loaders, they were stacked on a metal pallet nine boxes high by four across and six along, one every couple of seconds. 'The boxes must interlock correctly,' said Christine, 'If they are not, they can fall over when the *palette* is moved, spilling *champignons* everywhere.

If all went well, a waiting fork lift would roar in and uplift the full pallet, enabling one of the two guys to replace it with an empty one. This of course left the other guy trying to cope alone, often being overwhelmed by produce spewing across the floor. 'When this occurs; the boss he is not happy,' said Christine sternly.

125

There was a red button to press in an emergency, she said. However I couldn't imagine anyone wanting to be the one to press it. Oh boy, I thought, *this* could be fun. I finished the tour a thoughtful and much wiser man.

Seated back in the main office, Christine asked for my thoughts on the visit. Picking my way carefully through a minefield of 'Franglais,' I tried to appear positive, eager to begin work *'tout suite.'* However, Christine, in her blunt no-nonsense manner brought me sharply back to earth. 'The boss, he thinks you may be too old to keep up. If he employs you I will very soon see.'

She then told me, Maurice's brother-in-law had been given a trial. He didn't last a full shift. 'He does not invite hot water,' had been Armand's comment.

No, I didn't understand either. Maybe it meant he couldn't even be trusted to boil water. Who knows? But whatever it meant, it didn't sound like a compliment.

After saying goodbye, I walked back to the surface feeling deflated. Emerging gratefully into incandescent sunlight, I gulped in sweet fresh air, wondering how to explain it all to Diane without appearing negative.

Back home again, I picked up the kettle. 'Don't bother,' Diane said, 'you'll have to go back again.'

Apparently a letter to the *cave* had been miss-delivered to us, and she'd opened it in error. 'Can't it wait?' I asked.

'Well there's a cheque in there for almost four thousand euros. What do *you* think?'

Sighing, I trudged back to the office, where I caught the *secrétaire*. She was very grateful for the 'special delivery,' which couldn't do me any harm if I *did* get the job.

Home again I gave Diane a potted version of the tour. Then deep in thought, I mixed cement and attacked the outside wall, until the heat drove me indoors. Finding Diane making chutney in the kitchen, I helped her de-stone plums, both of us subdued.

At six pm I nipped over to Le Lavendu. Whilst updating Bertrand and Véronique on my tour, I voiced my misgivings.

Trying to be tactful, they said, yes I was older than all the other workers. But the guy I'd be replacing was about my age, and *he'd* managed the job for ten years so I should be okay. True, I thought, but he'd started out ten years younger than me.

I'd made my decision though. I had no choice, we needed the money. I told them I appreciated their vouching for me, and would happily be interviewed after Armand's vacation. If offered the job, I'd take it and make the best of it. I returned to Diane with my mind clear, and we sat down to our meal.

While we were clearing the table afterwards Bertrand appeared at the French windows. Following closely behind him, François carried what looked like a metal detector. Puffed up with pride, he explained that his work experience involved locating pipes. This was the machine he used, and he'd been allowed to take it home for practice. He could locate our pipes, stop-cocks and valves, then we could map them. Brilliant! The water pressure had dropped lately, as had the level in the well, so it made sense to check it out.

Wasting no time we set off, machine beeping. We found some hidden valves which François checked enthusiastically; then near the bottom of the field, we discovered one beside the storm drain. When François opened it the stench was vile. Nevertheless he bled the system, saying it was the first time on record since 1997. We only found two leaks, but I suppose every little helps in a drought. Moreover, François was ridiculously happy, solving this drain on the local water reserves with his scientific instrument.

Heading back on a high, Bertrand asked about the power cable that supplied the *mouton* shed and *cave*. I'd checked it out from switch room to sockets and it was dead. Puzzled, he asked if he could take a look. Confirming my findings, he suggested by-passing the cable, and running a new cable through an existing water pipe. Then I could re-connect it to the main fuse board. Water and electricity – I don't think so, insulated or not.

# Chapter 20

## Fêtes and fiestas

Friday the sixth of August heralded the start of *La Fête* in our *commune*. And as the whole area began to unwind after harvesting, each village mounted its own flower pageant.

On the Saturday morning, villages which were closed off to traffic welcomed lines of tractors pulling decorated floats. These floral masterpieces were crammed with excited children, waving and scattering flower petals as they passed by. Proud parents cheered enthusiastically, as the parade trundled through streets lined with sideshows and produce stalls. Celebrating this highlight in the community's social calendar, they vied with each other to produce the finest local show; with prizes being awarded for best float. But the most import aspect was, everyone got to let off steam.

We'd planned taking in some of these events; beginning with Château-la-Vallière's, which also had a large *brocante*. But first there was unfinished business to attend to.

The saga of the kitchen goods was nearing its conclusion. The delivery, which was due at ten am, eventually arrived at twelve-thirty pm. No worse than the UK then; and at least they got the day right.

Diane had agreed to wait in for the driver, while I shot off to the agency. Jane's renovations were complete; and with her house registered for letting she suggested we view it. However, she was out with clients so I arranged to return later. After calling into a *boulangerie* though, I decided to swing by her place to check it out. Devious maybe, but when *we* began renting she'd be our competition. All's fair in love and war, they say.

When I arrived, I found the house sited near a busy road and some derelict industrial buildings. It had hardly any *terroire,* or land, and her pool was small, with no terrace or garden furniture to enhance it.

Returning home, I told Diane what I'd seen. 'Why don't I check out her web-site,' she suggested.

Her web-page showed small, sparsely furnished rooms, a basic bathroom and kitchen, and the cramped outside area.

'No wonder she said our place would let easily,' she mused. 'And look what she's asking for a week in high season. 'No chance.'

Having checked her booking page though, we found it inked in solidly for the next three months.

Meeting Jane at the office later, we gleaned lots of interesting information. Of course we didn't mention my spying mission, or our on-line investigation. Actually she was quite open about it all, saying there was precious little holiday accommodation hereabouts, therefore enough business for us both. She was a really smart cookie. As a fluid French speaker with experience in property sales and rental, she had information and contacts unavailable to us. Yet everything we needed to know she shared readily. English TV and satellite installation, faster internet service, you name it. She was actually a really nice girl, and totally honest about what she offered. She'd done her research, and with no competition she had a captive market. Working on a shoe-string budget, she'd offered the best value she could. With us having lots more to offer, *we* should have no problem letting when our renovations were complete.

We left feeling revitalized, though guilt-ridden about our undercover tactics. But being realistic, we knew Jane had assessed us as future competition a long time ago.

After leaving Jane, Diane dropped me off home before going on to La Flèche. With her gone for a while I began sorting out the kitchen. As most of our electrical items were ex-UK, they needed E.U plugs or adaptors. And though our new French oven was electric, the hob was gas; so there was work to be done. Connecting up the gas hob was simple enough on paper; however, once assembled it refused to ignite. This was a bummer, as I'd re-set the jets from mains to bottled butane as per the manual.

On her return Diane found me fuming. Calming me down, she cast a fresh eye over the instructions. 'Could the factory settings have been mixed up?' she suggested.

And of course they had. Luckily the *oven* wasn't gas, or she might have found me with my head in it when she walked in.

The cooker debacle was soon forgotten though, when the peace was shattered by a horrendous squawking from next door. Concerned at the noise we dashed over; finding Bertrand and Véronique scuttling crab-like around the garden, trying to catch three large cockerels. But whatever they tried, they couldn't corner them. Bumping into each other and cursing in French, both they and the birds were becoming increasingly agitated. We could only watch gleefully as the scenario unfolded.

Sadly, (and much too soon for us) Bertrand brought the firago to a close. Utilizing two sheets of plywood, he shepherded the distressed birds into a corner. Then while Véronique took over the boards, he jumped over, grabbed the birds one by one, and wrestled them into a large box. He said they were for his parents; one for Christmas, the other unhappy duo destined for their freezer.

And *that* was when Diane made her mistake. My heart plummeted, when I heard her say we'd just installed our new washing machine. Of course Bertrand asked *how* we'd installed it. Then we all had to troop over to Le Ferronnerie, to see why it needed both hot and cold water feeds as per the instructions. According to him, the hot feed is blanked off in France. The resulting discussion obviously required a bottle of *rosé* to sharpen the mind; and of course a snack was considered mandatory. Then like most teenage boys, that was when François made his appearance.

After enquiring if he could join us he went to the kitchen; and while filling a plate, he peered inquisitively into a bowl.

'What is this?' He asked.

Diane had been baking earlier, and the bowl he was pointing to held molasses. She explained the recipe she'd followed, and the ingredients used. At first he frowned; then with his usual naivety, he came out with yet another classic.

'Ah yes! In France we feed pigs on this.'

At eight am on Château-la-Vallière's *fête* day it was already twenty-seven C. As I entered the kitchen barefooted, I stepped into a pool of water. 'Aw bloody hell,' I shouted.

'What's up?' said Diane, who then spotted the water. It was leaking from the brand new freezer, whose door we'd reversed last night. The simple process (in the handbook anyway) allowed us to open the fridge away from the kitchen door. But now the door seal was leaking. The best laid plans of mice and men eh? Shrugging, I mopped the floor then switched the damned thing off. There was little in it to spoil, so it could wait until we got back. We had a *fête* to attend.

Heading off a second time was more successful. Though by then, climbing into the car was like a Christmas turkey being slid into a pre-heated oven.

After a hot, sticky drive, we eventually found the show-ground. The site was heaving with attractions, including a beer tent and hog roast. Running along one edge of the field was a large *brocante*. And though we usually found something to buy, these stalls predominately sold children's clothing and toys. Nevertheless, we spent an enjoyable morning absorbing the uniquely French atmosphere; before heading back home to the joys of floor mopping; before reversing the freezer door again.

Sunday started badly, and early drizzle grew into a torrential downpour. But we'd promised ourselves we'd patronise

Bourgueil on their second *fête* day. Saturday's event had been a washout; but with a better forecast promised for the afternoon, and a clear evening for the *son-et-lumière*, or sound and light show, we decided to go for it.

Leaving Diane cooking breakfast, I thought I'd make a quick phone call first. And of course, that was when the gas chose to run out. With no spare cylinder at that time, I tried connecting a spare English bottle we'd brought with us. It didn't work of course, but it was worth a try.

Off I went to *Intermarché's* garage with the empty bottle. On arrival I found the pay-kiosk closed. No gas until Monday then! No sweat, we had alternatives – the microwave or the fire.

Breakfast was interesting at best, and we arrived at Bourgeil around nine am, just in time for the ploughing competition. Normally contested between tractor teams, this *fête* was different. Everything had a medieval theme. The ploughs in this contest were pulled by yoked oxen. Those bad boys were huge hump-backed beasts; placid on the surface, but possessing huge wickedly curved horns. And boy, they could pull.

By then the rain had stopped, and people were emerging from beer and food tents to spur on their favourites. After casting our vote with the judges we circulated; checking out wrought ironwork, weaving, pottery-making, and pole-wood-turning. And let's not forget the dedicated exponents of bees wax modelling. Favourite with the kids though were the archery butts; made evident by the long queue to have a go. All the skills shown were demonstrated with dedication and enthusiasm, by artisans dressed in medieval costume. My favourites – though not medieval, were the steam-powered threshing machine, and a 'Heath Robinson' creation that trundled along picking up and pulping apples for cider making.

Caught up in this heady atmosphere, the crowds were cunningly channelled towards a communal area, where tables and benches surrounded a huge bread oven. Once seated, it was almost impossible not to linger. In a salivating trance, your senses were battered not only by various breads, but by aromas from large *chaudrons* containing various *ragouts*. On a stall next to them, skewered chickens, roasted meats, and *saucisons* of all shapes and sizes sizzled. With your eyes streaming from the smoke, and your mouth watering at the aroma of cooked meats, it was a brave man who dared enquire about vegetarian options. We walked around twice, then left for pastures new.

Plumping for a relaxing drive, we meandered through deserted towns and villages; windows wound down and hair blowing in the breeze. As the sun reached its zenith in a powder blue sky, we arrived at La Touraint's lakeside beach. This man-made stretch of sand circled the lake like a golden necklace, fronting a stand of pine trees shading car parks and picnic areas. As a treat for both children *and* adults, a small-gauge steam train chuffed around the area, stopping at 'The *Auberge le Lac's* restaurant and ice cream parlour on its regular circuits. Being British, we naturally travel everywhere equipped for all four seasons. Gauging the weather, we moved damp umbrellas to one side of the boot. Then out came the swim-wear. Once changed in the communal facilities, it was time for a cooling dip, followed by an unexpected spot of sun-bathing. Who'd have thought it, after such a dismal start to the day?

We arrived home as the sun was setting; sunburned and content, but in desperate need of a shower. Pulling up we spotted François next door. Sat astride their ride-on mower, he was 'manicuring' the grass around the duck-pond. Waving to us, he shouted glumly, 'This is not good, we must have more rain.'

Only two weeks before he was wringing his hands, worried about us having too *much* rain. It would cause massive problems for the upcoming harvest, he'd moaned. That's farmers for you. But actually he was right to worry. When *would* we get some rain?

# Chapter 21

## Losing the will to live

I'm sure we've all heard the saying two steps forward one step back. It applies to us all sometime or another. Well this was one of those times. We awoke to torrential rain – thanks François! Five centimetres had fallen since the previous afternoon, with a lot more due according to Meteo's forecast. Our mood plummeted even further when Jorge pulled up in his mud-splattered van. He emerged clutching an official looking brown envelope, which invariably contained bad news. The rain sodden letter was from our English bank, stating that a cheque we'd promised them hadn't arrived. This was the second one we'd issued; the first having vanished somewhere between France and England. We'd cancelled that one, then sent another by French Special Delivery. That was over a week ago, and now *that* hadn't arrived either. I mean, what the hell do you pay the extra charge for? This meant a lost morning, trying to untangle the sorry mess by phone.

A really hacked off Diane handled the call this time, becoming progressively more agitated by the minute. I kept well away. I had my own problems. The white goods weren't fitting properly. All that planning; measuring twice and cutting once; where did we go wrong? Frustrated, I ended up planing down the unit to take the oven, then feeding the cable through. As I struggled to plumb in the washer, Diane was rapidly losing the plot trying to locate the cheque.

Taking time out, she adjourned to the *cave* to check on her preserves. AAGH! Mice had nibbled the tops off most of her jars, ruining the hard won contents.

Incidentally, we learned that our washing machine *did* only need one filler pipe as Bertrand said. In France the hot water pipe fitting is blanked off. Never mind, I thought, let's just get it installed and finish the damned kitchen. Hah! Life should be that easy. I ended up lying squeezed behind the units, feeding wiring and hoses by touch through a ridiculously restricted space. By then we'd both lost the will to live.

Dropping everything, we drove to Le Lude to find gas bottle connections and a regulator, but mainly to chill out. However, we still needed to trace the missing cheque. So when we returned, Diane took a deep breath and picked up the phone.

'I don't flaming believe this,' she said minutes later, shaking the phone murderously.

'What's wrong *now*?' I asked, dropping a spanner and coming in from the kitchen.

'What's *wrong*? I've been transferred to a call centre in Mumbai, that's what's wrong. Can this day get any worse?'

Eventually she calmed down – that is until she'd been kept on hold for ages and transferred four times. She finally snapped completely, after a guy who insisted he was in Manchester despite Indian street noises in the background, said no-one in his office had heard of the bank clearing house she'd been told to ask for. Hands up anyone who thinks call centres *anywhere* abroad are the way forward.

I thought it best if *I* made the next call to *La Poste!* When I got through, I spoke to a very helpful French lady, which was unique in itself. She said the problem might *just* lie with the erratic French postal service. She'd check into it for us, as 'special delivery,' timed to arrive the next day, could actually take more than a week. Hold on there! Here was a French person actually admitting to imperfections in the French system. We sat down and had a strong coffee to treat the shock;

stunned that someone was actually trying to sort out our problem for us.

But then it was *my* turn. The washing machine wouldn't fit under the worktop now. Right, what were the alternatives? Well, I could take off the moulded top cover, or I could remove the rubber feet, which seemed the most sensible option. It was a no-brainer then. Ten minutes later the feet were off; but then it wouldn't slide across the floor. An exasperated Diane said, 'Right, move out of the way. I've had enough of this.'

Sitting down on the tiled floor, she pushed firmly against the machine with her feet. Wisely, it slid into place.

After quickly coupling up hoses and electrics, I crossed my fingers as Diane pressed the button. 'Whoosh,' water squirted everywhere – and that was when François arrived.

Examining the situation, he sucked on his teeth. 'I see the problem,' he said. 'It is the fault of Monsieur Renard. He has cut the exit pipe too short.'

By saving a few cents on piping, the tight-fisted old bugger had almost caused a flood. Cursing the late Monsieur soundly, I fitted a new piece of pipe; feeding it into a 25 litre drum first to test the system. With baited breath I switched on. Eureka! Switching off again, I coupled the pipe to the washer. We were in business. With François translating the French symbols and programmes, powder, softener and clothes were inserted. Pressing a button the panel lit up, water gurgled, and our first wash was under way. Waving cheerfully he left us to it.

Leaving the washer humming away busily, we drove to *Intermarché*, where we bought a couple of bottles of wine to soothe our shattered nerves. While queuing at the check-out though, my peripheral vision picked up a movement to my right. Stood at the next till was our Nemesis Madame Renard. Comfortable in her dry new home, she smiled at me magnanimously, the old witch. Steering Diane through the checkout before *she* spotted her, I avoided carnage. And more importantly, our wine transfusion made it safely out to the car.

Mission accomplished we set off for home; just as a sudden shower began drumming off the car roof.

'Isn't this flaming typical?' Diane sighed. 'Now that I've actually *got* some washing to hang out, it's raining.' The wipers swiped frenetically at the screen, as if in sympathy.

Arriving home in a downpour we ran laughing into the house. Heading into the lounge I lit the fire, as we were both drenched and getting colder by the minute.

'Oh God, I don't believe this,' I heard from the downstairs bedroom; followed by Diane emerging in fresh dry clothes.

'What's up?'

'The rain's leaking through the bedroom ceiling, and running down the light fitting. What do we do?'

'Well, I'm still soaking wet, so I'll run out to the boiler-room and turn off the electricity. But first, why don't you put a bucket under the leak then light some candles. Next; pour out two huge glasses of wine while I build up the fire. I mean, enough's enough, right?'

Though we had to empty the bucket twice overnight, the ceiling finally stopped leaking in the early hours. In fact things had improved immeasurably when François called around at lunch-time. He'd arrived to tell me Armand had returned from vacation, and asked if I'd call in on Thursday at eight am.

'Can my muzzaire take back your reply?'

I said I'd be there. And turning to leave, he suggested ploughing the field, as it would be easier after the rain. It made sense of course, so I agreed.

Amid a cloud of black smoke, Bertrand pulled up on the tractor later. Behind him, François sat high above the plough. Jumping off, Bertrand asked, '*Ca va?*'

I said I was okay, but suffering from lack of sleep due to the roof leak. Shrugging, he said, old houses often leak, but he'd pop over sometime to conduct an 'inspection.' Then off they trundled to the field.

Two days later, I received a call from Eddie. I'd forgotten about him, thinking that he and his family had returned home. It transpired they'd had *three* weeks holiday, and he wondered if they could stop over on Thursday to break the journey home. He began making excuses for not contacting me after the last fiasco. However, it was pointless dwelling on what he should have done; life's too short. I just said, 'Yeh, that'll be fine. When will you get here?'

He said they were going to an adventure park first with the kids. Would seven pm be okay? I said yes, but I wasn't happy. Their initial invitation had been to an afternoon BBQ; a relaxing time in the garden for us all. We'd have had time to catch up while the kids explored. And Diane had also prepared rooms in case they wanted to sleep over. Now I know the previous debacle wasn't entirely their fault; but since then the situation had changed. I had a job interview on the morning of the proposed visit. Then to show the place at its best, the house and gardens would need sprucing up, and the Barbie sorting out; and all for what seemed like an afterthought on their part. To cap it off, he said they'd need an early night, as they had a long drive the next day. Maybe they had no option, but it felt like we were being used. Then, as a final body-blow, he casually mentioned that they were all vegetarians!

There was *one* good bit of news though. When Diane rang the UK bank, they said the cheque had arrived. Thank God for that. However, to keep our feet firmly on the ground, Jorge delivered a hefty phone bill at lunch-time.

Wednesday saw us headed out to Saumur. With our visitors arriving the next day, we did food shopping at *Aldimarché* and *Leclerc*, after scouring *Emmaus*, where we bagged six crystal sorbet bowls and a chandelier for a measly twenty-three euros.

As we left the sun was fierce, so we opened all the car's windows. And with the seat panels close to melting, we threw an old blanket across them to prevent third degree burns to the 'Gluteus Maximus.'

Entering the store after the blistering heat of the car park was a massive shock; hitting a wall of ice cold air as we crossed the threshold. Exquisite though it was however, the A/C couldn't mask the overpowering smell of fish. Now don't get me wrong. Everything looked fresh on the counters, and the range was formidable. Plus, with it being French, half of it was still alive, crawling over mini Matterhorn's of crushed ice. But the thing is, I've heard TV chefs say fresh fish shouldn't smell fishy, it should smell of the sea. Or are 'they' wrong?

Anyway, shopping done it was back to the overheated Peugeot. Gasping for air, we endured a frustrating crawl through Saumur's traffic snarl up; hoping to get everything home before it spoiled.

Safely home chilled drinks took precedence. While I poured them Diane began unpacking, returning soon after carrying huge fruit cocktails. What a star!

In the wee small hours I was shaken awake by Diane. She was convinced she'd heard footsteps outside. Maybe it was Jacques the giant and his mate Igor, calling by for a friendly chat. Having experienced some strange situations in the past, I kept a cut down pick-axe handle for such emergencies, and holding it firmly, I tip-toed into the lounge. After searching all the rooms from top to bottom, I checked outside – my loyal back-up following closely hefting a large coal shovel. Thankfully there was nothing. Declaring the all clear we made a cuppa, as understandably we were wide-awake by then. Leaving a security light on I packed Diane off to bed, while just in case, I spent the rest of the night on the settee with the pick-axe handle for company.

I gave up on sleep at five forty am; and after showering in an attempt at livening myself up, I had breakfast and dressed. At seven forty-five am I set off for my job interview bright-eyed and bushy tailed – Yeah right!

# Chapter 22

## Hello and goodbye – again

At last it was my interview. Striding into his office at seven-fifty five, I found Armand at his desk, his vacation a fading memory. Inviting me to sit he poured coffee; talk of his holiday and our house renovation breaking the ice. Then we got down to business. Knowing I'd been given the grand tour, he asked what I thought of the set-up. Of course I said everything was fine and I wanted the job, which seemed to please him. However, he voiced concerns regarding my age and command of the French language, saying it might cause problems within his workforce. He gazed steadily at me for a few seconds, tapping his pen on the desk; then he spun his chair around towards the window. For a while he sat deep in thought, staring at the yard below. Then swivelling back he bounced to his feet.

'Okay we'll leave it there,' he said. 'Let me think it over, and I'll ring you tomorrow.'

We shook hands, I said goodbye and left, frustrated at having no information for Diane or my neighbours. Walking back, I rewound the interview in my mind; then reaching the head of the drive my senses registered an, 'Ah Bisto' moment. The smell of grilled bacon hit me. I'd timed it perfectly.

Over a late breakfast with Diane I described the interview; going over everything in detail. In reply, she said our already hectic day had just moved up a gear. We'd forgotten an appointment with Jane, who was driving us to Noyant *Mairie's* office to check out French employment laws. She'd said that under revised E.U. rules, *Carte Séjours,* or work permits were no longer required. But we reckoned her fluent French would qualify the situation, and picking her brains on the journey would be an added bonus.

At the *Mairie's* office, they rubber stamped her story, and after saying goodbye she dashed back to the agency, promising to catch up sometime soon. We then drove home quickly to prepare for our visitors.

While playing catch up an hour later we heard beep, beep! I groaned as a familiar Renault pulled up outside. Henri and Annette had made an impromptu visit. Climbing stiffly out of the car, Henri tottered unsteadily towards Diane. Arthritis or *eau de vie* – who knew? Doffing his cap, he made to kiss her cheek, oblivious to Annette's struggles as she tried to get out of the car. He was halfway through a beer when she finally tottered in, looking fit to kill.

The reason for their visit of course, was to find out how my interview went. It was another sign of the bush telegraph in action. During our 'conversation,' I thought he said Armand had married into his family. That would explain the leniency towards Jacques and Jean. I didn't enquire too closely though. It was safer to just listen and agree. He appeared to be hinting that he'd spoken for me regarding the job; so I thanked him, hoping I'd understood him correctly.

In the yawning hiatus that followed, the conversation suddenly veered towards the weather; obligatory when talking to the British *anywhere*. Watching CNN news at breakfast, they'd seen 90 millimetres of rainfall in England over the past 24 hours. Footage showed widespread flooding and damage. Was this true Annette asked? Having been updated by family, I confirmed it. They were amazed. This region had 'endured' 30 millimetres over the past four days, he said; which to him was a monsoon of biblical proportions. Until CNN enlightened him, he'd thought God had visited a catastrophe on the poor long suffering French exclusively.

After ten exhausting minutes, spent mining every nugget from our French repertoire, Henri glanced at his watch. Then slapping the table, he said, '*Bien!*' and stood up. Apparently the visit was over. Sneaking three kisses from Diane, he shook my hand vigorously. Then saying '*Au revoir,*' he headed out to the car, waving as he crossed the drive. Her face puce with anger, Annette stood up painfully. Rolling her eyes, she whispered, '*Au revoir*' in a choked voice, exchanged kisses with us and followed him. Who said the age of chivalry was dead eh?

As the Renault vanished down the drive, Diane continued with her housework. Meanwhile, I set up the BBQ, before cleaning the patio table and chairs. By then, the heat that'd been building all morning was furnace like, burning through the soles of my flip-flops. But as I worked on the patio in stifling humidity, I noticed cloud building up in hazy blue sky. Glancing behind me, I noticed an ominous black rain-cloud headed our way. Oh great! Never mind, it could pass us by, I thought, positioning the parasol over the garden table.

Within minutes though, a blast of cold air hit me. Whistling across the garden, it overturned plastic chairs and shook the parasol. Rattling the shutters, a series of mini-whirlwinds scattered plant-pots. Soon the whole valley was thrown into shadow; the sky turning slate-grey and threatening. Piercing the cloud, a crackle of lightning was followed almost immediately by the crash of thunder. Then, as if orchestrated, a torrent of rain sheeted down, engulfing the area and making it impossible to see more than a few metres in any direction. From the safety of our kitchen sanctuary, we watched the drama unfold.

Dramatic though it was however, it was gone in five minutes. The rain-clouds passed, the sun re-emerged; and before long steam was rising from the grass. Out we dashed to dry off the furniture.

After that it was plain sailing; and before long we were relaxing on loungers, everything set up ready to go. Begging to be lit, the BBQ waited patiently. Fuelled by charcoal, it was topped off with pine cones to add extra aroma and flavour.

With the rain gone, the stifling air had been replaced by the tang of ozone, and the scent from nearby lavender beds.

With everything back to normal, Diane nipped to Le Lude for some last minute essentials. She'd just returned when the phone rang. It was Eddie's wife Sandra on her cell-phone; asking for directions while Eddie cursed vigorously in the background. As they were using satnav I'd been expecting a call; as so far, none of the providers had helped anyone find us. She apologized for arriving early, due to their ruined adventure park visit.

'Are you sure it's okay that we're early?' she asked.

'Yes of course,' I said, giving her explicit directions.


Thirty minutes later, a grey Peugeot 206 shot past the drive; too far away for the occupants to see our frantic waving. However, its brake-lights flared before the next bend; and reversing lights glowing, it whined its way back. Soon it rounded the head of the drive, and with a wrench on the hand-brake they parked opposite the kitchen door – on my freshly cut strip of lawn.

'Hey mate, ow'yer doin?' Eddie shouted, climbing out and whipping off his Raybans. 'Great place yer've got ere. Can Ah use yer toilet? Ah'm absolutely bustin.'

After quickly introducing me to Sandra, he dashed off. She then pushed forward their two kids Bella and Mark, who shyly said hallo. Introductions concluded, they carried their luggage to their rooms. Then Diane offered cold drinks.

'Ooh yes please,' said the kids.

'Tah, Ah could murder a cuppa,' said the relieved Eddie entering the kitchen 'Ah'm flamin parched.'

As we all got to know each other, conversation switched from their holiday to updates on my old workplace. Afterwards of course, there was the inevitable conducted tour; with lots of ooing and aahing about the interior layout. However Bella was completely mystified. She thought it was a hotel.

In a brief lull, I slipped out to light the Barbie. And engrossed in my 'ignition procedure,' I was joined by Eddie, a beer clutched firmly in his fist.

'Well mate, Ah've gotta and it ter yer. When yer left work to come down ere, everybody thought yer were mad, and yer'd fall flat on yer arse. Wait till Ah show everybody me photos of this place. They'll be right pissed off,' he said, in his Teeside patois; his hand patting my shoulder. Interrupting this embarrassing display of male bonding, the ladies joined us. Chattering away like old friends, they carried out trays for the veggie Barbie.

Before long the air was redolent with spices and wood-smoke. But the kids, restless after their long journey, couldn't be contained. Dashing off exploring, they grazed from the table when not running around. We forgave them, as they were in seventh heaven playing hide and seek; chasing bewildered lizards, and ... just being kids really. At one point, totally wound up, they brought grasshoppers and a praying mantis to show us. And after clearing the table we left them watching a video – the kids that is, not the insects!

Strolling around the lawns we pointed out various projects, including the spot we'd carved out for the swimming pool and terrace. By then the sun was a fiery red ball sinking behind the hillside; shadows stealing swiftly across the garden. Above all it was incredibly quiet; the silence hanging in the still air. That is, until Eddie shattered it with. 'Are yer sure yer'd not rather be back in the North-East?

'Are you completely mad?' Sandra quipped; clipping him gently around the ear. We all laughed; but the moment had passed, so we made our way indoors.

'Oh Ah forgot,' Eddie said, 'Is there anywhere Sandra could go for a run before breakfast tomorrer? We've all got bikes on the car rack, so Ah'l just follow behind er on mine – if yer wouldn't mind looking after the kids for us, like.'

Leaving the ladies to finish the washing up, I directed Eddie as he drove around the fields, then back through the village. It was seven kilometres in total. 'Is that enough?' I asked.

'Aye, that'll be fine,' he said, as we pulled up at the house.

By eight pm, desperate to stay awake though they were, the kids had finally flaked out. We adults then retired indoors, dousing the candles and leaving a cloud of disappointed insects. Continuing our chat over more wine, we eventually crept off to our beds gone midnight.

It was Friday August the thirteenth, and I was up and about at six thirty am. Not being superstitious – but hedging my bets, I made a cuppa and read until nine, without a sign of joggers or cyclists anywhere. Then Diane appeared – coincidentally, just after I'd made more tea.

Our guests finally surfaced at 9-30, kitted out in Lycra and raring to go. Yawning mightily, the kids followed them down in their PJ's. With the kids settled watching cartoons, the athletic duo vanished down the drive; re-appearing later suitably sweaty; ready for a shower and full English breakfast.

When we were all ready, we set off in convoy to Noyant market; bustling, ablaze with colour, and fragrant in the hot morning sun. The kids were fascinated by the chicken man, who they adopted as their firm favourite. Though I'm not sure how benevolent the birds felt towards him, being squeezed into tiny cages, prodded and poked by all and sundry.

After strolling around immersed in rural French ambience, we called into the agency to meet Jane. Yes, they'd fallen in love with the idea of a property in France. Do we Brits ever learn? However she was out on business; and with the weather turning 'iffy,' our visit to La Flèche's lakeside beach was shelved. Sadly, the beach games the kids had planned for us had to be cancelled. (Phew!) With heavy hearts, we returned to the farm, so the family could pack for their homeward journey. Poor Bella was crying, saying she never wanted to leave.

With everything stowed in the car and lunch eaten, they were more stoical as we set off to La Flèche in convoy. Visiting *Gifi*, they were soon absorbed in buying last minute presents for family and friends. After decimating the shelves, the car boot was straining at the seams. However, pulling away manfully, they followed us to the *Route Le Mans*, the main artery to the motorway. Turning off at the intersection, they shouted and waved as they headed off to catch the ferry. And do you know what? We'd already begun missing them.

Obviously we'd some tidying to do, but that could wait. First we drove to *Brico* to check out materials; though work wasn't foremost on our minds. The last couple of days had taken its toll on us. Living in rural France had slowed down our body clocks; making us so laid back that having guests quickly tired us out. Visitors expected to party and be shown around, and who could blame them? They were on holiday. We did our best to entertain them, but we were constantly aware that we had an agenda to stick to, and it was too easy to get distracted.

A case in point was a *brocante* we saw advertised on a tatty wall poster in town. On it, Nogent looked like a really pretty village, so we made plans to find it. On the day of the event we ambled along empty roads, passing fields of sunflowers stood like soldiers on parade facing the sun. In other fields, stunning red poppies peeped out from waves of golden corn. It was all so rich and earthy, food for the soul. That is, until we were catapulted back to the 21$^{st}$ century with a bang. Entering the suburbs, we found them to be shabby and industrialized; with graffiti and tattered posters brutalizing grimy buildings.

We hadn't called at an ATM before setting off. We'd rashly presumed that the other was carrying enough cash. On arrival, we found we had a total of five euros between us. And though the small town had a bank, it seemingly had no ATM. Well that wasn't strictly true. They *had* one; we'd spotted it in the foyer through tinted glass. However, a sign on the door said the bank was closed for the weekend. Shuffling through jostling crowds, we looked longingly at the stalls, unable to buy a thing. We felt like kids pressed up against a sweetshop window, until we passed the bank on our return. That's when we saw someone approach the bank, and whoosh, the glass doors opened and he entered.

Speechless, we looked at each other. Then we trotted over quickly, in case we'd witnessed a mirage which might vanish at any moment. But no; we'd missed a sign on the door handle saying '*pour entrer poussez,*'or, for entry push, and an arrow pointing to a green button beside the door. Doh! The *bank* was closed; but the foyer was left open for ATM users. Sheepishly, we pushed the button as instructed then sneaked inside. Murmuring, '*Bonjour,*' to the guy using the machine, we tried to look nonchalant as we waited our turn.

The day then changed completely, as we sauntered around with a wad of euros. But awash with cash, the stalls seemed full of the usual crap. Hungry and thirsty we broke off for *frites* with mayonnaise and cold drinks. Then, languishing on a bench in the town square, we soaked up the sunshine.

Enjoying the buzz, we sat people watching; until we were distracted by a commotion. Curious, we wandered over to the source; joining a crowd surrounding a ring of hay bales in the town centre. Inside the ring stood four llamas, looking incredibly bored but infinitely patient; yellow teeth chewing contentedly. Each animal sported a number, different coloured racing silks and matching jockey's cap. They seemed set to race through the streets. But with or without riders, who knew? We didn't stop to find out. I mean, who thinks these things up?

Though intrigued by the race build-up and flagrant on course betting, the heat was just too oppressive. Plus, the flies from the llamas had become attached to us – literally. Itching furiously, we made our way back to the car, jumped in, and headed for the cool lakeside of La Touraint.

Picturesque and tranquil when we arrived, the setting would've normally provided the perfect afternoon; if it weren't for a cringe-worthy family of English holidaymakers who landed up nearby. Loud, obnoxious, and oblivious to anyone else, they reinforced the stereotype of Brits abroad. Stomping onto the beach, they were led by a red-faced slob of a husband and father. Leaving his wife to sort out the kids, he laid down his towel and clothing over a French girl's things while she was off swimming. Why I ask? When she emerged from the lake, she looked around puzzled. But, eventually spying her clothes peeping out, she politely asked him for them. In turn, he scowled at her with a look that could kill. Sometimes I really despair of my fellow man.

Otherwise it was a gorgeous afternoon, spent on a rug spread over the fine white sand under a blazing sun. With it being so perfect we nearly nodded off, so we decided we should call it a day. Without sun cream it was just asking for trouble.

Arriving home around six thirty pleasantly tired, I parked the car in the barn out of the sun. This was a big mistake, as nesting swifts took great delight in crapping all over it.

After taking turns under a cooling shower Chris rang, giving us a laugh with news from home. With the call ended, watching the same old videos didn't hold any appeal. Neither did guzzling wine. So we retired to our 'boudoir' with a good book each. Tomorrow is another day we agreed.

# Chapter 23

## Stranger than fiction

In the cool of early morning, I hand-mixed cement; then with my new balletic style of delivery, I began hurling it at the house-wall. Meanwhile, Diane was doing the 'house wifey' bit. (Oops, she hates me saying that.) Later, with the cementing finished I turned my attentions to the garden. In a well rehearsed manoeuvre, I blitzed the terrain. Resembling a no-man's land invaded by some mutant life force, it needed drastic action. On the plus side; although, our melon plant had also run riot, it'd produced two football- sized fruit under a canopy of large leaves. You win some, you lose some I guess!

Muttering to myself I waded into chest high weeds, wielding a long handled tool with a viciously curved blade. Possibly used on the battlefields at Agincourt, it was my star buy at a local *brocante*. Employing my 'Whirling Dervish' technique, I'd soon cleared a wide swathe. Encouraged, I prepared my second line of attack; spraying insect repellent on cultivated plants. Unfortunately, whilst tipping up the canister to read the manufactures instructions, I realized it was leaking. The contents had dribbled onto the 'fly' of my shorts. Not the flies it was meant for, I suspect.

I suggest this so-called repellent should be re-branded, as it actually *attracted* flies. I was surrounded by a cloud of tiny mites with burning stings. Those little buggers couldn't get enough of it.

Since I'd been forced to shower and change, Diane thought it a good time to hijack me. Driving into Le Lude we posted some letters; then, parked up in a side street, we strolled around town checking out *Immobilière's* windows. Meandering past the château, we crossed the river bridge to check out the camp-site. As its facilities were also open to the public, the pool and bar had become a hang-out for teenage Lotharios keen on meeting foreign girls – or boys. Who knows anymore?

Walking back to the car, a disturbance in a nearby apartment block caught our attention. Two little girls ran screaming into the street chased by a woman – hopefully their mother. As she led them back crying, a man climbed from a Renault Megane and followed them in. Shortly after we heard crashing and shouting. Next, the main doors crashed open, disgorging a stream of people, presumably tenants. Some looked decidedly shady, carrying items which looked to have been 'appropriated' during the disturbance. Scuffles and arguments then flared up on the pavement, which were quickly drowned out by the 'eeh aw' of approaching police sirens. Oh-oh, It was time to make our escape!

But embroiled in the drama, we'd left it too late. As we turned away from the melee two squad cars barrelled into the street, blue lights strobing. Skidding to a halt outside the tenement, the lead car disgorged armed officers who ran into the building. Colleagues from the second car then pushed back 'rubberneckers,' while trying to curtail the fracas and interview witnesses. This task was made harder by curious tenants from other buildings who'd wandered over to have a look. What *was* this – a re-make of *The French Connection* with us as extras? Where's Popeye Doyle when you need him? However, we couldn't wait for Gene Hackman to turn up. We needed to leave right then.

Unfortunately, being parked on a one way street, the only way out was to mount the kerb and squeeze past the squad cars. Hands on gun holsters, the police didn't seem too happy with this manoeuvre. Thankfully, our GB plate got us waved through, albeit angrily. Well, what a nice gentle stroll *that* turned out to be.

Back home sipping coffee, we conducted a post mortem of the afternoon's events and possible consequences. A bottle was then opened to help 'ze little grey cells,' and inevitably the night spiralled into a music filled haze. By two am, bed seemed a highly attractive proposition.

We arose shakily, unsettled after an overnight storm. At one point during the early hours, I glanced out of the window and thought I saw a torch flashing. I kept watch for a while, before deciding it must have been lightning flashes. But you never know right?

After a late breakfast, a young woman in a white van pulled up with a squeal – the van, not the woman. I opened the door to a hot looking young woman. (Another Freudian slip.) Wiping away perspiration from her brow, she introduced herself as Cecile, an agent selling kitchen equipment for a catalogue company. Now as a rule we discouraged callers, but she'd been referred by Annette, so we invited her in. Over coffee we discussed her job, telling her *we* were seeking work. She said a *pomme* farmer near Marcilly was recruiting workers for the upcoming *ramassage;* maybe we should try there.

When she left clutching a token order, we followed her directions. But forty kilometres later we hadn't seen any sign of an orchard. You wouldn't think it would be so difficult to spot, now would you?

We viewed the next few days through a veil of rain. Trapped indoors we prepped for painting, and we'd just covered everything in the lounge with dust-cloths when François arrived. His mission was to ask if they could visit that afternoon, as Bertrand had something to show me. Curiosity piqued, I said yes, and off he shot back to Charpentier H.Q with my answer.

At four pm, a hesitant knock on the window heralded their arrival. I'd just tidied up; so with us all settled the 'visiting ritual' began. First they presented us with some home-grown vegetables, which of course we praised highly. Then somehow a bottle of wine appeared already opened. (How *does* he do that?) Next, the real purpose of the visit was revealed.

Like a naughty child, Bertrand sneaked out a grainy old black and white photo. Smoothing it out, he pointed to a tall gawky figure with jug-like ears. '*Monsieur Renard,*' he said solemnly, '*A quinze ans*' at fifteen years. We all looked at each other; biting our lips and striving desperately not to laugh. But unable to contain it any longer, we all erupted hysterically.

When we'd calmed down Véronique changed the subject, saying she'd spoken with Armand, who said he hadn't forgotten me. But knowing him, he could call at any time and just expect me to attend for work the next morning.

François then pulled out a map, showing the location of the Marcilly *pomme* farm we'd looked for. According to him, we'd passed within half a kilometre of it. Really?

'Finally,' he announced dramatically, 'we must be at all times cautious from today. The gypsies have been seen by my fazzaire near our fields. This could be dangerous.'

Over the next few days a couple of problems arose. Just a couple, I hear you say! When I rang Michael, he mentioned Dylan's christening. He asked when we'd be returning, as Miranda needed to make plans. We'd actually suggested a date on our July visit, but they must have forgotten. And now, with a desperately needed job in the offing, I couldn't let him know immediately.

My second problem however was an *absolute hammer blow*. After a whole day spent treating ceiling beams against termites, my right shoulder had seized up. A hot soak and painkillers didn't help, as the shoulder muscle was frozen. The timing couldn't have been worse.

To add to our problems; the next afternoon a weather front materialized, with dark clouds rolling in out of nowhere. Following a terrific thunderclap, we were showered with marble-sized hailstones, which completely decimated the garden. It was a freak storm from the North we were told later – but hailstones in the third week of August?

That night I lay awake racked by pain; my shoulder throbbing in an improvised sling. After breakfast Diane had to finish off the beams, while I looked on frustrated.

The following days couldn't have been worse. Hot baths and painkillers achieved nothing, and sleep came in fits and starts. Thankfully though, Saturday saw a change for the better, both in the weather and my condition.

Driving us to Saumur, Diane coaxed me around some small shops, timing our arrival at *Emmaus* for the two pm opening. Standing behind dealers who'd assumed 'pole position,' we waited. Two o'clock came and went – nothing! No-one arrived to open up, and no-one knew why. Confusion reigned, with most people turning away angrily. Stoically, we crossed over the road to Euro 2, a French Pound shop. After a brief look around we drove to *Aldimarché* and *Gifi*. However, the day out didn't help my shoulder or my mood one iota.

Even more determined to fight it the next day, Diane packed a freezer box and flask, and off we went to Le Flèche's lakeside beach. The weather was 'middling' as they say in Yorkshire, but we still had a pleasant afternoon despite the sling.

Arriving back at tea-time my shoulder was throbbing; so I tried the age old whisky remedy. Well that was *my* excuse anyway!

With no improvement, I rang François the next morning, asking if he could recommend a doctor. He said he'd ask his parents and get back to me.

I couldn't wait too long though, and getting no reply from François, I asked Jane if she could help. She gave me *her* doctor's number. He practiced from home near Noyant apparently; and his wife, a nurse-cum receptionist was British. Ringing the surgery, an English voice told me to turn up early the next morning and they'd squeeze me in.

Diane drove us to a large Napoleonic house the next morning. Arriving at nine exactly, she decided to wait in the car while I entered a musty old sitting room filled with dark furniture. As locals arrived and exchanged *'Bonjours,'* we gathered in the gloom. And there we sat, avoiding eye contact while awaiting a call to the inner sanctum. The same as in UK waiting rooms really – except in this community, people addressed the whole room with a *'Bonjour'* when they arrived. Whereas no-one even acknowledges you in most UK surgeries I've known.

My turn came quickly which was a blessing. Have you ever struggled to open and read a glossy French magazine one-handed, with it balanced on your knee while sitting on an upright chair? Called into the office, I was greeted by the bespectacled elderly doctor. But I was taken aback when his wife sat next to him as translator. Jane had said they'd been married for ages. Hadn't he learned any English from her? Or maybe he required 'exactitude' for his diagnosis. (The French way, don't forget.)

I must admit though, I received a thorough examination; followed by his wife making an appointment at Le Baugé for an X-ray the next morning. I then received a prescription for powerful pain killers, and a request for twenty euros for my treatment. After debiting my bank card, his wife swiftly ushered me out of the mausoleum into welcoming sunlight.

Back at Le Lude, I paid a pharmacy eleven euros for prescription tablets. The extremely helpful pharmacist then said the *Laboratoire* would charge me forty euros for the X-ray, which would be processed while I waited. I'd then return with it to the doctor (another twenty euros) then maybe I'd receive a cortisone injection, (another twenty euros.) Now can you detect a certain pattern developing here? Whoah! This was beginning to sound a tad expensive.

My friendly pharmacist advised me to register with a doctor. Then, as a resident home owner, I could apply for a *Carte Vitale,* entitling me to a 70% reimbursement on all treatment costs. Medicines unfortunately had to be paid for in full. Until then, using the E111 visitor's card, I'd have to pay up then claim it back from the British N.H.S. We said thanks and left. Soon after taking the tablets I noticed an improvement; and for the first time in over a week I slept like a baby.

Feeling much better when I awoke, I began gently exercising the shoulder; and after two hours it felt so much easier that I cancelled the X-ray appointment. Diane said it was because I was too mean to pay for the treatment. Too right, we needed the money for other things. I just hoped I'd recover, before a possible job vacancy occurred at the *cave.*

As part of my improvement we visited Noyant market that Friday. Unfortunately we bumped into Annette and Henri straight away. Stupidly, I had a conversation with Henri before going our separate ways, which left us both baffled as usual.

'Until you're absolutely sure what you're saying, keep it simple,' Diane advised. Wise words that came back to bite me in the ass later.

Visiting *Emmaus* the following afternoon I was as happy as a sand boy. Now what *does* that mean? Or – as happy as Larry? Larry who?

I cared not a jot! I was just happy rooting amongst the detritus of a bygone France. We did manage to pick up a couple of things, but nothing to write home about. Now there we go again. I mean, why would I want to write home about it? And would anyone care if I did? Learning French can be difficult, but English often presents its own problems. Help! I'm losing it. It must be the tablets.

With the forecast looking decent, Diane thought a Sunday BBQ would perk me up. But this time we thought we'd go crazy. Let's try some meat. Getting back by six pm, I rang Véronique, asking *sans un interpréteur,* would they like to join us for this cookout the following afternoon. I even suggested a time. After a squeaky '*Oui,*' from Veronique, the line went dead.

'Are they coming then?' Diane asked.

'I *think* so. But who knows for sure. Anyway, if it's fine I'll light the Barbie. If they don't arrive soon after, I'll have to go and get them.'

In the twilight next morning, I heard a vehicle grinding slowly up our drive. Nipping out of bed, I peeped through the blinds, spotting a car without lights. About halfway up it stopped, turned around, and drove off again. I didn't think it was our gypsy friends. It looked more like Henri's car. But it was too far off to be sure. Oh oh! If it *was* Henri, he may have misunderstood me at the market. Could he think we were expecting a visit from *them*? But if so, why turn up at such an ungodly hour? Oh Hell, not another cock-up. What if they arrived in the middle of our Barbie? Assuming of course that *Véronique* had understood me and *they* turned up. Worse still, if both couples turned up it would be disastrous, as the two families had history and didn't get on well.

Though breezy the weather wasn't bad later; so up and dressed I struggled to erect the gazebo while Diane prepared food. With me having limited success one-handed, Diane came out to help. Then just as we seemed to be winning, the cover blew off across the garden. Dammit!

At one o'clock, with Bertrand and Véronique due any minute, we *still* hadn't sorted it. Giving up on it we reverted to plan B (the one without a gazebo.) By one thirty I'd decided Véronique must have misunderstood me. But with the whole thing spiralling towards a social cock-up, they arrived fashionably late carrying the customary bottle of *rosé*.

Like most potential disasters it turned out well. The rain held off; and though it took a long time to cook, the food tasted great. During the meal François turned up like a sniffer dog; I swear he must have been fitted with food radar. But most importantly, Henri and Annette didn't turn up.

While Diane and I cleared up, François spoke quietly with his parents. Then mysteriously, he asked, 'Would you like to see our fishing lake? It is nearby; only a short trip by car.'

Intrigued, we said yes, so excusing himself Bertrand nipped off home, returning soon after in his Citroën. We all piled in and he drove towards Noyant, turning after a few kilometres onto a dirt track. Bumping along through a field of sunflowers we came upon their lake; a small backwater feeding off a nearby river. With his usual flourish, Bertrand produced fishing rods, tackle, and chairs for us all from the boot. Arms full we staggered down to the river bank, passing a huge pen containing a flock of squawking *Volailles* or mixed fowl. Eventually we stopped, as François pointed dramatically towards 'the lake.' Then with a grin uncannily like his Dad's, he spoke. 'We can also fish in the river. But the man, he must not see us.'

With the sun sliding gently behind the trees, we picked our positions. Enclosed in our peaceful little world, we watched dragonflies dance on the water. Surrounded by midges, contentedly chatting to each other, (us, not the midges) we had a great afternoon. Though we competed for perch, François said some big carp lived there. I wouldn't know as we never caught one. But we had a great time trying, and my shoulder didn't spoil my day at all.

On the drive home, it was decided we'd call at Anna's apartment near Le Lude. Entering the building we climbed to the first floor, where Bertrand asked everyone to hide as a joke. Then pressing the doorbell *he* hid, pushing me out to surprise the old lady. By then it was dusk; and despite nearly having a coronary Anna invited us in. With aperitifs poured she produced snacks, served on fine china with lace doilies. In contrast to this finery, we were then served rough Normandy cider and the inimitable *quarante-quatre*.

Our fishing trip was then described tongue in cheek; with tales of huge fish caught and others that got away. Anglers must be the same worldwide.

After a while though we sensed the old lady was flagging, so giving and receiving kisses we left. Tired out ourselves, we were also ready for home.

I crawled into bed awkwardly that night. Yes my shoulder was sore; but considering the strimming, mowing and furniture shifting that I'd subjected it to it was hardly surprising. And let's not forget catching all those monstrous fish!

All in all it'd been a great day, and well worth the effort. Now, forgive me if I sound pessimistic at times; but whenever we'd had a good day there'd often been a heavy price to pay for it. Now what could it possibly be *this* time I wondered?

# Chapter 24

## A comedy of errors

Why can't I leave well alone, I often wonder? After the recent misunderstandings with the Plombières, I stupidly decided to clarify the situation. I say stupidly, because when we tried speaking French to them, they most often looked blank. As for us expecting *them* to speak or even understand English, there was no chance. Furthermore, Annette was really beginning to annoy Diane, as she'd begun tugging at her arm impatiently if *she* wasn't understood. Not advisable!

In retrospect I should have let sleeping dogs lie, I suppose, but I felt things needed resolving. Therefore, using dictionary and phrase-book we composed a letter.

While engaged in this project Bertrand arrived, intimating that Armand had tried ringing me, but he'd possibly written down my number incorrectly. Could I re-write it and pop it in the *cave* letter box? Like a drowning man clutching at a lifebelt, I dragged him in to check over my letter. While pointing out the odd mistake in grammar, he laughed at my concern, saying Henri and Annette had only a rudimentary education, and probably wouldn't understand anyway. Maybe I was opening up a can of worms best left alone. Sighing inwardly I thanked him; but like it or not I had to try.

Well, what happened next reminded me of an old Whitehall farce. (Feel free to Google it) Armed with a bunch of hand-picked flowers, the letter and our French dictionary, we set off.

On the way I dropped off my phone number at the *cave*; then having doing everything possible to delay the inevitable, I drove on to La Minoterie. Parking near the windmill, I knocked tentatively at the door. Frankly, I was hoping they were out. However Annette answered, admitting us with a welcoming smile. Seated in their conservatory we were then offered coffee; after which Annette looked at us expectantly. Taking a deep breath I held out my bouquet and the letter. Looking bemused, she took the flowers, put on her specs, and read my message. Then getting up slowly, she walked out of the room. She returned minus the flowers, but accompanied by her two little granddaughters whom she was baby sitting. *They* were then shown the letter; and understanding immediately one girl explained the contents to her. Annette then relayed the message to Henri who'd just walked in. This was becoming ridiculous. However they both turned to us beaming. As spokesperson for Annette, the eldest girl then thanked us in English for the flowers. This was actually going better than I'd dare hope for. She then said, her grandpa hadn't misunderstood about Sunday after all. (Phew) But he wished to know if I still wanted Jacques' house.

*What*? … Oh God, what had I gotten myself into *now*? I tried telling her we didn't want, nor could we afford '*un résidence secondaire*,' and I was sorry if I'd somehow misled Henri. In the silence that followed, the little girl tiptoed forward. Reaching up she handed me back my letter. Then, with a grave look on her cherubic little face, she said, 'If *you* don't want it; who is it who wants the house of Uncle Jacques?'

I almost whimpered. It *had* been Henri, who'd driven up early the previous morning. Apparently, when he and I were chatting at Friday's market, he'd mentioned that Jacques was selling his house. And like many country French, Henri believed that the English are all rich. I was '*un millionaire*' in his eyes, simply because I was buying a run-down farmhouse with a few acres of land. He must have asked if I wanted to add another property to my burgeoning property portfolio, and taken my inane nodding as a buying signal. Oh boy! Thank God the girls were there to help us. It was ludicrous really; but due to the language barrier, two primary school kids were mediating in a house buying dispute.

When François and Philippe rode by later, they enjoyed the tale immensely. Laughing out loud they both agreed, '*Cette normale pour Monsieur Plombière.*'

They'd visited so that François could invite us for aperitifs later, as he was returning to college the next day. As usual, the aperitifs preceded a five course meal, enriched *this* time by the Henri fiasco. After the story Bertrand attempted to speak English – which sounded uncannily like Dick Van Dyke's atrocious Cockney accent in the film *Mary Poppins*. Coupled with the experience of seeing Véronique tipsy – a first for us, the night was a memorable experience.

While still sober, Bertrand broached the subject of their oak dining table, chairs, and matching *armoire*. They'd bought the set when they married 20 years before, and it was in remarkable condition. We'd mentioned liking it; and as they'd decided to replace it with modern custom built items, were we interested in buying it? Oh yes we said. Our dining room was finished, the beams were treated and stained; it just needed the right furniture. The timing was perfect. Like many French people, they were moving away from a traditional look. Conversely, the English were buying into it to create French ambience. One man's meat is another man's poison eh?

We left around 10-30pm, as by then Véronique was beginning to flag. Never mind; she could enjoy a lie-in in the morning, as they were on vacation. Though, they weren't sure whether to have a few days away, or to catch up on work. Ever resourceful, I offered to help Bertrand with his jobs – if he taught me to drive his tractor. It could prove invaluable if I got the job at the *cave*. He looked at François who translated for him. Backed into a corner, his reply was translated as, 'We will see.' We left it at that.

161

The next day was such a lovely day, that I decided to nip out and leave Diane to her beauty sleep. (Not that she needed it of course.) Pushing my luck, I decided to visit Henri again. Yes, I know, I was a glutton for punishment. But as a close neighbour and friend, I felt it necessary to clear the air with him.

At seven am, with my arm strapped up, I set off under a clear blue sky. Passing the *cave*, I headed across the road and down La Minoterie's long drive. Approaching the old mill all was peaceful; but nearing the house, I heard dogs barking and chickens squawking. Then, following some crashing noises, I heard shouting and screaming. Suddenly a cry of '*Merde*' rang out. Bloody hell, I thought, they're being attacked by those thugs we'd seen hanging around.

My mind racing, I thought of Henri's son Jean. His house was back across the B road; but he was too far away to hear the pandemonium. And without my cell-phone, I couldn't contact the police. Anyway, if I could have rung them, would they have responded, or even understood me?

There was only one thing for it. This was an emergency. Picking up a broken branch, I sneaked up to the end of the building, my heart thumping. With my best arm in a sling, God only knew what I hoped to do. But I had to do something. Not knowing what to expect I counted to ten. Then taking a deep breath, I jumped out from behind the wall, arm raised and shouting loudly.

Clutching at his chest, a startled Henri turned towards me in shock, nearly dropping the wooden gate he was holding. He looked at me mouth agape, while I, feeling stupid tried to hide my improvised club. It'd been *him* shouting at Annette; who was stumbling around the muddy chicken pen in her wellingtons. With her pinafore dress tucked into knee-length bloomers, red-faced and dishevelled, she resembled a cartoon postcard character, as she swiped at frenzied chickens with a fish landing net. She was screaming, the traumatized chickens were squawking, the cats, dogs and new puppy were yowling and running in all directions – and Henri our hero? Well he was holding the gate; while shouting at Annette, the chickens, and any other animals that strayed into his path. It was pure theatre, and the absolute bedlam that I'd come to expect by then.

I tried vainly to explain my quixotic intervention, while noting that Annette's job seemed to consist of netting the chickens. Then grabbing them by a wing, a leg, their neck or whatever else that came to hand, she passed them to Henri. It seemed *his* task was to clip their beaks with de-beaking clippers. After this treatment, the traumatized birds were casually 'tossed' into the next pen. The procedure was to stop them from pecking each other's arses, he said, and to prevent them becoming distressed. Really! Well good luck with *that!* If it wasn't so comical it would have been tragic. The poor birds, some with bleeding beaks seemed freaked out by the whole experience. Let's face it; as performed by Henri it wasn't an exact science. They probably wouldn't lay an egg for ages, if ever again. However, chicken shit – well there was loads of *that* to go around.

Stepping up to the gate, I instinctively grabbed one bird which was making a bid for freedom, and was immediately deputized into 'the team.' Fielding chickens one-armed at Henri's side, a hectic ten minutes flew by. But at long last they were all accounted for, and a red-faced Annette had regained her modesty. Retiring to the kitchen for coffee we passed the utility room, where Henri pointed at a victim of the dreaded 'arse pecking.' Stiff with rigor mortis, the chicken laid on the bench seemed set for a post mortem, in a surreal episode of C.S.I.

'*Voilà,*' he said with a flourish, '*comme ça.*'… End of conversation.

While Annette went off to change and make coffee, I re-opened the subject of Jacque's house. Pleading with Henri to listen carefully, I spoke slowly. I just *had* to make him realize.

'I'm not rich,' I said, 'and *Le Ferronerie* is my only home. Furthermore, I don't want or need another house.' All of this I enunciated as carefully as possible in reasonable French.

I could almost see his mental synapses engage. He thought for a while, then replied gutturally, 'You say you don't want it, your family and friends don't want it; so who *does* want it?'

Almost sobbing I gave up. But luckily for me his short attention span saved me. Swiftly changing tack, he decided to show me his new aluminium granary. Once there, he proudly displayed his flock of doves, newly-hatched ducklings, chicks and goslings. I've never been so passionate about looking at birds before – well not the feathered kind anyway.

After inspecting this avian 'sanctuary,' I was about to make my escape, when I was offered the mandatory garden tour. This one involved scrutinising a pile of potatoes – some weighing half a kilo. Then before I could make my escape, Annette caught me at the gate; presenting me with a large bag containing beetroot, tomatoes, and two of her enormous potatoes. In her other hand she held a large bunch of flowers.

'*Pour Deeana,*' she said smiling sweetly.

This was really kind of her. However, it all had to be lugged home one-handed. Thanking her profusely, I gave her three heartfelt kisses, before staggering off clutching two carrier bags in one hand. Setting off in scorching sunlight, I turned into the farmyard scattering cats ahead of me. And with the new puppy yapping at my heels, I crossed the bridge and assessed the long walk home.

Drenched with sweat, my shirt clinging to me, I trudged up that long road with teeth gritted. Finally I arrived at '*Chez nous;*' the carrier bags slicing into my fingers and shoulder muscles screaming; just as Diane sashayed downstairs yawning. 'Have you had a nice walk?' she asked ingenuously. 'Would you like some breakfast?'

I looked at the kitchen clock. It was just coming up to eight am. Oh my God! I felt like crawling back into bed.

# Chapter 25

## The pint-sized assassin

After demolishing a full English breakfast and some very strong coffee, I'd almost recovered from my traumatic visit to the Plombier's, when Bertrand and François rolled up on the tractor. They'd arrived to conduct my driving master-class. It was no good saying my shoulder was on fire, or that I wasn't up to it right now. That didn't cut it with them. Their *modus operandi* was, just get on with it.

As I dressed wearily Véronique arrived to chat with Diane. Then we hairy-chested guys strode off to fire up 'the beast'. After a fleeting introduction to a bewildering array of knobs, dials, switches and levers, I mounted the machine. Lowering my posterior onto what looked like a colander, I checked that the gear-stick was in neutral, then fired up the engine. Engaging first gear I let out the clutch and off we lurched. I say we, because François was hanging on for dear life behind me. Hey, no bother mate – a piece of cake.

Crunching into second gear (no synchromesh) we bounced down to the main road. I must admit, by then I was enjoying myself hugely, my shoulder blissfully forgotten. And François was even looking happier with *his* position. With the wind whistling through my hair, I opened her up; the revolving orange light clearing my way. We rumbled along for a while trailing a cloud of smoke in our wake, before turning off-road again. After completing a circuit around the two farms, I braked reluctantly in a shower of gravel next to Bertrand, who seemed impressed. Well he was grinning anyway.

Next, I was told to take the machine around the bottom field flying solo. Leaping across furrows François ran alongside me – until I lost him off. After five minutes of bouncing around, and avoiding the storm ditches, I was waved off the field into 'the pits.'

Dismounting, I ribbed them mercilessly, saying the French drive on the wrong side of the road. While disputing my claim hotly, François couldn't understand how I drove my right hand drive car so easily on their roads; saying neither he nor his father would have the nerve. To prove my inherent British superiority (only joking guys) I asked François for his car keys. He handed them over reluctantly. Despite having no knowledge of his left-hand drive Peugeot, I climbed in, started it up and drove off with panache. Through the hamlet I went; around the farms and back again. No problem.

'French drivers, pah,' I said, clicking my fingers in front of François' nose. It was just as well those guys were my friends, and understood my sense of humour. Joking apart, I now felt comfortable driving a tractor if asked to start work, which was the point of the exercise.

As François was returning south later we wished him a safe journey. With kisses and handshakes given and received, we left the family to their personal goodbyes.

Allowing for road-works, we set off early the next morning for Saumur. Driving towards La Touche with the sun in our faces, the roads were clear and life was good.

But things can go wrong very quickly – and did, as I was suddenly forced to brake sharply. An extremely old guy had suddenly lurched into the road from a nearby garden. Waving a stick in the air, he tottered towards my side of the car. Leaning in through the open window, Methuselah began ranting at me in garbled French, punctuated with flecks of garlic tainted spittle. Striving to appear sympathetic wasn't easy, as he had a wild, haunted look in his eyes. And grinning without the benefit of teeth, he looked to be at least a hundred and ten years old. Oh oh! Loony alert, I thought, as he scrabbled to open the car's rear door.

At that point, a lady ran out of the garden, shouting something like, 'Come now papa; you mustn't bother the nice English people.'

Or then again, it could have been, 'Get back in the house you crazy old bugger.'

Who knows? But that's the joy of living in a foreign country, isn't it? Anyway, as well as being woefully lacking in the denture department, he also seemed as deaf as a post; so whatever she said was irrelevant anyway.

'Ah well, here we go again,' I thought, giving Madame my humanitarian look; quizzical eyebrow cocked at just the right angle. Roger Moore would have been proud of me. Eyelids fluttering coyly, she steered Hannibal senior back into the house; perhaps explaining that I wasn't the getaway driver he thought he'd organized for his great escape.

With a cheery wave I wished Madame, '*Bonne chance,*' before driving off with a toot of the horn.

'I don't know why, but this sort of thing only seems to happen to *us*,' Diane whispered; as if our nonagenarian friend might suddenly appear in the wing mirror – or worse still, rear up off the back seat.

Setting off again, shaken (but not stirred) we arrived in Saumur, just in time for Wednesday's free for all at *Emmaus*. Being old pros by then, we burst through the doors alongside the best of them. Splitting up to cover ground quickly, our practiced eyes and 'rubbish radar' picked out the best items. Then jostling with the French we went after them; the bargains that is, not the French!

Not for us a genteel stroll around. No siree. After snaring a couple of small items, Diane grabbed a crate of Kilner jars for her preserve making; saving greatly on store prices. Meanwhile, out in the yard, I unearthed two large sun loungers priced at ten euros each. I got both for fifteen. A steal, as they cost eighty euros each when new.

Arriving home after a fun day out we had our meal, then decided an early night wouldn't do us any harm at all. While toying with the idea of a relaxing soak before watching a video, the phone rang. It was Armand from the *cave*. Would I 'attend' on Monday morning at six am? I would begin on a month's trial. If satisfactory, I would continue working on monthly contracts. Well that was it then; I had to get my shoulder sorted out – and fast.

Holding a council of war, we decided I'd better get household jobs cleared up first, so I dug out the mower the next morning. After giving it the once over I fired it up. Despite a temperamental start it was soon buzz-cutting the lawns to receive my new loungers.

I'd just set them out when Bertrand appeared. He'd heard the lawnmower blade catching the odd stone or root, and wandered over to advise me how to do it correctly. However, his heart didn't seem to be in it this time. Sitting on a wall, I asked, '*Avez vous une problème Bertrand?*'

Putting on a brave face, he said he was missing François down in Bordeaux. Until recently he'd attended the local school, and spent most evenings working the land with his father. They were very close, and I sympathized with him as my sons were living in England. How was Véronique coping? I asked. Sitting next to me, he flicked pebbles half heartedly at scurrying lizards. Shrugging, he said she obviously missed François, but summoning inner strength, she was keeping herself busy with the dispatch. Puzzled, I asked him, 'What is the dispatch?'

It was when they filled the *congélateurs pour hiver,* or freezers for winter, he explained. By then I understood most of what he said, and guessed the rest. This method hadn't worked for Henri though. It probably never would.

'*Véronique coupe les poulets et canards,*' he said, drawing a finger across his throat.

Sharing a family venture, the guys procured newly hatched poultry, then helped tend them throughout the year. But when it came to butchering them – step forward Véronique the smiling assassin. Though pint-sized, she was rock hard when it was called for. Apparently she'd begun as soon as Françoise left for college, by 'despatching' four large cockerels. 'The moment of truth' had now arrived for four mallard ducks. Getting up to leave, he invited me over to witness these executions, as if it were some form of treat.

'Hmm, maybe the next batch,' I suggested.

Shrugging, he said I could have admired Lupé's new look. Seemingly the cocky little mutt had received a radical new haircut. Shorn like a sheep, he was half his normal size – and apparently quite depressed after the experience.

As Bertrand wandered off dejectedly, I continued grass cutting into the late afternoon. Trudging inside, I collapsed knackered. Coming to with a start at eight thirty pm I felt ravenous; and after wolfing down a snack, I went to bed and read until two am before nodding off.

The phone rang while I was enjoying breakfast. It was Armand. Could I take my birth certificate and passport to the *cave*, so everything could be set up for Monday? Best do it now, I thought. Strolling down to the office in brilliant sunshine, I caught *Madame Secretaire* in her office, where she photocopied my documents. As I left she wished me '*A bientôt,*' and I realized, I was officially on the books.

Back home again, Diane suggested we visit Noyant market to inspect the chickens. We'd fancied keeping some, but when we got there and saw the sad looking specimens on offer, we decided against it. Moving on, we perused the *Immobilière's* window, where we spotted Jacque's house advertised. Underneath the photos and imaginative blurb was the asking price. Well good luck with that, we thought. However one stunning house we saw could have tempted *us* into moving. It was reasonably priced, well decorated and complete. We could have moved straight in, unfortunately the owner had signed the '*compromis-de-vente*. Besides, the grass is always greener etcetera.

Driving back towards Le Lude we saw the doctor's wife out walking. Though seeming well off and blessed with social standing, she was strolling along looking thoroughly miserable. Ah well, it just goes to prove … Fill in the rest yourself – or send your answers on a postcard please.

Approaching the Broc turn-off on our return, a slow moving cavalcade of tractors and trailers slowed us to a crawl. Awash with ribbons and flowers spelling '*Comice d' Agricole,*' they turned off in convoy onto the Chigné road.

As it was such a beautiful day we decided to follow them, and let things take their course. With trailers brim-full of ebullient children they entered the village, drivers tooting their horns crazily. In response, a ragged cheer went up from the waiting crowd, while we followed behind basking in reflected glory, waving like royalty as we passed by them.

Most villagers had made a stupendous effort for this annual event, their houses and gardens a riot of flowers and ribbons. One garden we passed sported a gigantic wire framed horse, its whole body interlaced with blooms.

As the floats continued on through the main street, we turned off and parked up. Finding a choice spot, we watched the festivities for a while before peeking into *L'eglise St. Pierre*, a lovely old church. This Sunday's service was special, a time when locals gave thanks for a good harvest, while invoking good luck for the next year. Though the *fete's* roots sprang from pagan beliefs, those hard-working communities deserved a reward no matter which deity it came from.

The inflammation in my shoulder had worsened. But popping painkillers I tried ignoring it, concentrating on picking damsons in the cool early morning.

It was Saturday, and at two pm we dived through the doors at *Emmaus*, once again hot on the heels of the dealers. Diane began by lifting some blue and white pottery from the window display, and having it set aside for her. I was close behind, asking Louis, a harassed assistant to ticket two cupboards. Diane then took the lead, nabbing two exquisite Turkish coffee sets. Slowing down a little, we bagged a bisque-ware bowl and two superb crystal goblets, which completed our shop-a-thon.

After collecting our purchases we joined a long queue. Stepping up to pay the *'caissier,'* we were told one of my cupboards had been damaged since ticketing. After much shoulder shrugging, we reluctantly loaded the pair onto our trailer. Five kilometres down the road while checking her receipt, Diane noted we hadn't been charged for the crystal goblets. Hey ho! The spoils of war, we thought.

Arriving at Le Ferronnerie, we unloaded before I tried a hot soak. I'd never had a strain injury last so long before; and with me starting work on Monday, I decided a couple of medicinal brandies might prove effective. Oh Yeah!

At the end of a *very* long night, I'd vicariously fronted at Status Quo, Meatloaf and Bon Jovi gigs. Now, my taste in music is fairly eclectic; but this time I was definitely a rock hero. Come two am, I retired unsteadily to my rock-star's trailer (the bedroom.) Despite my wild gyrations I was feeling no pain at all. Sorry fans, no autographs.

This time we were off to Chiné's *fête,* where we arrived just as the ploughing competition began. Standing alongside the locals, we studiously inspected the arrow-straight furrows like experts. With judging complete, we left the show-field and wandered around the village. Plonking our asses on a bench in the village square, we sat in the sun absorbing sights, sounds, and smells like sponges. We were then informed by a wizened old guy,

171

that the parade wasn't due until two pm. Since it had just turned noon, which was lunch-time almost everywhere, we drove home for a siesta.

At one thirty pm we set off again, passing a tractor and driver constructed from hay bales which marked the way to the village. Arriving, we parked in a designated field and joined the crowd. After a significant wait, the parade could be heard approaching, signifying the beginning of the festivities.

Local *communes* were vying for best float in the show; with secondary competitions taking place later. The first was for best, or weirdest costume. Then there was best band. Each *commune* had one; and they competed enthusiastically for best at the *fête*. The formula for success seemed to hinge on playing off key louder than the others, while being hopelessly out of step. And a degree of intoxication appeared almost mandatory.

It was at that point that the day took on a surreal quality. First we spotted Henri and Annette on the other side of the events field. Then, as we casually sidled away to avoid any misunderstanding, I turned – and standing nearby like one of Macbeth's witches was Madame Renard.

That definitely put the tin hat on it. Skipping the finale; a chaotic version of 'It's a knockout' contested between rival *communes*, we beat a hasty retreat. We never found out who'd won. We thought it best not to ask Henri when we saw him next.

We laughed for most of the trip home. Then later, after tea and a bath, I rang Chris, updating him on our latest foray into village life. His reply was, 'Dad, you're living the dream man.'

However, it was pointless ignoring the inevitable. With a feeling of impending doom, I laid out my work clothes ready for the morning. Setting the alarm clock for six am, I took some pain-killers and went off to my bed. Who knows, maybe I'd even get some sleep for a change.

# Chapter 26

## A harsh reality

After chasing sleep unsuccessfully all night, I climbed out of bed well before daybreak. Diane insisted on getting up with me for my first shift, making me a cuppa and some toast that settled like concrete in my stomach. As dawn stole softly across the fields, I said goodbye to her at the door. A kiss for luck; then like a child on his first day at school, I set off to Le Lavendu.

Feeling responsible for me, Véronique had offered to drive me in on my first day; though after that I intended to walk as the *cave* was just down the road. However, Véronique always took her car to maximize her lunch-break. After a snack, she'd hang out overnight washing, before starting off the evening meal in a slow-cooker.

Pulling into the works car park at six-forty, we climbed out and joined a trickle of mainly female workers, some of whom stared quite blatantly at us. One shouted out something to Véronique which caused a burst of ribald laughter. Blissfully ignorant, I dared imagine it might be, 'Why've you brought George Clooney along with you?'

Well a guy can dream, can't he? Anyway, whatever she replied it broke the ice; and like a grinning loon, I was led into the cavern like a lamb to the slaughter.

Leaving the pale dawn behind us we descended down an incline, meeting the harsh glare of artificial lighting. Rounding a bend we made for the time clock, where Véronique found my punch-card and we both clocked in. Then joining a group gathered inside the office, we were greeted with a ragged *'Bonjour.'* Most of the others, I suspected, were like me; wishing they were somewhere else but needing the money.

Emerging from the main tunnel just before seven, Armand entered followed closely by Christine. Shouting a general *'Bonjour,'* he received a half-hearted response back from the crowd. He then introduced me to my co-workers, who seemed friendly enough. And of course, I knew Véronique and the Plombière brothers which helped.

After being allotted jobs people drifted off, picking up a cap and lamp on their way. Véronique headed off with a cheery wave and, *'Bonne chance,'* and I was left with Armand and Christine. Handing Armand the documents he'd asked for, he thanked me; saying he'd sort out my contract later. Then wishing me good luck he strode off, leaving Christine and I standing together.

In French, sprinkled with a little English, she explained safety procedures. Then handing me a denim cap and safety-lamp, she showed me how to check the battery pack and where to charge it. I was then told it was the most important piece of equipment, and my lifeline to the surface. If my lamp failed deep underground I'd be blind, lost in a maze of tunnels. With dawning apprehension, I realized my interview was history. This was reality.

Glancing at her watch, Christine picked up a cap and lamp. Then setting off with a firm stride she entered the main gallery; me following like a lapdog. Pointing to a pair of massive double doors daubed with a huge number four, she said, *'Chambre quatre.'*

Not rocket science so far, I thought, as she opened the huge doors with a squeal – the doors, not Christine. Donning her cap and lamp she said, *'Allez,'* and marched off into the tunnel. At this juncture the wall lighting ended, so following her lead I switched on my lamp. In her purposeful manner she strode over to a large piece of equipment. An outlandish platform measuring approximately two by one point five metres, it had one wheel at the front and two legs at the back. With a set of front loading forks and wheelbarrow handles it was a hybrid loading platform. Pointing to it and a metal pallet nearby, she said, '*Poussez la brouette dans la palette, et suivez-moi.*'

Doing just that, I pushed the barrow into the pallet and followed her. Heading off into the tunnel she set a rapid pace, while I was acutely aware that the height and width were reducing alarmingly. In fact, there were places where I bumped my head on roughly hewn limestone. And let's not forget, we weren't wearing hard-hats. So much for the safety talk.

Concentrating ferociously, I followed my mentor, trying to avoid the walls with my *brouette* as we marched onwards. Rounding blind corners we twisted and turned; sometimes ascending sometimes descending; and occasionally splashing through puddles leached from the walls.

Eventually, after trudging hundreds of metres and passing numerous side passages, I noticed a larger gallery ahead. As we approached, the faint illumination fragmented into dancing light beams from a group of women's cap-lamps. While picking tiered mushroom trays, they'd obviously seen our lamps approaching, and were consequently working furiously as we arrived. Lowering my *brouette* I flexed my shoulders gratefully; sweating freely, though I'd heard the temperature underground held steady at 13C. After asking the crew if everything was okay Christine turned to me. With a sweeping arm, she indicated many filled *panniers* stacked next to emptied beds. Pointing to my *palette* she grabbed a couple of the *panniers*. She then showed me how to stack them so they interlocked. I should load them four wide by six long on the first layer; then alternate them on the second and third to interlock them, she said. She then pointed back towards the gallery; lost in the darkness through the labyrinth of tunnels.

175

Dusting off her hands she strode away, having imparted all the information she thought I might need. Meanwhile, the girls continued picking the beds rapidly; laughing, chattering, and gradually pulling away from me. Soon I'd be on my own; one small light in a sea of darkness.

Well I'd asked for the job, so I'd better get on with it. National pride was at stake. I began collecting *panniers;* loading them carefully and interlocking them as shown. Engrossed in my own little world, and being quite methodical (or OCD as Diane would have it,) I became totally absorbed. That is until I stood back to admire my handiwork. Bloody hell! It stood almost two metres high, about two point five long including the handles, and over a metre wide. Having lost track of time I turned around, and ahead of me yawned the empty tunnel, dark and forbidding. The faint light and sounds from the team were an alarming distance away by then; the near silence and brooding darkness a palpable threat.

'Right, that's me outta here,' I thought, grabbing the *brouette* handles and taking the strain.

'Christ, this is some weight,' I muttered, staggering into an awkward rhythm. Like anything in life though it was a learning process; and often painful, as I lurched along the tunnel with muscles straining and lamp-beam bouncing off the walls. On more than one occasion I scraped the wall, almost toppling the stack. And God only knows how often I hit my head off that gnarled ceiling. Apparently, the *caves* were chiselled out in the 17th century when people were quite small. Now I'm no giant, but with almost all my work-mates being smaller, the confines of the tunnels were more suited to them.

After the first lung-bursting push, I stopped to rest my aching back, and was shocked to see no lights ahead of me at all. Looking around me, my light-beam flickered over ominous side tunnels on both sides. Feeling disorientated, I thought, is it left, right or straight ahead? Aware that my light was the only one in the tunnel, I wondered what it would be like if I lost that comfort. I decided to switch it off to find out.

I was hit by the most absolute blackness I'd ever known. Feeling totally uneasy, I stood it for a few minutes; imagining what it would be like having a dead battery. Spinning around a few times I tried to find the walls, but I'd totally lost my sense of direction. Without my light I was helpless. Disorientated, and feeling that everything seemed to be closing in on me, I switched on my lamp again; but though I felt relieved, I now wasn't sure which direction I should take. I thought there's only one thing for it. '*Aidez-mois, je suis perdu,*' or 'help me, I'm lost,' I shouted.

My voice echoing around the tomb-like walls was unnerving. I had a vision of my skeleton being delivered to Diane sometime in the future, on a funereal *brouette* perhaps. Thankfully, while conjuring up this grisly prospect, I spotted a beam of light flickering towards me, and soon one of the girls arrived. '*Vous êtes perdu, oui? N'est pas grave. C'est votre premier jour,*' she said sweetly, or 'You're lost yes? No problem. It's your first day.'

I was actually on the right track, but grateful for her directions all the same. With a shy smile, she disappeared wraith-like into the darkness.

Staggering up to the drop-off point a lifetime later, I felt like I'd already worked a full shift. Lowering my *palette* gratefully, I straightened up, watched with amusement by two seasoned pros. Cigarette in his mouth one of them sauntered over, and using a pallet lifter he moved my load. With a wry smile he pretended to wipe his brow, indicating sympathy for my plight. However, he glanced pointedly at my tunnel and grinned. Ah well – *Once more unto the breach dear friends,* I thought.

Collecting an empty *palette,* I set off again; this time taking note of directions. My one consolation was the next trip would be slightly shorter, as I'd cleared the area furthest away on my inaugural visit. Unfortunately, there were many such trips to be made, plus side tunnels to be explored, before my shift ended. Thankfully, once they were emptied, the job would become simpler. But the brutal truth was, however fast I worked the women were pulling away from me remorselessly; unable to help me if I became lost again.

After the initial trauma, the morning settled into a monotonous routine of loading, pushing, unloading and returning. Complacency was never an issue though, as there was always the chance that I might lose my direction again. But finally I could see 'light at the end of the tunnel,' as at long last I was working in sight of the main loading area.

Early on in the shift, Christine had turned up to check on my progress. Nodding to herself, she'd walked away without speaking, so at least I hadn't been sacked. Stretching my aching back and with my shoulder on fire, I wasn't sure whether that was a good thing or not.

On the last section, Jacques arrived with a *brouette* and *palette* to help me, as the old hands in other tunnels had finished. Slapping my back, he said, '*Il fait chaud oui?*'

Wincing after the slap, I agreed. Yes, it *was* hot.

Pretty soon though we'd offloaded the final *palette*, and at last, for a few precious minutes I could relax. Thinking I hadn't done badly on my first morning, I watched stacked *palettes* being loaded onto a transporter platform then towed away by a small tractor. Two of these machines worked virtually non-stop all shift, their engine noise reverberating throughout the tunnels. Racing to and fro horns blaring, they delivered the pallets to the surface to be off-loaded at the weigh station for onward shipment. With exhaust fumes dissipating through roof vents, the drivers quickly cleared the area in a well-practiced 'balletic' routine; flowing forwards, backwards and spinning around with mechanical grace.

As I stood absorbing it all Jacques turned; and pointing at his watch he mimed eating. It was almost *midi,* and with noon approaching fast, we hurried up the slope to clock off. Then

178

joining the others, we wended our way to the surface like lemmings.

Making for the *cave* entrance, our breath became visible as it met the thirty-eight C temperature outside. Summoning up a brief spurt of energy, I reached the *cave* mouth and freedom. While noting most workers headed off to their cars, I watched stunned as some actually cycled home. Oh those heroes, I thought, as I trudged off wearily up the hill. Only another two hundred metres to Le Ferronerrie, and the absolute bliss of getting those damned boots off.

Well, I was in the house by 12-15pm, my boots were off by 12-16pm – and I was asleep in my chair before twenty past.

Diane woke me just in time for a quick cuppa and sandwich, before we both struggled to squeeze the boots onto my swollen feet. God only knows how we did it. Then stupefied, I trudged back down the hill to clock in again.


'*Stewaard, lavage des palettes,*' shouted Christine as I arrived in the office with some other workers.

Mystified, I was led away by another guy. Shaking my hand he said, '*Je suis Jean-Luc.*'

Zombie-like, I turned, and trudged off towards the tunnel doors. '*Non Steward, suiveze moi,*' or, 'No Stewart, follow me,' he said. Turning back, I followed him up the ramp, emerging into glorious sunshine. What fresh torture was this? I wondered, as we headed towards a terrace overlooking the valley. Then it hit me. I'd been here on my tour. It was where emptied beds were pressure washed.

I was told to don waterproofs, while Jean-Luc set up the power washer. Then standing back, I watched a huge forklift roar out of the *cave* carrying a stack of trays. After dropping them off; the top tray was loaded onto a tilting frame by a smaller forklift. Then after checking below, the operator pressed a green button. With a clang the frame swivelled over, tipping mulch onto a pile below. The tray's plastic liner was then discarded, and the forklift spread the emptied trays in line where they were pressure washed. Following that, they were hoisted on chains, plunged into a tank of solvent for ten minutes, then stacked to dry in the sun. This was to be my new domain.

Once I'd been shown the ropes, I had a whale of a time. I was a kid again with my own giant water pistol. Of course there was a serious side to it, but I soon developed a rhythm with the forklift drivers, while practicing my French on them as we worked. They indicated I should wash the beds *vite*, but *propre*. If not, the next spores laid down could be contaminated.

Oh my God! That afternoon was heaven compared to the hell I'd experienced underground. Working *'pleine aire'* was fabulous; with excellent views to be enjoyed over the surrounding countryside. And as an added bonus, I could even see my house and Le Lavendu next door. With the odd driver or cyclist waving as they passed, it seemed life couldn't get much better.

All in all then it'd turned into a great afternoon, though Armand just had to appear out of the weigh station and show me the most efficient way to *lavage*; even though I'd already been shown at length. It must be something embedded in the French psyche. Everyone can't help telling you how to do everything the French way. However I listened carefully – it was his business after all. Besides which, I didn't want to kill the golden goose and get sent back underground.

With the last trays done I pressure washed the machinery. Jean-Luc then hosed down his forklift; and finally, I hosed off the terrace, sluicing waste onto the pile below. After locking the equipment away, we made our way back into the *cave* to clock off.

Well that was it; I'd survived my first day. Walking out with my new work-mates I already sensed a bond transcending language barriers. However, I noticed Armand studying me shrewdly as we passed him on the way out. Maybe he was surprised I was still standing! Not wanting to show how desperately tired I was, I tried conveying a spring in my step as we all went our separate ways. Once out of sight though the weariness washed over me, as I faced a daunting walk up the road, before joining our steep drive.

Ten minutes later I staggered through the door completely knackered. Kicking off my boots, I grabbed a beer and stumbled outside, relishing its icy bite as I sprawled on a sun-lounger. This routine became known as having a Judith, after the time Diane asked, 'Do you want a beer?'

And, with a saying current back then I replied, 'Does Judith Chalmers have a passport?'

For the younger reader, Ms Chalmers was a well-known travel correspondent back then. And yes; that was sarcasm.

Dragging myself back inside I had a meal and a soothing bath. But watching a video afterwards I found myself nodding, so it was early to bed and oblivion. However, my shoulder had started to throb again. After tossing and turning for ages I crept out of bed; spending the rest of that painful night on the settee. When would my shoulder improve I wondered?

# Chapter 27

## How to lose weight – quickly

After tossing and turning all night, I was just drifting off when the alarm clock jangled. Eyes puffy and swollen, I thought, *Oh God, I can't do this.* I could barely lift my arm; my shoulder throbbing painfully as I staggered to the bathroom. *Please make today easier*, I prayed.

However, once again Sod's law reared its ugly head. In her infinite wisdom, Christine decided today was the day I should learn the intricacies of cross-over box loading. Leading me to the work station she explained the process briefly, before introducing me to Michel, a strapping young lad less than half my age, blessed with bulging biceps and flashing teeth. '*Pas de problème,*'or not a problem, he kept repeating.

We began by prepping our work area at the end of the line. Then glancing along the conveyor belt, I saw the rest of the team were ready. The girl feeding us empty *panniers* had also loaded up *her* conveyor belt, and we all stood nervously, like racehorses waiting for 'the off.'

With a bellowing roar, a huge Komatsu forklift careered into the building. Bouncing past us on gigantic tyres, it carried six trays stacked vertically. After loading the stack into the automatic feeder system, an alarm signalled the start of the run.

As the first tray tipped its contents onto the belt, I tensed, hearing a faint rumbling sound. Standing there transfixed, I dreaded what was to come.

A moving shadow slowly appeared. Reflected against the aluminium mainframe, it signalled the arrival of a large pile of mushrooms. Rounding the angled bend, the fungi tsunami bore relentlessly towards us; and just before it reached us, a crashing noise marked the tipping of the *next* tray. We glanced at each other, Michel resigned, me aghast. After pressing our buttons to bring forward two *panniers* we tensed. Then, as my heart plummeted into my stomach we were deluged.

Jesus! In seconds our *panniers* were full. Slamming them onto the *palette*, we grabbed empties quickly. It was gruelling back- breaking work. Plus, once the stack was nine boxes high, it became impossible to stack the rear *panniers* without spilling mushrooms – unless you happened to be two metres tall.

With the *palette* filled, a small forklift rushed in to snatch it away. But replacing it without interrupting our rhythm was impossible – though no-one ever acknowledged that. When the process inevitably went 'tits up,' mushrooms spewed all over the floor, and were trodden underfoot as we worked. We *could* of course press the red button to stop the belt; but doing so would bring either Armand or Christine rushing over, moaning about lost time. So, sliding around on squashed *'champignons,'* the only respite from the onslaught was if the process malfunctioned in some way.

We endured this torture for three hours; the end of production leaving us exhausted, sweating, and steaming; like the aforementioned horses after a gruelling race.

At that point Christine strode over, tut-tutting at the sea of spillage. Delegating one of the girls to box up what she could salvage, she beckoned for Michel and I to follow her. Dreading what might come next, I fell in line behind her.

Heading down into the *cave* we were designated different tunnels. And arriving in mine, I was told to grab a *brouette* and *palette*. Further in, the girls were picking at a furious pace; outstripping the loaders who needed help catching up. I don't know what Christine was shouting in French, but whatever it was, she wasn't a happy bunny.

At noon we all trooped off for a well-earned rest. Surprisingly, considering I'd worked like a mule, I felt much better than the previous day. Plus my shoulder seemed to have been shocked into recovery. It really hadn't an option.

The afternoon saw us down in the *cave* again at one thirty sharp. No hanging about talking; no cigarette, tea or toilet breaks. (A toilet was finding an unused tunnel somewhere.) And this was for minimum wage. Pretty much like Victorian England basically. Unfortunately, with little work available in the area it was an employer's market. And with only basic French language and I.T skills, there was little else available.

We laboured on with Christine hovering over us; then surprisingly at four fifteen pm she shouted me over. 'You have caught the pickers,' she said. 'Leave early, but do not forget to punch your card.'

Damn, a short pay already. Still, it was wonderful to walk up that gradient and emerge into glorious sunshine. Striding up the drive to the house felt great. Everything looked so fresh and bright. Even the birds sounded more tuneful.

After a quick shower I changed into shorts; then grabbing a cold drink and a bowl of ice cream, I laid out on a lounger enjoying the late afternoon sun. Diane left me to it, driving into town to *La Poste*, then on to *Intermarché* for fresh produce.

She'd barely returned when Henri and Annette pulled up. With a sigh I headed off to the fridge for Henri's beer, while Diane made coffee for Annette. It was a well-rehearsed choreography by then. Let's face it, we'd been unofficially adopted by those kindly souls.

With a cheery '*Bonjour,*' Henri shuffled in, offering me freshly picked vegetables from his garden. While thanking him, I noticed Annette was walking badly and looked drawn. I offered her a seat; but when I asked how she was, she just shrugged. Deciding that she needed fussing over, I offered her some English biscuits as a treat. Bless them; they'd struggled to visit us, to ask how my first couple of days had gone.

While agreeing that the work was hard, I said I was pleased to have the job and was enjoying it. (No harm in a little white

184

lie, I thought.) I also said that their two boys were looking after me, which pleased them immensely Concentrating fully we chewed the fat (figuratively speaking,) and when Annette mentioned a large *fête* at Le Lude the coming Sunday, we said we'd probably attend. They didn't mention Chiné's *fête d'agricole*, so maybe they didn't spot us after all. It was sad that speaking to them could cause such complications. They were kindly souls, and we didn't like having to avoid them to prevent mistakes.

Well I'd made it to Wednesday, and my baptism of fire continued, working flat out on the cross-over boxes. Then adding insult to injury I spent the afternoon in the *cave*, where I hauled *brouettes* for the rest of the day.

The next morning promised even worse, as my shoulder was really inflamed. It was no day for the cross-over boxes – so what I was working on? You've guessed it. However, I couldn't ask to be moved, as I'd have to say why, which could end my contract. Then joy of joys! I was teamed up with Deni, the smallest guy in the whole team at 1.5 metres tall.

Explaining my shoulder problem to him in French, he waved dismissively, saying he'd show me a method he'd developed to combat being vertically challenged. He'd named it the *escalier* or step method. This would help us both, he said.

It was complicated, and frowned on as 'not correct,' by the others. All I knew was, it got the job done easier, which was all that mattered to *me* right then. It was just as well we used this method though, as the mushrooms were the gigantic *Champignon-de-Paris,* which filled the *panniers* so quickly that we scarcely had time to breathe.

After lunch everything went haywire; beginning when some trays became de-railed, putting us way behind schedule. While Armand commandeered a tractor, Christine climbed aboard the huge Komatsu; and between them they lifted trays back onto the track. I had to admire the way everyone worked as a team;

quietly and efficiently getting the job done – well most of the time anyway!

During the general commotion, one guy ended up injured, and had to be transported home. While using a large pry-bar to help lever a tray back onto the tracks, he'd collapsed bent double. Poor Jean ended up working both sides of the cross-over boxes single handed. God only knows how he managed it. Even on the slowest setting, I know I couldn't.

But at long last the run ended. It was four forty five pm when Christine told us to leave early, saying we should return at seven the next morning. I for one didn't need telling twice.

When I arrived home unexpectedly a surprise awaited me. Diane had been busy cutting grass; the lawns, orchard and driveway edges. In total it'd taken four hours of heavy mowing and strimming. But after I'd praised her hard work she just had to spoil it, by asking, 'Do you notice anything else different?'

Now ask any man, and he'll tell you he dreads *that* question. Having failed this test miserably in the past, I had to be extremely careful. Had she changed her hairstyle since I'd left that morning? Was she wearing something new? My eyes darted around feverishly, trying desperately to find some sign.

'You mean to say you can't tell the difference?' she asked a little peevishly.

With a feeling of impending doom, I said, 'Ok I give in; what is it?'

Well – she'd only ripped out the kitchen sliding doors and framework, plus the dangerous structure enclosing the stove. And totally exhausted and pre-occupied, I'd walked blindly past both jobs without noticing either. Oh-oh!

'Where's it all gone?' I asked lamely.

'I've barrowed it out and loaded it into the trailer,' she said through gritted teeth.

'Aw look, I'm sorry I didn't notice, but I've had a really hard day.'

And *that's* when I wished I'd bitten my tongue off!

'Oh – so *you've* had a hard day have you?'

Well, there was only one way *that* conversation was headed. After we'd both let off steam, I helped her clean up the remaining mess before dinner.

At last it was Friday, and the end of my first week at work. Arriving at the *cave* at six forty five though, I found it strangely deserted. Usually there was someone around by then. It felt weird standing there alone, but then I heard footsteps. Christine walked through the door and did a double take. 'Ah Steward,' she said, looking surprised to see me.

Recovering quickly, she asked me to collect a cap, lamp, *brouette,* and *palette* then follow her. Catching her up as she headed into tunnel 14, I was told to team up with Jacques-Noël He was waiting with his equipment ready to go. Go where? What was going on? *'Ou sont les autres,'* or where are the others? I asked him after she'd walked off.

Shrugging, he said everyone else had been asked to start at six am. So why wasn't I then? I had no time to dwell on it though. We began loading, with Jacques-Noël issuing a running diatribe of instructions – most of which I missed, as he sported a huge bushy moustache which covered his mouth. This hirsute curtain made it impossible to read his lips; a skill I'd had to master to overcome the noise underground. Feeling excluded, and with my shoulder giving me gyp, I really didn't need what happened next.

Struggling to pull the *brouette* forks out of a full *palette*, my feet slipped on the wet limestone and I fell flat on my backside. Luckily it was only my pride that was hurt; and thankfully no-one was around to see it happen.

Midday arrived and I downed tools, which provoked outrage amongst the girls. Shouting at me they pointed at their watches. In passable French I shouted back at them. 'I'm going for lunch. You began work at six am, so *you* should have gone home at eleven am.'

Walking over to me, Véronique said, I should continue working, as on Fridays everyone worked straight through to finish early. I hadn't been asked in because my hours were too high. Most French businesses operated a strict thirty five hour week back then, and I'd worked an hour more than the others. Because I was always winding them up, I thought, *I'm not falling for that*. I was about to leave when Christine strode up. 'I forget,' she said. 'You leave at three pm, the others one hour later. You will return on Monday, yes?'

'*Oui, je retour,*' I sighed.

Well I'd made it. And I felt my workmates were surprised. After all, French guys half my age had failed to hack it. All things considered, as an out of condition 58 year old, with a history of two hernia operations, I'd done better than I dared imagine. Though, despite eating like a horse that first week, I'd lost six kilos in weight. It seemed impossible, but it shows how unfit I was. However, despite the weight-loss, I wouldn't recommend it as a diet.

Much to Diane's surprise, I arrived home unexpectedly at three fifteen pm. After drinking a litre of water– the first thing to pass my lips since six am, I luxuriated in a hot bath for ages. Climbing out feeling almost human, I grabbed a quick snack before we set off for the *bureau de pomme verger,* or apple orchard, to check on Diane's job prospects. With bad weather delaying ripening though, *le secrétaire* couldn't help us. Could we call back? Or maybe she could ring us?

Arriving home we chilled out, as the temperature by then was overwhelming. As I nodded off in the crippling heat the phone trilled. It was Chris saying he'd passed his driving test. After we both congratulated him, he said, sadly he was still jobless. However, he had *some* good news. His old firm had been sued for wrongfully dismissing its apprentices, so he was due a settlement. All in all then it was something to celebrate; giving us an excuse for a 'session'– as if we needed one back then. But as it happened, we only had one glass of wine each, as we'd planned to visit Saumur in the morning.

Changeable weather greeted us when we awoke, so shelving the Saumur trip, we visited La Flèche instead. Feeling cheated though, we planned a late meal and a few drinks. After all it *was* Saturday night – though that doesn't mean much in rural France. Apart from Sundays, bar-cafés open early, serve alcohol all day long, and mostly close early in the evenings. And while it's no secret that some ex-pats enjoy a lock in at certain bars, social drinking generally happens with friends or family at home. In retrospect, that's not a bad thing, considering problems caused by drink elsewhere, though I suspect French city life might be a lot livelier.

One salutary warning we were given regarding alcohol, was from a retired English nurse we met in *Emmaus*. She said the greatest danger for ex-pats was excessive drinking, caused mainly by cheap alcohol. Especially at risk were retirees. With extra time on their hands, boredom often caused habitual drinking at home. This trait had added to the high incidence of heart disease and liver cirrhosis prevalent throughout the French health system.

We took on board her well-meant advice – then went on to ignore it. We thought we knew better. It could never happen to us. However, much later we realized just how right she was. Gradually we drifted into a routine of social drinking. Then, a glass or two at home turned into, 'The sun's gotta be over the yard-arm *somewhere* in the World,' which began most nights before dinner. She was right, it'd become a habit. So we made a determined effort and cut right back.

Therefore, to anyone contemplating a move like ours, I offer the advice that *we* were given. Here endeth yet another lesson. But take note – there may be more.

# Chapter 28

## An apple a day etcetera

Visiting Le Lude that Sunday was a spur of the moment decision. *La Fête* was heaving when we arrived; but with hundreds of people to pick from, we just had to bump into Henri and Annette almost immediately. Annette was looking worse than the last time we'd seen her; something which seemed to have escaped Henri's notice. Ambling along way ahead of her, he stopped only to shake someone's hand and chat. Shockingly, her legs were heavily bandaged, and she was following him leaning on a stick. She had serious varicose vein problems according to Véronique; which for some reason her doctor attributed to poisoned water. Being old school though, her husband came first, then her children and grandchildren. And occasionally she might just get a little time to herself. Whereas, Henri believed a woman's place was in the home; his home looking after him.

The *fête* was an enormous spectacle sprawled throughout the town's streets; a cosmopolitan event where anything from plough shares to baby clothes changed hands. Having evolved over the years into a diverse melting pot, it drew people from far and wide. Meeting up with family and friends, it gave locals an excuse to trot out their Sunday best clothes. Conversely, tourists whose feet had screamed enough, soaked up the ambience whilst people watching. Sat in the shade under awnings, they topped up the tills of bars and cafés.

The sun was beating down fiercely when we arrived. Finding a parking space near the municipal *boules* club, we walked into town. Closed off to traffic, the streets were packed with a noisy throng, trawling through the bizarre range of items on display. Spilling out across the main street, they gathered in groups to chat, while seeking any shade possible.

Even this early, food-stalls were doing a roaring trade, some selling rotisseried chickens and huge *saucissons*, while others ladled out *cassoullét* from huge cauldrons. With smoke and steam wafting through the still air, the heady aroma of spices beguiled both visitors and locals alike into trying a portion.

Melting into the crowds we meandered around – a leisurely stroll being all that was possible in the circumstances. Inevitably we encountered both English and French people we'd met since our arrival; Henri and Annette included. Even Jorge our postman was treating his family to a rare day out. Hands were shaken and kisses exchanged in this happy atmosphere, where haggling over the odd item seemed almost obligatory. But after two hours we'd had enough. So escaping the noon-day sun, we headed home for lunch.

After our meal and a snooze, we decided to visit Luche-Pringé. Often, when driving to La Flèche, we'd noticed a sign for the town and its 11th century *église,* or church. Turning right, we joined a minor road leading to a wooden river bridge. With its hand rails sporting baskets of crimson geraniums, it made for a startling red-carpet welcome for visitors.

We parked under shady plane trees near the church, which was unfortunately locked. Moving on we found an impressive sports complex, complete with open-air pool, gym and disco-bar; surprising for such a small town.

Leading off from the centre, a riverside walk passed the municipal park, a caravan site, and a boat hire company. But with the exception of some anglers, a couple in a rowing-boat, and a woman walking her dog, the place seemed deserted. I often wonder where they hide all the people in these towns!

But for me, that's the charm of France. More than twice the size of the whole UK, its population is roughly the same; so huge swathes of open countryside allow peace, quiet, and a chance to contemplate the meaning of life.

Setting off at a leisurely pace, we followed a narrow path along the river's edge. Startled by our passing, dragonflies skipped away across the shallow water, tempting lethargic fish to the surface. Rounding a copse of willow trees further ahead, we were surprised to come across a large wooden sculpture. Climbing over a stile next to it we skirted a cornfield, spying a ruined old mill on the far bank. Sadly its working life had come to an end long ago; its broken water-wheel allowing the current to swirl by unchecked, before tumbling over a weir.

Resting for a while on some welcoming rocks, we sat mesmerized by the tranquil scene. Ahead of us, like figures in a Constable painting, two young boys with rolled up trousers were using stepping stones to cross the river. Their adventure, made possible by low water levels, would normally be too dangerous to attempt. But there was no talk here of hose pipe bans, or political correctness which stopped kids from having fun. It was how I remembered *my* childhood; when common sense and the school of hard knocks was allowed free reign.

All too soon though we had to head back, as dark clouds gathered overhead. Who knows, with a little luck, the parched landscape might soon find relief.

Passing the apple orchards on the way home, we saw large wooden crates at the head of each avenue of trees. As festooned netting had also been removed and a tractor parked up nearby, it meant picking wasn't far off.

With the weekend over it was back to 'mushroom 101,' where I stood waiting to be allotted my *'travail de jour.'* Fingers crossed, I watched Christine approach with her clipboard.

'Steward, you *lavage,'* she said, moving on. I set off quickly before she could change her mind.

However, the *lavage* proved to be a poisoned chalice that morning. When I emerged onto the terrace it was teeming down, and I'd picked *this* day to wear a tee-shirt and jeans. Of course I'd be wearing waterproofs – but at seven am in heavy rain I was more than a little nipped, I can tell you.

Once underway though I soon warmed up; but due to another cloud-burst later, we took a ten minute break. Holed up in a shed out of the driving rain, I chatted with my latest workmate about his holiday. This was his first day back poor sod, and he looked thoroughly miserable.

By midday; numb with cold I belatedly realized my trousers and socks were sodden. I'd been so chilled I didn't even notice. Back home at lunchtime, I towelled off, changed into dry clothes; then after a quick snack it was back for more of the same.

The afternoon continued along similar lines, until around four pm when a full-on storm erupted. Luckily we were almost finished; and with my hours checked by Christine I left.

Arriving home absolutely drenched, I found Diane tending a blazing fire. As I changed into dry clothes, she drove off to Le Lude for a few things.

In France it's common to buy fresh food daily. For example, the local *boulangerie* baked twice daily, and one old lady neighbour cycled into town each morning and afternoon, returning with just a mini *baguette* in her basket each time.

When leaving, Diane had suggested I have a long hot soak, saying she wouldn't be long. 'Good idea,' I said. 'See you soon.'

Five minutes later, my drenched clothes lay discarded on the bathroom floor. With mixer taps frothing up a herbal additive, I stretched over to adjust the flow, muscles rippling manfully. Yeh right! Anyway, there I stood as naked as a Jay bird, when 'click,' the electricity cut out. Well thank you God! That meant the pump was out of action.

This'd happened before during bad weather; and being on the power grid from Le Mans to Tours the fault could lie anywhere. It could take anything from five minutes to five hours before power was restored, based on past experience.

Standing in the cold gloomy bathroom, I sighed in resignation. After thinking about it briefly, I shrugged fatalistically, then lowered my cringing buttocks into ten centimetres of lukewarm water.

The electricity came back on at seven pm as we read by candle-light. It could have been worse I suppose.

Seven am Tuesday and my luck was out. Nursing my throbbing shoulder, I was hiding at the back of the crowded office. Alas Christine spotted me. 'Ah Stewaard, you are working on cross-over boxes with Jacques Plombièr.' Oh crap!

I worked flat out for two hours alongside Jacques, before we were transferred to the *cave*, where we loaded '*palettes*' until midday. By then I felt ready to quit. When I trudged in cursing at lunch-time though, Diane justifiably berated me, saying, my mood wasn't just due to the job. I'd been hell to live with since my shoulder injury. Ignoring my grumpiness she prepared lunch; but I never got to eat it. I had to ring England to sort out a banking glitch. Due to the time difference I had no choice. Gulping down a quick mouthful afterwards, I headed off to work again.

The nightmare continued in the afternoon, loading *panniers* alongside Jacques and Jean. They were both nice lads, but like Henri they were barely understandable. Leaving at five fifteen, I felt that with the language problem and general noise level, I'd *always* have difficulty communicating. Though nothing had been said, I felt I was slowing people down. Maybe they thought I wasn't pulling my weight, and were making allowances for me. The thing was, *they* all seemed to know exactly what to do – meshing together like cogs in a gearbox. While on the other hand, *I* felt like a spanner in the works. When I told Diane how I felt, she said I was being too hard on myself. After all, I'd only been there a week. She agreed that communication was difficult, and she understood my frustration. But the *real* problem was my shoulder. 'Relax while I nip to Le Lude,' she said. 'We'll talk when I get back.'

She'd just left when the phone rang. It was the secretary from the apple orchards. Could Madame attend for work at eight o' clock on Thursday?

When she returned, I said to Diane, 'What do you want first? Good news or bad.'

'Go on then, give me the bad first,' she sighed.

'I hope you like apples,' I said, grinning.

When the news registered, she was pleased that we now *both* had jobs. But then she began worrying about language problems and what to wear. 'I've got another pair of safety boots somewhere,' I said.

'Safety boots? Why would I want safety boots?'

'Well, high heels and a handbag won't be much use in the orchards, now will they?'

Deep in the *cave* the next morning things had begun badly. Moved to a new tunnel, my team encountered uneven terrain and water seepage. Gradients became even more dangerous than normal; catching the unwary out, especially when the track turned sharply at the bottom. Twice that day my *brouette* slid off downhill, with me hanging on behind in a skier's crouch.

The first time it happened I dug in the metal legs; desperate to slow down what had become a sledge. However, the immutable laws of physics wouldn't be denied. As I tried desperately to turn into a blind bend, the heavy load continued remorselessly forwards. With my heart plummeting, I watched helplessly as the stacked *panniers* toppled over, sending many kilos of fungi cascading across the floor. It'd been inevitable really. Jacques had said it would happen sometime, but I'd ignored him, thinking this is Jacques, 'the walking accident' talking. It would never happen to *me*.

Well, pride definitely comes before a fall. A cheer rang out as the girls watched my initiation; as they'd no doubt watched others before me. Taking pity on me they helped pick up the spillage – which of course contained their tally markers!

It happened again later. But this time I took a theatrical bow when the girls cheered. Apart from those two disasters though, it wasn't a bad day at the office, considering I'd had less than four hours sleep. With stiff upper lip I walked home, dignity intact, if a little bruised.

Arriving at the farmhouse, I found Diane seemingly blasé about her impending baptism in the orchards. She'd rung to confirm her starting time, and was told she'd be working alongside various other foreign workers. Most were experienced and returned annually, but this season she was the only Brit on the workforce. Well what a coincidence!

After tea I regaled her with my disasters, trying to take her mind off any worries she might be having. But as the morning would roll round inevitably, we decided a long soak and an early night would benefit us both.

Waking with a start I glanced at the clock. I thought I'd slept in – but no, it was almost six am and I'd woken up ahead of time as normal. Switching off the alarm I dressed quietly, made tea and a slice of toast. Then just before leaving, I took Diane a cuppa. Shaking her gently I wished her good luck; making sure she was fully awake, and not about to crawl back under the duvet. With my good deed done, it was off to *my* hell on Earth for another day of fun.

As it turned out, the day was short-lived. I was sentenced to the dreaded cross-over boxes with Jacques. Angry about a previous tongue-lashing, he made a monumental error of judgement. He'd obviously decided that whatever happened on his watch, he wasn't going to be the one to stop production.

Well, what happened next was like a flickering old black and white comedy movie. With Véronique feeding us boxes the run got underway; Jacques having set the belt at top speed.

196

Almost immediately we were deluged with mushrooms; and with arms going like pistons we worked flat out. But finding it impossible to cope, we fell hopelessly behind. As mushrooms were pouring across the floor by then, I shouted at Jacques□. Getting no reply *Véronique* then shouted at him. But ignoring us both he continued working furiously.

I had no choice. Climbing over the rapidly mounting pile I hit the red button. Amid shouting from down the line Christine appeared, scowling at the scene of devastation that met her.

'Why the bloody hell didn't you stop this sooner?' (Or the French equivalent,) she shouted at the three of us. But being in charge, it was Jacques who had yet another bollocking added to his 'rap sheet.' We were told to clean up the mess; after which Jacques was sent down to the *cave* as a punishment. Being honest, I think he was happier down there anyway. Luckily I landed an easier job; clearing off trays with a *raclet* or rake. Meanwhile, mechanics stripped down the choked belt drive.

At 11-45 Christine called a halt to proceedings, saying the machinery needed a complete clean-out. We should go home, she said, but return at six the next morning to finish the order.

Dropped off by Véronique, I was just 'peeling' off my boots when Diane roared up the drive. My virgin apple picker was home, fresh from her first mornings toil. I made her a cuppa, while she collapsed with a groan onto a chair.

'Come on then, tell me all about it,' I said.

'Hang on a minute. Help me get these damn boots off first. Ah lush! Right, now where should I start?' she said, rubbing her feet. 'Well, the owner's called Dominic and he's a real shit. Then there's a supervisor called Céline. She's an alcoholic, and looks like a half-a-gadgie. (a Geordie euphemism for a transvestite back then) She's built like a brick outhouse, has a foul temper, and shouts at *everybody*. But apart from her, nobody's spoken to me all morning, I've never stopped for a minute and I've been working like a bloody horse. Otherwise, everything's just fine. So what's for lunch?'

197

Sat down with a cuppa she got it off her chest. As usual it was all about the 'the French way.' She'd been lectured by Céline, on how to *carefully* pluck the apples by twisting them in a particular way. Then she learned how to inspect them before placing them *carefully* into her *pannier;* a large metal basket slung across the chest. Finally, the full *panniers* were to be tipped *carefully* into a large wooden crate called a *ballox*.

'What a load of crap. It's not rocket science. Not when you watch the so-called professionals anyway. They *rip* the apples off the branches, *drop* them into their *panniers*, and *pour* them into the crates. Apart from the French, most of them are Moroccans and Poles working on piece-work rates, so they couldn't give a toss about 'the French Way.'

As I helped her off with her boots, she drank another cuppa and devoured a sandwich, while giving me a snapshot of her first morning as a *cueiller,* or apple picker.

The first thing she'd been told was, she was a *cueiller* – not a *cuiller,* which is a spoon. It was another instance of two words sounding similar, but having two entirely different meanings; something she'd had drummed into her repeatedly.

From the off, the work was fast and brutal; and the huge nets slung overhead to deter birds, had become a haven for flies and wasps. These critters had then made it their life's work to occupy every orifice available on, or in the human body. Coupled with the intense heat, it made conditions 'interesting,' she said. The Moroccans just plodded along, laughing and chattering, accustomed to the heat and flies; while the *'Polonaises'* or Poles were awesome. Working flat out on piece-work, some didn't even stop for lunch. The faster they worked, the more money they could send back home.

Unfortunately, by working so fast they made mistakes, sending bad or misshapen apples to the factory. When this was discovered, it'd sent 'half-a-gadgie' into an apoplectic rage. Furious, but unable to pinpoint the culprits, she'd dished out threats indiscriminately. She was constantly hyper, as Dominic (a real shit you may remember) was on her case all the time.

Diane had already experienced all of this, and it was only her first morning. Now I could've been mistaken, but she didn't seem to be relishing the afternoon.

Picking blackberries from our hedgerows occupied me after Diane left; followed by collecting and stacking wood. I also discovered that the red marker in the bottom field was actually an enamel coffee-pot, stuck jauntily on a pole. Rusty, and riddled with bullet holes, it must have been used for target practice – right next to the road.

After foraging, I decided to cut the grass around the *poulét* pens. But when I dragged the mower out it wouldn't work. I cleaned the plug and filters then changed the fuel, but it still refused to start. Sod it, I thought, pushing it back in the shed and collapsing onto a sun-lounger.

Diane arrived soon after, saying Céline had gone completely ballistic after lunch. Apples that were acceptable that morning weren't in the afternoon. Diane then got to experience the censorious wagging of the finger – something I'd come to hate with a passion. Tut-tutting, Céline had said, *'Non, non Deanna, non bon,* or – no, no Diane, not good.

Diane just kept her cool and carried on, so Céline turned on someone else. 'Look at this,' she said. She was pointing to her *pannier* which held ten kilos of apples. 'What do you think of *that* then?'

'Nobody said it would be easy,' I replied.

# Chapter 29

## Hunting, logging and gathering

By the third week in August Diane had settled into her job, and we *both* arrived home weary. After Friday's early finish and with the house to myself, I washed up after lunch then prepared to indulge in a little 'Me' time. Carrying a novel and cuppa out to the patio, I relished this rare opportunity to slob out on one of my bargain sun-loungers.

Carefully setting down my tea, I opened my book and leaned back with a decadent sigh. 'Crack,' the back of the lounger collapsed. Over I went flat on my back, ass in the air and the book flying off into the flower beds. 'Oh for Christ's sake,' I gasped, standing up and rubbing my scraped posterior.

Dismissing any ideas of chancing the second lounger, I analysed the comfort factor to be had from the smaller upright chairs. Sighing wistfully, I realised that my sybaritic afternoon had just evaporated. With weary resignation, I located the book, picked up the cup of tea; then took both them and my pet lip back into the house.

Shortly after five pm, the Peugeot pulled up with a screech of brakes. Muttering incantations against Céline, Diane climbed from the car and slammed the door. Her afternoon had been crap, she fumed. After making a cuppa, we sat down and compared notes. But it wasn't long before she was sniggering, as she pictured my unscripted acrobatics. A relaxing soak in a herbal bath completed her recovery.

By then a blood red sun was sinking below the horizon. Enjoying the warm still evening, we sat with the French windows open. Between us, a bottle of Pinot Noir nestled in a champagne bucket – both us and the wine chilled to perfection.

Home from college for the weekend, François paid us a visit, where we discussed his course and our projects. When I mentioned the bullet-ridden coffee pot, he smiled wryly, saying, 'It was *normale* for Monsieur Renard.'

Talking of shooting, he said the hunting season, or *'la chasse'* was due to begin. We'd already noted the distant baying of hounds most mornings. Over in the next valley a large pack was caged, eager for the beginning of September, the start of the red deer season. Roe deer however were *really* unlucky, as their season opened in June. Each *commune* was allocated a quota of deer to be culled, with all kills to be reported to the authorities. The numbers were enforced rigidly, as the local deer population was dwindling. For instance, the limit placed on *cerfs* or stags was seven in our area. And as few as that seems, does were even more jealously protected; as most had given birth, and were still weaning their young.

Hunting *sangliere* was totally different; as they were savage and damaged crops. Considered a menace, their season was officially June until February, with a break in October. But as they tasted delicious when smoked, it was virtually open season on them.

September was generally the start of tree felling season; and this year teams were harvesting swathes across our valley. Using log skidders, these professionals dragged out machine-felled trees. But working nearby were other hardy individuals, prepared to cut their own firewood. Bertrand was one of them. Day after day he'd return from his early shift driving; and after a quick lunch, head out on his tractor.

In this densely forested region, he and others had banded together to buy a stand of trees, mainly *chêne* (oak,) or *châtaigne* (chestnut.) After felling them, they sawed them into two-metre lengths, before loading them onto their trailers manually. Bertrand made many such trips day after day, vastly reducing the cost of his winter fuel. I'd feel sorry for him when he arrived home looking weary, and gave him a hand unloading whenever I could.

I'd read that in France, seventy percent of fuel used was wood. Often changing hands as payment for work, it avoided the dreaded '*taxation*.' Bought by the cord (three cubic metres,) or *stere* (one cubic metre,) it could be delivered in two-metre lengths, or cut logs which cost more. A *stere* cost eighty euros delivered. But if Bertrand felled and hauled his own, a *stere* cost him twenty-eight euros plus his fuel. Multiply that by three for a cord – of which he used many, and you know why.

Hauling the two-metre lengths back to Le Lavendu, they were stacked in large piles, covered with tarpaulins and left to season for three years. In his woodshed he stacked one metre lengths, measured with a metre long hazel wand. Those were sawn in half when needed for his stove. (What a palaver!) Many stacks were needed, to have seasoned logs available at all times. And it was a matter of prestige, as to who had the most, and best stacked logs in the area.

That first year, I was ignorant as to the amount of wood *we'd* need. Using my shiny new chainsaw I cut up old poles and fence-posts lying around the property, then attacked fallen trees in our wood. To my untrained eye, this growing pile in my wood-shed looked impressive, and more than enough for our needs. *Anyway, this is France*, I reasoned. *With unlimited sunshine, why squander our limited funds unnecessarily?*

I'd live to regret that later.

Mounted on a pharmacy wall in Saumur, the giant thermometer read thirty-one C in the shade. We'd just toured the market; found Diane a cheap watch for work; then after food shopping returned home totally frazzled. Pulling onto the drive, we saw Bertrand and François striding out with exaggerated footsteps along the bottom field. Waving me over, François said, 'We have a problem with this field you are renting us.'

Warily, I asked what the problem was. He said they'd been measuring it carefully using an industrial tape measure. 'Oh *have* you now?' I said bridling up. 'So what's wrong with it?'

'There is no problem with the *land*. But you have given us more than is shown on the deeds. What do you want to do with the extra?'

Touched by their honesty, I said, the narrow strip left over was no use to me. They should just treat it as shown on the deeds. Going on to discuss preparation and planting, they pointed out furrows gouged in the turf by *sanglier* tusks. Then, with raindrops beginning to fall, we shook hands and went our separate ways.


A heavy mist shrouded the valley the next morning, defying the sun's attempts to break through. But with work looming the day after we drove off quickly, determined to enjoy our day off. If the mist cleared we'd probably feel guilty, and find something that needed doing.

By then the roads were back to normal; almost deserted on this Sunday morning. Departing tourists had given us back our freedom; and meandering through deserted little villages at our own pace was sublime. As if magnetized, we were drawn to Château-la-Vallière where we strolled around the lake. Invigorated, we returned to the deserted beach and set down a rug near some chained-up pedalos. Like the shuttered life-guard station and ice cream kiosk, they looked abandoned and forlorn.

At peace with the world we basked in autumn sunshine, watching the odd car pass by or people strolling around the lake. But as shadows lengthened, we stood up, shook sand off the rug then returned to the car.

Back at H.Q, we sipped strong bracing coffee, before nipping over to wish François a safe journey south after his visit. On our arrival, Véronique served us *more* coffee with some dainty little biscuits. Awash with caffeine by then we waved off our young student. Then wishing Véronique *Au revoire,* we left with Bertrand as he prepared to go rabbit shooting, 'assisted' by his trainee hunting dog Lupé.

Returning to our garden, we began picking quinces from our manic looking tree. Being ugly looking, with a tough waxy skin, (the fruit not me) they were virtually useless until cooked. But after Diane's kitchen alchemy, they evolved into fine jams and preserves. Having picked enough to supply her production line, I took a basketful to both Véronique and Annette. A thank-you for the many veggies they'd given us recently.

I felt blessed being assigned to the *lavage* that Monday, though it proved a mixed blessing, as the morning was dark, cold, and required warm clothing. Uncomfortable though it was, I found it infinitely more preferable than working underground.

My team-mate that morning was a burly guy named Luie; one of three brothers at the *cave,* and not into stimulating conversation – well *any* conversation to be honest. Slogging on robotically, I became lost in my own private world; until with spirits soaring, I spied Diane driving out to work. As usual when '*lavaging,'* I kept an eye out for her; waving the spraying water in an overhead arc when she approached. The spray reflected the the car's headlights, which she then flashed in return. A meaningless gesture to some perhaps; but to us back then it was priceless, and a sign of solidarity.

After enduring a morning of grunts and shrugs from my work-mate, I arrived home cold, wet, and tired. Diane appeared soon after looking withdrawn. She'd been placed with the French contingent; and though she'd tried speaking to her co-workers, they'd all ignored her. It must have been a long lonely day, ostracized for no apparent reason.

We discovered why later. The new phone directory had just been issued. We received one and saw our name in it. Rumour had spread that we'd bought Le Ferronerie as *un domicile secondaire,* or second home. As wealthy foreigners (in their eyes,) we'd priced out locals. They'd presumed that Diane didn't need to work in the orchards; and being rich, we'd both

204

taken French people's jobs which we didn't need. What a load of rubbish! Did they really think we were working like mules for *fun*?

What they didn't know was; we'd sunk everything into this venture. And with restoration costs increasing rapidly and a short term mortgage to pay, our funds were dwindling fast. The hypocrisy of their reasoning, and why foreigners were *able* to buy properties, was many French buyers won't renovate houses. Young people were buying new builds; often sited near older properties which were just left to collapse. Meanwhile, French opportunists were jumping onto the property boom, and selling at inflated prices to foreigners.

Topping off Diane's morning; under pressure from Dominic, Céline had come down hard on the pickers. Shit rolls downhill, they say. While trying to up her pace, Diane slipped on the wet grass, and gouged her shin on her *escalier*. 'At least it makes a change from all the bruises I've got,' she shrugged.

But at least she'd received her contract; which stated her hours, though not her pay rate. It also mentioned a production bonus – which never materialized. Meanwhile, I still had no contract. Though frustrated, we knew some of our problems were due to poor communication skills. We could live with that. But it didn't excuse the misguided prejudice that Diane was enduring. She said she'd be better off working with the Poles or Moroccans. At least they tried speaking to her.

A gloomy lunch-time was spent changing into dry clothes and socks. Then wrapping plastic bags around dry stockings, we slid on damp wellingtons and set off for the afternoon shift. I was hoping for a five pm finish, but was informed by Armand mid-afternoon that I was required to work until six thirty pm on an urgent order. Destined for Parisian restaurants, it had to travel overnight to arrive early the next morning.

Working on the rain swept lavage at five forty pm, I flagged down Diane as she passed; saying I'd be late and to keep everything warm.

Leaving the *cave* bone-weary around seven pm, I set off alone on the long walk home. Battered by rain on the unlit road, I was spotted by Lupé and Hermé, who took great pleasure in barking at me until I passed out of sight. I could have done without that right then.

Incidentally, plastic bags didn't solve my wet feet problem. Striding out, I squelched up the drive, drawn towards the welcoming lights of home. Staggering through the door I, could smell odours wafting from the oven. Needing no further encouragement, I bathed in record time, then received a glass of wine in my eager hand. Both the wine and meal were unbelievably good. And as Billy Connolly strode across a Glasgow stage to manic applause, I melted blissfully into the settee, remote control in hand.

On my first day walking to work, I'd set off hugging the hedge on the dark unlit road. Waving a torch behind me, I tried to warn approaching vehicles. Whether this'd been taken as a sign of distress I'll probably never know. But the next morning a Citroën BX pulled up, and a girl from the *cave* offered me a lift. After accepting her kind offer it'd then become routine. Any language issues were avoided by discussing the weather or work; and with the journey being short, it never became awkward. If I was feeling down and didn't feel like talking, I could always set off late and miss her. But if it was raining I was always there on time.

By then I'd proven myself at work, and been generally accepted. However Diane was still having problems. But it wasn't with Céline who'd calmed down a lot. It was the other French girls. Diane believed that Marie, a 'mouthy cow' (not my words) was the instigator; stirring it against '*la femme Anglais.*' But as things stood, she could only grit her teeth, keep her head down and get on with it; hoping things would improve with time.

Over the next few days life rolled on as normal – until the morning I was paired on the cross-over boxes with the phenomenon known as Christopher Borelle. As it was his first day back after recovering from a severe back injury, I reasoned he'd be taking it easy. But no. Nodding to me, he hung up his jacket, set the lever at top speed, pushed the start button and we were off.

With a cigarillo clenched firmly between his teeth, he hit a furious pace which the box-feeder and I found difficult to live with. Then alarmingly, he got into his stride and began to speed up! Soon the *palette* was full. But did that stop him? Of course not! While the fork lift driver tried in vain to get to it, 'Iron man' began stacking boxes on the floor, indicating that I should do the same. Before long *panniers* were stacked everywhere; despite the forklift driver's efforts to get at them. This superhuman, wearing a surgical support corset, actually worked the machine to a standstill.

Thankfully, after three hours the run finished. We'd missed a possible break *ages* before, because he'd refused to stop. But what was this? He was waving me to follow him. Muttering '*Brouette*,' he strode off. What the hell was he up to now? I wondered.

Shouting '*Toilette*,' I took a quick slurp of water at the fountain. Wiping my mouth, I saw him disappear into a tunnel, pushing a *brouette* and *palette*. Was he for real? Hurrying to catch up with him, I too grabbed a *brouette* and *palette*; arriving to find we'd been assigned to work with the Plombière brothers. And there the nightmare continued, with Borelle setting the pace for everyone until noon arrived. Christine then said, thanks to our furious pace we could take a half day off – unpaid of course. Thanks a lot Iron Man!

The kitchen door burst open at lunchtime, and Diane found me flat out on the settee, steam rising from my abandoned boots. She reported that she'd had a much better time that morning, as finally her life seemed to be improving. An elderly French couple had joined the team and been chatting to her; and a woman named Yvette walked over from her terrace to praise her work. She appeared to be related to Henri somehow, and mentioned us visiting his home. Even Dominic finally spoke to her in broken English, which was unusual to say the least.

After lunch she returned to the orchards, while I changed into my other work gear. Braving the fierce sunshine I began mixing cement. At one point, stepping back to mop my brow I thought I was hallucinating. The mix was moving! Poking it carefully with a trowel encouraged a huge sorry-looking toad to the surface. Sluicing it off I carried it to the flower-beds. Then getting into a rhythm, I applied two barrow-loads to the walls.

While hosing out the barrow later Diane pulled up. She was aching from head to toe, which was par for the course, but she'd also pulled a back muscle. Running her a hot bath and administering painkillers, I nipped over to return Bertrand's trowel. There I found Véronique, who'd also finished early and collected Anna for a visit. Concerned when I mentioned Diane's back they wanted to pop over; but I knew Diane hated being fussed over. Thanking them for their concern, I said she was sleeping. Then I left to proceed with the next stage of my mission.

When I'd last saw her, Annette asked us to pop down, as she had some veggies for Diane. With the invalid resting, I plucked up courage and set off to collect them, forestalling a visit while Diane was laid up. On the way I passed Henri, supervising Jacques in his garden. Waving to me he continued his vigil.

Arriving at the mill house I met the long suffering lady, her arms full of vegetables. I suggested carrying them – a gesture which obviously surprised her. Declining politely, she invited me in, offering me a beer which I accepted gratefully.

Adjourning to the sun- room, I asked about her health, and as usual she assured me she was fine. The subject then switched to our families; and without Henri's presence it became our first decent conversation. When she heard about Diane's bad back, she gave me some strong painkillers for '*le mal de dos,'* along with a pile of veggies. She was really a very nice person, and much easier to talk to on her own.

After pondering on other people's relationships while driving back, I was unloading the vegetables when Armand pulled up. He'd lost my phone number again, and had driven over to change my start time the next morning. Not to an earlier time though, but to nine o' clock. He'd just completed a tunnel inspection, and said the *champignons* were too small to be picked right then. He wanted everyone to start two hours later in the morning, to catch them at their very best. No problem I said; though God knows what difference two hours makes to the growth of a mushroom. Mind you they'd be fresher I suppose. Ah well, back to my patient.

Toot toot! Oh no, it was Jacques. He and Henri had brought a basket of peaches, fresh from Jacques' tree. Staggering off to the bedroom, Diane said, 'Tell them I'm sleeping *please.'*

As it was, they hadn't arrived for a long visit. They were keen to get back to their evening meal. However, they wouldn't mind having a quick look at our garden.

Headed down the path, Jacques inspected my plasterwork on the house façade, and nodded his approval. This was praise indeed, as he informed me proudly that he was a *maçon* by trade. Also, the garden seemed satisfactory, as I didn't receive one 'tut, or any advice on the correct way to tend it. With beaming smiles they left soon after. Returning to Diane, she said I resembled a stunned mullet. It was the constant strain of trying to master the local dialect, I told her. But our French was improving by leaps and bounds, and at least people were taking the trouble to look after us. So we must be on the road to acceptance by this little community, mustn't we?

# Chapter 30

## Much ado about nothing

Though it seemed like an eternity to Diane, Friday saw the end of her second week in the orchards. And with a month's hard graft under *my* belt, I'd returned that afternoon proudly clutching my first pay-note. However, I was amazed to find sixteen off-takes, including union fees. Where *was* this union? I checked with Véronique and the note was correct. Most of the off-takes were various taxes. However, every cloud has a silver lining, they say. As an incentive, everyone received two kilos of free mushrooms per month. Whoopee!

Diane was also overwhelmed to hear, that as a privilege, pickers on the terraces were allowed to eat the odd apple while working. One or two could even be taken home on occasion, she was told with a furtive wink. Wow! Who needed the stresses of being an International Banker or Investment analyst, with rewards like those on offer?

By then work had settled down to a hard routine; enduring aches, pains and niggling injuries as par for the course. On the plus side however, we'd both lost weight and were generally fitter. But however hard we worked; to the French we were still outsiders. The word had spread that we'd used influence to get our jobs, which many believed should have gone to French people. Yes, people did let me know a job was available, but I was interviewed, and I only got my job because the French wouldn't, or couldn't hack it. As for Diane; her name was on a list, and was picked in order. Also, none of the French would put up with being treated the way she was. Knuckling down in the job, she worked hard while being 'sent to Coventry.' And though he meant well, it didn't help Diane's cause one iota, when Dominic singled her out for praise one day. *That* went down like a lead balloon with her French co-workers.

On the plus side though, she finally made a friend, a young woman from Le Lude named Chantal. It was a huge leap forward for Diane, and they contrived working together whenever possible; conversing in 'Franglais' and taking the mickey out of Céline, whose name translated as Moon Goddess. 'Moon-faced more like,' Diane commented dryly.

Steadily and predictably life rolled along in our commune, the days growing shorter as people prepared for winter. And with unpredictable weather, our workload at home grew even heavier as we pushed hard with the renovations. Coupled with our day jobs, work seemed never-ending. Plus, with increased rainfall, we discovered the wood-shed's corrugated roof leaked badly. What had been a welcome source of ventilation in the summer had morphed into a water feature, drenching the bone-dry woodpile, which then had to be moved.

Another job requiring attention was replacing missing planking on the barn. Using Monsieur Renard's ladder, it promised to be interesting, to say the least.

However, all outside jobs were eventually sorted, and it was time to move indoors. Considering our options, we decided to add insulation panels to the larger downstairs bedroom. For some inexplicable reason, one wall was decorated in pink tiles, leaving a sixty centimetre gap at the top. Why? Maybe the old skinflint had just run out of tiles. Bertrand thought the room may have been used for cold storage; but whatever the reason, we'd relished the cool bedroom during the summer, with its glass door leading out to the patio. In winter though it would be untenable, and might even develop damp problems. Therefore, a date was set to begin work, and materials assembled. But first on the agenda was picking fruit and veg. for bottling and storage.

While giving our lawns a final cut, Bertrand arrived to harvest the meadow grass, his tractor towing an ancient cutting attachment. Once cut, he and Véronique raked the swathes into long windrows to dry in the fierce sun; and a few days later, his friend appeared with a hay-baler. Though contracted to local farms, he made time to trundle up and down our fields, his machine disgorging large bales of hay like some giant metal insect laying eggs.

By the time he'd driven off the denuded fields, golden *rondelles* stood proudly amid the stubble. Wasting no time, Bertrand uplifted the bales from the fields; then came back to begin ploughing. And that's when the secondary side of the mushroom business took off.

Throughout the season, trucks collected waste mulch and fungi from the *cave*. Normally, a mere handful appeared during any given week, but now traffic increased exponentially. No longer were trucks just supplying a local fertilizer manufacturer. Farmers now wanted bulk deliveries before ploughing. And not to be outdone, the public began arriving on-site with *their* trailers.

That Friday I'd landed my plumb job '*lavaging*.' Teamed with Jean we began working towards an early finish; but like a magnet he attracted bad luck. After coming loose repeatedly, one of the forks actually fell off. Running late by then, he drove off to change machines; and being left to tidy up, I got a rare chance to study my fellow man in secret.

Overlooking them from the terrace, I saw people thinking themselves unobserved, cramming mulch into their trailers and tamping it down ferociously. Then 'innocently' by-passing the weighing platform, they went to pay at the office. We're all the same under the skin, I reckon.

In the event, we didn't get the early finish we'd hoped for. Jean desperately tried to catch up, but he should've changed machines much earlier. Worried about Christine's reaction though, he'd tried to muddle through. We were only half an hour late, but I got home to find Diane with only five minutes of her lunch break left.

Once she'd gone I checked our *dépendances,* seeking bricks to construct a fire surround. I only found three; but with them as a pattern I could estimate type and quantities needed. Unfortunately, I'd let Diane shoot off with the car so I was stymied; I'd have to nip down to *Brico* the next day to check out their stock. Changing tack I marched off to the wood-shed, where I continued moving and re-stacking sodden logs.

Readying the trailer the next day I was ready to go, but I was informed that instead we needed to visit Saumur. Diane required specialist waterproofs for work, which were only available in Saumur apparently, and on sale for a limited period only. I knew when I was beaten so off we went.

After driving like a maniac to get her there, Diane just managed to secure the exclusive waterproofs. We were lucky mind you. When we dashed into the shop, they only had about *two hundred* pairs left! After buying these rare items we ransacked *Intermarché's* shelves for yet more food. Oh sorry, I forgot! I nipped next door to *Bricomarché* and treated myself to a bath-plug and spark plug. How extravagant was I?

Driving back through Broc, we passed two English looking pedestrians. Rumour had it that *un Anglais* had bought the huge house at the end of the village, for a highly inflated price. I bet that really cheesed off the natives. Short on time we tooted and waved, as they'd noted our English plate. We'd bump into them sometime no doubt.

Meanwhile, back home, Diane informed me that the toilet wouldn't stop flushing. Removing the cistern cover to check the valve, I found a deodorant block wedged under the ball-cock. Smiling inwardly, I thought, I may as well fit the new sink plug while I'm here.

With supper over, we settled down to watch a video. Wine in hand and feet up, I pressed the remote control – nothing! Aaaagh! Diving behind the TV and video, we fiddled with cables. 'Dah-dah,' on it came. Phew! Diane then admitted she'd been vacuuming behind the unit earlier, and *might* have dislodged a cable. Shattered nerves called for more wine; and to hell with the comedy we'd agreed on. Dig out the rock videos.

Vernante's Sunday market seemed like a great idea at first, but on arrival we found there wasn't a stall to be seen anywhere. We'd checked our little red book of market venues before setting out, and it was definitely listed for today; so where was it? Perplexed, I asked a passing local. It'd been cancelled, he said. Trying to be charitable we forgave the stall-holders, with it being near the end of season.

Heading on to Saumur, we decided to take a river cruise instead. Yes, you've guessed it; the last one was the previous weekend according to the timetable. Frustrated, we wandered aimlessly, before finding a gallery displaying old photos of the city. Shot in yellowing monochrome, the faded images were fascinating. Feeling perkier after that, we ate our packed lunch watching anglers along the river bank; the normally packed car park yawning emptily behind us. Yes, the holiday season was definitely over.

Lunch finished, we criss-crossed deserted streets lined with closed shops. Let's face it; they'd never really embraced Sunday trading anyway. But it was a further sign that autumn had arrived.

Wandering into an unfamiliar side-street we discovered an art shop. After spending a pleasant fifteen minutes and a few euros, we left with sketch pads and pastel pencils. With the house now coming along nicely, we intended sketching *en plein air* again on the odd occasion. Our jobs though, they were a different matter altogether.

Monday saw me paired with Iron man Borelle on the cross-over boxes. Yet again, kilos of mushrooms cascaded over the floor as he refused to 'stick with 'the programme.' At one point Armand was forced to intervene; edging a massive excavator in to scoop up piles of spillage, including perfectly saleable mushrooms. He was shouting at Christopher to slow down; but in the zone, Iron Man wasn't listening and carried on remorselessly.

Clocking off at noon, I found that only five workers were needed that afternoon. Most had worked their weekly quota, while others were taking a lieu day. Me? I was one of the lucky five. I arrived home for lunch as Diane drove up, drenched from her morning on the terraces.

Problems had resurfaced, testing her fragile relationship with the French yet again. They'd been told to back-pick rows for missed fruit; and as Diane's team-mate hadn't shown up, Céline removed her *plaquets* from the *ballox* that Diane was filling. Then of course the errant team-mate arrived late and began arguing with Céline; glaring murderously, and pointing at Diane as if *she'd* removed them.

Meanwhile, my afternoon went swimmingly – almost literally, as we worked the first hour on uneven puddled limestone. What about health and safety, I hear you ask. I'm not suggesting it was ignored. But like industry everywhere, production often took priority.

I spent the late afternoon alone in a side tunnel; the continuous hard slog leaving me worn out and dehydrated. While trudging home, Armand pulled up in his Lamborghini. Would I like a lift? You bet I would! While he drove we discussed the job. It wasn't a long discussion – then again it wasn't a long journey, and he was a very fast driver. Casually, I mentioned that my contract was almost up. Equally casually he said, 'Yes I know, I'm thinking about it.'

Oh oh, now what did *that* mean? After he'd roared off, I entered the house deep in thought, to find Diane peeling off wet socks before enjoying a hot bath. It'd turned into a bleak afternoon and promised no better for the evening; so while she soaked I lit a huge fire.

After dinner I phoned England, while relaxing in front of the crackling logs. Meanwhile, my freshly scrubbed *sommelièr* refreshed my wineglass whenever the level dropped. Aaaaaaah!

My luck was out the next morning, as I was asked to set up the cross-over boxes. Yves joined me, and once we were underway the pace was brutal. But we were working well together until Christine came over. 'Come with me Steward,' she said ominously.

Looking puzzled, Yves held out his hand for me to shake. I thought, *This doesn't look good. What's happening here?*

With the spectre of unemployment staring me in the face, I asked should I pick up my coat.

'If you want to,' she shrugged.

Oh boy! She headed off towards the office, me following blindly thinking, *Bye everyone.* But instead we passed the main office and headed down into the *cave.* Arriving at the charging station, she told me to grab a cap and lamp, and follow her into a huge tunnel I'd never even *seen* before. I was told to find a *brouette* and *palette* then begin clearing *panniers* at the tunnel's end. Jacques-Noël would arrive soon to help me. Off she strode without another word.

With her gone, I just stood there flummoxed. Though clueless, I thought I'd best keep my head down and work. If anything was wrong I'd find out soon enough. Emerging from my trance I examined the tunnel, noting the uneven floor. In fact, once I'd loaded the *palette* a few minutes later, I couldn't move it. With my feet slipping on limestone slurry, I offloaded a layer. Able to get moving at last, I delivered three more loads in the same manner. But then Jacques-Noël arrived and saw my reduced loads. Rather than praising my ingenuity, he shouted *'Non, palettes pleines seulement,'* or 'No, full pallets only.'

He then fully loaded his palette and set off without a problem. However, he was pulling the load, not pushing it. I'd tried it that way myself once before, as it was much easier. But I'd been told by another team-mate, *'Non,* that is not the correct way to do it.'

Yet another case of do as I say, not do as I do.

Later in the morning Iron man rocked up on a tractor. Jumping off, he helped with the last *panniers.* And in no time at all we'd finished, spot on 11-55am. Just then Christine arrived with her afternoon list. 'Stewaard your hours are high, you are not required this afternoon.'

Yippee, I had the afternoon off, plus some gossip for Diane over lunch. The *Secours des Pompières* had been called to the *cave* earlier, and carried a woman out on a stretcher. Why I didn't know. News would doubtless hit the orchards in the afternoon, as everyone knew someone at the *cave.* Diane could fill in the gaps later. Good God I thought. How sad am I? Was that really the highlight of my day?

Véronique gave me a lift home at noon. *'Bon après midi,'* or 'Have a nice afternoon,' she said jealously, as she dropped me off. Diane on the other hand was slightly less charitable saying, 'Oh you lucky bugger.'

A little harsh I thought, but who could blame her? It was a gorgeous day; warm for the time of year, and far too nice to be at work. Of course we both knew that I wouldn't be frittering away my afternoon sat in the sun with a beer. Oh no, there was a lot of cementing to be done, and as quickly as possible. Jane had rung earlier, asking, could we accommodate a family the following week? We'd had to decline as the house wouldn't be ready, but if we were serious about this B & B malarkey we'd better get a move on. The season was almost over.

It was business as usual over the next few days; with the Plombièr brothers making their usual quota of mistakes, and Iron man causing mayhem if left unchecked.

On the Thursday Jean sauntered into my tunnel, asking if I'd received my free mushrooms. I said no. And since I was apparently the only one who hadn't, he asked Christine why. Looking shifty, she said she didn't know. Oh the shame of it! Maybe Armand had made his mind up. Was it 'bye bye Stewart?' I continued working on autopilot, my mind in overdrive. If I was sacked I'd have to work day and night to finish the house as we'd be a wage short. However, if I was mistaken and my contract was renewed, I'd be eligible for the *Carte Vitale,* my entry into the French medical system. Either way, the decision was out of my hands.

Just before noon Christine appeared with two brown paper bags. Placing them on the fork lift counterweight, she began chatting to some women. Thinking, *I've had enough of this,* I sneaked over and peered into the bags. Just as I thought – mushrooms; for her mates probably. It looked like I *was* the only one missing out.

*So I'm not even worth a bag of mushrooms eh? Well sod you, and sod this bloody job,* I muttered.

I'd just made it back to my work station, when Christine turned and walked over, saying. 'Ah Steward, here are your *champignons.*' Handing me both bags, she added, 'I am sorry, I forget. Oh, and your hours they are sufficient. You can go home now.'

I wandered away to clock off feeling totally bemused, hugging the precious mushrooms to my chest.

# Chapter 31

## The only way is up

Needing the car to collect cement, I drove Diane back to work after lunch. That was my first close up view of the terraces, and I was amazed at how extensive they were. As we drove, Diane pointed out different apple varieties growing on separate terraces. Keeping them apart limited cross-pollination, and allowed staggered harvesting, she said. Each section was sign-posted, and as we approached the terrace she was working on, I finally laid eyes on the vision that was Céline.

In the shaded rear of an old baker's van, a thick-set figure sat devouring lunch. With shoulders straining bib and brace overalls, cropped hair, and a bulldog face flushed from heavy drinking, she was every man's ideal partner. That is, if your dream woman was an alcoholic all-in wrestler. She looked like she'd been catapulted through the ugly orchard, and hit every tree on the way.

As I pulled up with a squeal (the car, but it *could* have been me,) Diane introduced me to this creature. Holding out a tentative hand I introduced myself. Unfortunately, my attempts at *entante cordiale* were met with a grunt from behind her baguette. Retracting my hand carefully, I decided my time might be better spent loading bags of cement.

After swallowing though, she growled that her husband (*she* had a *husband*?) was a lorry driver, who often travelled to England. I waited for more – but apparently this sentence had exhausted any interest she may have had in me. Checking my watch, I said, 'Is that the time?' and made a hasty departure.

Slightly unnerved, I left Diane to her fun filled afternoon. But traumatized by my encounter I took the wrong turn. I then had to reverse; before heading off again watched by that scowling red face. Now *that* was a woman. Actually, that was the question I put to myself on the way home. 'That was a *woman*?'

Compared to meeting Céline, humping bags of cement was a doddle. Loading done I went inside to pay; waiting as a *chasseur* bought cartridges then signed the ammunition register. At last, a piece of red tape I agreed with in our increasingly violent society.

Returning home I unloaded; then as I headed in for a cold drink the phone rang. It was Helen, saying she'd just begun maternity leave. With five weeks until her due date, she'd been told to prepare for a big baby, and been advised to take it easy. After some chit-chat, I said I'd get Diane to ring her later.

When I finally got around to cementing all went well. That is until I encountered my first ever viper. With its black zig-zagged back and greyish underbelly, it lay basking in the afternoon sunshine. Now animal lovers amongst you may want to skip the next bit – the bit where I whacked it with my shovel! But those were deadly creatures, and were dealt with accordingly by the locals. Alongside posters describing edible fungi, pharmacies also warned of the dangers of viper venom, showing in graphic detail a pump sucking it from a bite. The poster stated, 'This suction *must* take place within the hour, as in rare cases bites have proved fatal to children.'

Sorry animal lovers, it was them or us.

When Diane returned from work I was cementing. Mentioning my reptilian run-in, I was surprised by her acute reaction. I soon realized why though. While hanging out the overnight washing before daybreak, she'd heard a rustling noise near her feet – those feet wearing only flip-flops.

It was amazing how quickly the days had shortened since I'd begun working. That morning, Jean-Ives was my partner on the *lavage* as we worked under floodlights. The fork-lift was making good time, the beams from its 'mast' spotlights guiding Jean around the site – until they cut out. Fortunately it was just a loose wire, and with it fixed we pushed on hard, aiming for the Friday early finish.

At seven-forty Diane passed by, flashing me as usual. (Steady now, just her headlights.) I waved my arc of water in reply, but I doubt she even saw me. Then just before noon Christine strode purposefully towards me, her face devoid of expression. 'You finish at Midi, and do not return on Monday,' she said, in her clipped tone.

What? My heart plummeted. Sacked! And just like that. No job, no more wages. Oh shit!

But then she said, 'You have Monday at *repose*. Return on Tuesday at seven hours.'

Spirits soaring, I set off again at a furious pace. At 12-45pm she returned, saying. 'You begin a contract for one month on Monday. Have a *bon* weekend.'

Fantastic, now there was only Diane's job to worry about. Squelching home in wet socks, I arrived just as she was about to leave. Eagerly blurting out my good news, I didn't pick up on her pensive mood; until she replied quietly, 'That's good.'

Realizing something was wrong, I asked, 'What's up?'

'It's Marco the tractor driver,' she said. 'He's been sacked.'

Bullied mercilessly by Céline, the little guy had finally retaliated. Dominic had then got involved; and after a heated argument, he'd screamed, 'Finis, finis,' and stormed off. Marco had then left the terraces, probably never to return. Diane liked the cheerful Marco; but like the other workers she'd kept out of it, as a furious Dominic tore into anybody that caught his eye. Eventually he arrived at Diane's *ballox*, where he lectured her and her workmate, for pulling twigs off the branches along with the apples. 'It is not good,' he'd said. 'They hold buds for next year's growth.'

'Okay,' she said, 'I'll allow him that.' But then Céline had returned after receiving a dressing down; saying they must work faster and fill *balloxes* to the brim. Of course she was just venting her anger after *her* tongue-lashing. Everyone knew that Dominic treated her badly because he knew he could. She'd have problems getting work anywhere else due to her drink problem, and they both knew it.

Commiserating with Diane, I reminded her the season was almost over. She wouldn't have to put up with it for much longer. Shrugging her shoulders she glanced at her watch. Then saying she had to go, she jumped into the car and shot off back to work. Watching her drive off, I felt heartily sorry for her. But I knew she was a strong character and would rise above it.

Noticing that rain looked likely, I put my wall rendering on hold and did house-work instead. With less to do when she got in, Diane could relax in a hot bath then put her feet up. As it turned out, she got in at four forty-five totally wrecked, following Dominic's idea of an early finish.

After a well-earned Friday night of debauchery, Saturday shopping took place at Le Lude's newly opened Lidl store. Feeling rough, we decided to chill out in the afternoon then turn in early. However, what actually evolved left us hitting the sack at two am on Sunday. Status Quo and Tina Turner had a lot to answer for.

Idly scanning a magazine over an early breakfast, I was thinking how to avoid visiting Henri's, when there was a knock on the door. Who the hell was calling at *this* time on a Sunday? I decided to find out, as the knocking continued, which wasn't helping my headache at all.

I was greeted by a tall grinning black guy. Attired in a long dark frock-coat, he just stood there beaming; a starchy-looking white woman and a young boy standing at his side. He began speaking rapidly in French, to which I replied, '*Pardon monsieur, je suis Anglais.*'

'Ah you are English,' he replied. 'I speak English very well.'

Well wasn't *I* the lucky one? My day then got even better when he said he was a Jehova's Witness – and a very enthusiastic one at that. By the time I'd gotten rid of him, clutching pamphlets in my sweaty hands, I was almost looking forward to visiting Henri's ... Almost.

Nerves twanging we drove to the mill-house; where Annette met us enthusiastically. Henri was busy in the garden; but as Annette poured coffee he entered, his arms full of vegetables. Spotting Diane he tossed the veggies aside; then lumbering over, he managed to doff his cap and kiss her cheek in one fluid movement. Belatedly, Diane realized he'd refined his technique since we last met. With a beaming smile he went off to wash his hands; returning minutes later with a bunch of freshly rinsed vegetables. These he presented to Diane with a flourish; proving yet again, that to Henri the age of romance wasn't dead. However, the Interflora advert, 'Say it with flowers,' did spring to mind.

Following the usual enquiries about health and families, our fund of small talk was rapidly dwindling. As we floundered in joint ignorance, the conservatory door suddenly burst open. Jacques, Rosaline and their kids swept in on a wave of noise, and we were engulfed in hand shaking and cheek kissing. The children then lined up politely to be introduced to us, which we found refreshing. They then sat quietly while the adults spoke.

After a while they were allowed into the garden, while Rosaline my co-worker flicked through our dictionary, trying out her schoolgirl English on us. This was a rare event, and soon a mix of 'Franglais' banter had us all laughing. Jacques was as always, big hearted and friendly, but Rosaline was a real surprise. She showed intelligence and an enquiring mind which she'd previously kept hidden. It proved the old adage; don't judge a book by its cover.

With a clatter the door opened again, and another couple entered with *their* children. In the general melée we were introduced to Henri's eldest daughter and her husband. Though unable to catch their names, Rosaline said they'd sold their house in Dissé to an English family. The daughter had been hired to act as caretaker while they were in the UK, and house-keeper when they visited. Oh oh! Alarm bells began tinkling faintly. Was it coincidence that they'd arrived just after Jacques, who'd recently moved from Dissé and was keen to sell *his* house to an English buyer? We were afraid this might happen sometime. Had we been set up? Did Henri ring them after we arrived; or was this my paranoia surfacing?

Abruptly the second family took their leave; and in the silent void that remained, we were left sitting with Jacques and his family all smiling pleasantly. Then 'the sting' unfolded, as Henri suggested we drive over to Dissé to inspect Jacque's empty house. Now what a surprise! With fixed smiles we climbed into Henri's car, as if entering a *tumbrel,* en route to *Madame Guillotine.*

After the short trip made in stony silence, we arrived at the house, following Jacques and his family in their car. On arrival, we reluctantly appraised it; then after making polite responses we were invited to visit their new abode in Le Lude. Oh come *on* now!

Off we went again, oohing and aahing on cue when we got there. Finally, after a tour of the garden and an inspection of the chicken-coop, we were plied with beer and coffee during general chit-chat. Before long though, the conversation veered smoothly to the French housing market. Well how awkward was *this?*

After a few moments there was a lull – then an embarrassing silence as we all looked at each other. Was that when I was supposed to leap forward cheque book in hand, eager to snap up the Dissé house? How many times did I have to tell them?

As patiently as I could, I reiterated. I wasn't a millionaire living in a *'résidence secondaire,'* and I didn't want or need another house. Furthermore, I didn't have any friends or family who wanted one. In fact I didn't know anyone *anywhere* who was interested in buying a house.

There was a stunned silence after that; and though my French wasn't perfect, I could see by the hurt looks on their faces that they'd gotten the message. Then of course, I felt like I'd kicked a puppy.

After making awkward farewells to Jacques and Rosaline, we were whisked back to Henri's in silence. However, back at the mill-house Henri completely side-swiped me; beckoning us to follow him up a track. We then felt really bad, when he encouraged us to fill a trug with walnuts from a nearby tree. Then following us as if nothing untoward had happened, they waved us off cheerfully at the front gate; both of them beaming from ear to ear.

We drove off totally confused. Was it possible that we'd misunderstood them? Might it just have been innocent friendliness? We honestly didn't know. But we couldn't help thinking; however long we lived here, we'd never completely understand these people.

# Chapter 32

## Rain, rain, go away

The first week in October marked a distinct change in the weather. Following a sharp drop in temperature and increased rainfall, life became even more uncomfortable for Diane in the orchards. By then, she was working most days in wellingtons and waterproofs as Dominic strove to harvest his crop. Tempers flared as he pushed the team relentlessly. Then one day Céline finally snapped, when he refused to let the teams stop picking during a storm. With thunder and lightning rolling over the area, she'd led them off the terraces soaking wet. But sensing rebellion, Dominic pulled up in his Mercedes and ordered them back to work. Céline refused; stressing the danger of using metal steps and *panniers* during an electrical storm. Reluctantly he gave in – but only if the pickers rode out the storm in their cars. Some of the French refused to mess up their vehicles; suggesting temporary shelter should be arranged. Either that or they should all go home.

In the depths of the *cave* however, the rain wasn't a problem; except when increased seepage caused slippery conditions underfoot.

Outside on the *lavage* of course, it was a different story altogether. Dressed in bulky sou'esters, jet-washing trays in torrential rain seemed absurd; and the danger of lightning strikes with all the metal equipment on site was high.

Throughout the afternoon conditions grew even worse, as strong winds scoured the exposed site. But we continued working. There was always the alternative of course – cross-over box loading inside. Enough said.

With a lunch-time finish on Monday, I drove Diane back to the terraces. Then heading into Le Lude, I bought birthday cards for Bertrand, and my grandson Dylan. Returning home I worked peacefully in the garden; that is, until Henri and Annette arrived from Baugé market. They'd come to inspect the quince tree; and after an examination and much discussion the crop was pronounced '*Bonne.*'

Looking gnarled and bent (the tree not me) its fruits were misshapen, hard and blemished. Personally, I couldn't see the attraction; but Diane the culinary wizard, said stewing them produced peach coloured preserves. I needed convincing, but if Annette wanted some, she could have them. I'd already formed the opinion, that after Madame's departure the orchards had been ransacked. With their inspection finished, the duo arranged to return later for '*deux kilos.*'

As I was getting ready to pick up Diane later, the Renault and trailer rattled up, halting next to the tree. A couple of kilos eh! It looked like they were about to strip the tree bare. I strolled over, and after the usual hand-shakes and kisses they sized up the job. Then completely out of left field, Henri asked if I could get him the white table. Puzzled, I asked him if he'd rather not have a ladder. Equally puzzled he looked at Annette – then back at me. '*Non merci!*' he said; could he just have the table.

It seemed strange to me, but I said that I'd get it. Though it was full sized, it was made from pre-formed plastic, which was strong but lightweight. Off I went to the patio where I'd sited it, and picking it up I lugged it back. Placing it under the tree, I said, '*Voilà,*' and pointed at the branches.

Looking mystified, they glanced uneasily at each other. They looked at the tree, then helplessly back at me. Belatedly, I noticed two baskets standing at their feet. It was the usual comic opera I'd come to expect by then. I realized the baskets were for the fruit, but the table wasn't to stand on to pick them. Seemingly, because we'd put it in the garden and not the kitchen, they thought we didn't want it. I then felt awful that we'd assumed it was a gift. I apologized and thanked him for the extended loan, before helping him load it onto the trailer. Right, so now we needed a garden table.

Standing back I then watched in admiration, as shaking the tree vigorously between them, those determined octogenarians dislodged enough fruit to fill their baskets. Collecting some of the remainder, I filled two orange boxes, handing them over as part of my guilt trip. With a beaming smile Annette thanked me; then said I should take six kilos of sugar and some jars down to the mill-house. She'd then make a batch of jam, decant it into jars and split it with us. At least I hoped that was what she'd said!

With a cheery wave they climbed into the car; and after a hairy three point turn they drove off. Earmarked for the picking, the ladder stood unused against the barn. After they and the table had disappeared down the drive, I put it away again. Smiling to myself, I wondered if we'd *ever* understand the Plombièr's.

Driving to the orchards, I picked up Diane; who climbed stiffly into the car after throwing her *pannier* into the boot.

'God, what an afternoon I've had. What have *you* been up to?' she asked.

'Well, you're gonna love this,' I said. We arrived five minutes later still laughing.

While relaxing in the lounge later, there was a tapping on the French windows. There stood a beaming Bertrand clutching a bottle, followed closely by Véronique carrying a cake. Waving them in I put their bottle in the fridge, then took out a cold one while Diane laid out snacks. It was his birthday; therefore it required a little fuss, plus a surprise rendition of 'Happy Birthday to you' in French, which completely baffled them both. After receiving his card with childish delight, we all settled down to a slice of gateau and a chat.

François was due home at the weekend, and it was obvious how much they'd missed him. I said we'd also be pleased to see him; then the conversation turned to the weather, our leaking roof, and finally the universal grumble at escalating insurance costs. In fact it's amazing how much we could discuss, using basic French and a dictionary.

Steering the conversation around to our renovations, Bertrand said their dining room furniture could soon be ours; that is if we still wanted it. Oh indeed we did! After polishing off both bottles of wine, they left as darkness closed in.

Feeling pleasantly mellow by then, accompanying Billy Connolly on his Australian tour seemed a fitting way to end the evening – until I tried to play the video that is. The quality was poor, and tweaking the VCR's tracking button didn't help at all.

Months later Nadine gave us her discontinued Satellite TV system; a revelation at the time, as we could finally view English stations. Once it was set up, we sourced a spare box, as ex-pat friends said it was always handy to have a backup. Believe me; you only had to watch French TV for five minutes to see how dire our situation was.

However, that was later. Right then we'd lost patience with Mr Connolly's tape. The mood had evaporated, so we trooped off to bed for a good night's sleep.

We were well into October, and it was raining when we dressed for work that morning. Donning my waterproofs, I waved goodbye and set off walking; but sensibly I climbed in when my lift pulled up. While clocking on, I noticed some workers eying up my English waterproofs, so in French, I said, 'They are for the pedestrian who has everything.'

Then copying a male model, I strutted up and down in front of the office; much to the amusement of my team-mates. I had the last laugh though when Christine sent me to the *lavage*. I couldn't help feeling lucky, even though it was dark and raining hard. Unfortunately my state of euphoria didn't last for long. While bending to zip up my right legging, the casually discarded jet-washer snaked around, spraying icy water into my left wellie. Oh bliss!

Once underway, I spent the morning working alongside Jean-Ives, who wasn't a happy bunny. He was wearing torn company waterproofs, and complained to Armand who'd arrived to tell me my contract was finally ready. Examining the tattered waterproofs, Armand fobbed off my unhappy colleague with, 'Don't be an old woman. Get on with it.'

Alas, when I went for my contract it *wasn't* ready, though he said, 'At midi your workday is over.' which wasn't the worst news I'd ever been given. Soaked to the skin despite wearing my waterproofs, I masked my profound joy, kicked off my footwear and wrung out my socks. Then pulling on my clammy socks and wellies, I set off home with Jacques, Jean and Deni. As we parted company, I sighed, '*Je suis finis.*' Looking stunned they turned towards me. They thought I'd been sacked, or had resigned. I hurriedly re-assured them that I was only having an unexpected afternoon off. A relieved looking Jacques said jokingly, if he was the boss he'd sack me, because I was like an *escargot* to work with. 'Cheeky bugger,' I said, punching his arm. Despite the language barrier he got the message. Laughing, I squelched off, and was picked up by Diane as she drove home.

It wasn't long before I was stripping off my wet clothes – in the house of course. From the kitchen she saw me lighting the fire, and said, 'What's the point of that? 'You're gonna get wet again this afternoon.'

My evil chuckle told her the worst.

'Oh you lucky bugger; I could cheerfully throttle you,' she groaned.

I must admit, I felt guilty watching her go out in that rain. But then I thought, it's no good us *both* getting soaked, is it?

The last horse-chestnut had fallen; and along with a bountiful hazelnut crop, they'd provide food for hibernating animals. Leafless trees swayed in whistling winds, as rook's nests clung onto branches precariously. Wheeling around leaden skies, their squawking tenants mobbed each other. With autumn waning fast, winter was just around the corner.

Playing catch-up, we harvested peaches, damsons, cherries and blackcurrants; Diane turning them into preserves, which we bottled and stored in our *cave*. Remaining vegetables were then dug up, and the earth turned over exposing it to cleansing winter frosts. Any surpluses were swapped; or given as gifts to friends and neighbours.

Celebrating our first autumn, we'd bottled cherries in brandy, and damsons in *eau de vie*. Tucked away in the cool dark *cave*, they'd mature into warming liqueurs, useful for the festive season. At last we were ready for what Mother Nature could throw at us.

Mushrooms and apples however, were a different story. By then I was well into my second contract, with no signs of my predecessor returning. With mushrooms being an all year crop, I reasoned that a full-time job might be available. However, with the apples almost harvested, and casual workers being laid off in mid-October, it was a worrying time for us. If Diane lost her job we'd be in a pickle. But if my job also went belly up, we'd find it hard to make it through the winter. We didn't relish having to take out a loan; but missing a mortgage payment wasn't an option, as French building societies are ruthless regarding defaulters. With re-possession and the auctioning of properties a possibility, it was both worrying and frustrating. We were so close to letting out the house and getting back on our feet again. But until we did, what other options did we have?

# Chapter 33

## Chestnuts roasting on an open fire

As the landscape became bleaker, and autumn rolled relentlessly into winter, we travelled to and from work in darkness. Our jobs became even harder, and the daily grind was rarely alleviated. One exception was the morning I was saying goodbye to Diane at the doorstep, when something large brushed past me in the darkness. As it disappeared up towards the brooding woods, I wondered was it a fox, a deer, or even a wild pig? God only knew.

Walking down the drive on another dark morning, something shot out of the hedge and fluttered furiously into my face. When I'd recovered from a near cardiac arrest, I shone my torch around. Its beam picked out a wounded pigeon lying way off across the field. I debated whether to clamber over the furrows to neck it. But it got a reprieve, as I'd have been late for work. However, when I returned at lunch-time it lay there dead. Ah well, that's life – or not in this case.

As October established itself, Diane was retained to help finish the pick. All other foreign workers had returned home; and finally, albeit grudgingly, she was accepted by the French. She was even given a nickname, *La Pompière,* or the fire-lady; based on our Peugeot being the same model and colour as the Fire Chief's car. And due to its alarm going off regularly for no apparent reason, the name was a no-brainer. According to English garage mechanics I've used, French cars are prone to electrical problems. But try telling that to the French.

By then Dominic had begun cracking the whip. And though the weather was worsening, he still wouldn't let the teams stand down during torrential rain. He made sure they didn't, by sitting in his car above the terraces watching them. But he had to relent one stormy day, if only to avoid a riot. However, he demanded they come in at six am the following day to make up for lost time. It was crazy, as for the first hour they were picking in the dark.

On October the sixth I rang to wish granddaughter Lydia a Happy Birthday, and to check that her present and card had arrived. Then satisfied with both postal services for once, we shot along to the bank to deposit our work cheques. The vivacious Anne-Sophie, our favourite teller processed them. Her English was excellent, but she always encouraged us to speak French. Happy to see us as always, she was pleased we'd both found work.

Banking done, I nipped into the *tabac* for an English newspaper, but even this early they'd sold out. Determined to find one, we drove to Le Lude where we were told '*Non, pardon,*' at both The Kiosk, and *Intermarché*. We came up with two possible reasons. Shopkeepers were ordering less after the tourist season had ended, or an ex-pat explosion was causing greater demand. As lovers of solitude we hoped it was the former rather than the latter.

Visiting *Brico* next we bought Diane new wellies, then nipped into *Intermarché* to buy a few kilos of sugar for Annette's jam making enterprise. However we'd developed a cunning plan. To preserve our sanity, Diane would stay in the car while I called into the mill-house. I'd then drop off the sugar and make my escape, saying we'd frozen food to take home and hadn't yet eaten lunch. This should appeal to common sense, and the French occupation with the stomach.

However, Annette was having none of it; insisting she must speak to 'Deanna.' However, when 'Deanna' materialized, Annette simply wanted more jars for her production run. But we couldn't stay irritated with her for long. When we got home, we found a basket of walnuts at the kitchen door.

Fresh home from college, François and I traded news. He had English projects requiring our help. In turn, I asked if his father could help diagnose our roof problem. It was puzzling, as it only leaked when rain was blown from a certain direction – like the previous evening. Waving cheerfully, he then left; unaware that the trug of walnuts he was carrying as a gift to his mother were from Henri's trees.

Leaving Diane prepping the evening meal, I drove off with jars for Annette. Arriving at the mill, I heard a riotous barking and clucking coming from an old caravan behind the house. God only knew what was going on in there!

Hearing me knocking Annette opened the door. She'd been expecting Diane, but shooed me into the kitchen with the jars. Though she insisted it was important she saw 'Deanna.'

Returning I collected a slightly peeved Diane, who'd been busy in the kitchen. When we returned to the mill, we found she'd been summoned just to tell her the jam was ready. Annette had made us eighteen large jars, and she'd lots of quinces left. If we wanted extra, we must provide more jars and sugar, she said. Assuring her that eighteen jars were more than enough for us, we insisted she shared the rest with her family. Beaming, she accepted the offer with childish delight.

The coffee ritual was then invoked, *eau de vie* graciously declined, and with Henri stomping in fresh from gardening we resigned ourselves to a 'wee chat.' Surprisingly it turned into a decent conversation for once, which was a real pleasure as we often felt we neglected these good hearted souls. As we left Henri stepped forward; and with a conspiratorial wink he held out a box – filled with walnuts.

Having promised to collect the jams the next morning, we arrived home with our second box of walnuts that day. Plonking them onto the kitchen table we sat down to relax. But it wasn't to be. 'What the hell was that?' I said, hearing a clattering noise.

Slowly a metal ladder inched into view, followed by a grinning Bertrand. As the ladder emerged fully François appeared, holding the end of it while carrying the crawler ladder. Surprisingly, the team also included the Grand Dame Anna. Taking advantage of Bertrand's inspection plans she'd decided to visit 'Deanna,' while sneaking a look at our *projét* at the same time.

Welcoming the old lady, Diane whisked her off for coffee and a guided tour. Meanwhile, Bertrand had climbed onto the roof, and received the crawler ladder from François. After scampering around like a monkey, he descended inspection over. The diagnosis was then relayed by François. A repair was needed under a ridge tile. A weatherproof patch would be required. Having some sheets of aluminium in the barn, I cut a piece, and was invited to take it up to Bertrand. Despite misgivings regarding Monsieur Renard's roof, I accepted the obvious dare and ascended. Bertrand seemed impressed with my Sherpa Tensing impersonation. I could tell by the smile on his face. Well it was more of a smirk really.

After 'fettling' the patch into shape, sealant and nails made a secure repair. But of course it wasn't that simple. It never was. Apparently the end tiles hadn't been fitted correctly; and the roof insulation which was clearly visible, was the minimum required by building regulations. Well, what a surprise!

Fortunately, the Charpentier's had taken us under their wing. And like Henri and Annette, they'd helped us get through those tough early months. In return, we'd always helped them without question. Nothing since Concorde had induced the British and French to work together so well.

We woke up coughing and feverish the next morning without knowing why. However, we decided to push on; and based on the maxim, 'feed a cold starve a fever,' we forced down two large cooked breakfasts.

While clearing the table, a yapping noise announced Lupé's arrival. Bertrand, shotgun in hand said he was off rabbit hunting. But I thought he was joking, when he said Lupé was training as his gun dog. Now *this* I had to see.

Hermé his previous gundog had fallen victim to old age. His eyesight was failing and he was almost deaf. Often, something would claim his attention, and he'd bark without really knowing why. Unfortunately, being in a valley the echo came back to him. He then thought it was another dog he was hearing and barked again. Yes, you've got the picture! He'd spend many an afternoon yelping relentlessly, until someone stopped him. Sadly, his time as a gun-dog was over.

Inviting myself along for a breath of fresh air, we climbed the field together. Hanging back, Lupé the young pretender couldn't care less. He'd rather be somewhere else – anywhere else really.

Now I'm not suggesting he was scared of rabbits, but when Bertrand decided his tuition would begin by flushing them from a gorse thicket, Lupé wasn't happy at all. Whether he didn't get the idea, or he just didn't want to get dirty, I don't know. But after pointing at the thicket and repeatedly shouting '*Allez Lupé,*' all that Bertrand received back was a blank stare. Giving up on being Mr nice guy, Bertrand decided to 'encourage' him a little. Picking up the mutt, he launched him into the gorse bushes. Yep, that did the trick! A combination of rustling gorse, pitiful yelps and whining marked Lupé's painful progress. It soon became apparent (and no surprise to me at all) that no rabbits would be flushed – that is, if there'd ever been any in the first place.

When Lupé eventually emerged, he crept out shivering wretchedly, his coat matted with gorse twigs. After such a miserable performance, it was obvious to us all, especially Lupé, that the position of gun-dog was unlikely to appear on *his* curriculum vitae.

After all the commotion, Bertrand gave up on finding any rabbits. By then, any that might have been there would be sprawled out miles away sunbathing. However, it was too nice a day to go straight back. Untangling the shivering Lupé we meandered up to the woods, where Bertrand pointed out a man-made hide in a large tree. Accessed by a ladder, it was where he lay in wait while pigeon shooting. It was also near our fence-line, which we found had been cut and pulled aside. After he'd inspected some massive tyre tracks, Bertrand deduced it'd been E.D.F accessing the electricity pylon. He shrugged as if to say, 'What can you do?'

Switching subjects, he pointed out the wrecked Renault 6, shown me previously by François. Moving on, we burst through a thicket into a clearing carpeted with gleaming chestnuts. Many of the shells were split, the amber coloured nuts gleaming like jewels in the sunlight. Scooping up a few, Bertrand mimed chewing and licking his lips. Obviously they were the sweet edible variety. He intimated that Diane and I should harvest this unexpected windfall, for roasting throughout the winter months. I didn't say anything, but I'd already decided to give some to Henri and Annette in return for their walnuts. *Yes*, I thought, *they'd appreciate that.*

Breasting out of the brush we stood rooted to the spot; gazing across the roof of the valley for a few precious moments. Below us, wood-smoke curled up lazily from both farmhouse chimneys; the next hamlet barely visible in the distance. With just the keening of the buzzards wheeling high above us it was peace itself – until a pitiful whine from Lupé broke the spell. It was time to head back home.

# Chapter 34

## Things come to a head

In most of the UK, the growing season is over by the end of September, but not in the Loire valley. Not only are second crops still growing, but insect life continues to thrive. Waking each morning, spider's webs could be seen through windows; dew-drops sparkling on their lacy structure like crystal droplets. A nuisance maybe, but at least they held a certain charm.

Much harder to live with than a few harmless arachnids, were a plague of horned beetles that swarmed in one day like a plague of locusts. But of all the 'critters' we encountered, the most difficult to eradicate was an armadillo-like beetle. Endowed with a plated exoskeleton, they resisted all attempts to kill them, including guaranteed sprays. We tried swatting them, we tried stamping on them – they just walked away. Sometimes, if we caught one just right, we'd be rewarded with a satisfying 'crunch' as it burst. However, the cure was worse than the disease, as the smell released afterwards was foul. So it was no surprise that their name translated as stink beetle. Apart from those rare occasions however, they strolled off nonchalantly, just going about their business.

We seemed to have won *one* battle however, as the ant population, prevalent throughout the summer had disappeared. We smugly attributed this to the pesticide war we'd waged against them. Jet black, and much larger than their brown UK cousins, they resembled soldier ants when on the move. Throughout the summer, they'd march across the land in regimented columns; and if disturbed, they'd administer a fierce bite which quickly became inflamed.

Thankfully we had our resident lizard population on hand which dealt with most small insects. At first they'd seemed a nuisance; but we soon realized they were our unwitting allies. Sheltering from the sun in our flower beds, they'd dart out and grab anything that settled.

Moving up the scale there were the huge hornets, some over three centimetres long. Those airborne antagonists seemed most active when the sun was at its fiercest, droning around like distant aeroplanes but easily avoided.

The most disturbing insects we encountered were small brown scorpions; which were best avoided, not knowing how dangerous they might be. Others including grasshoppers and crickets were harmless, and bounded all over the garden. However, all of the above, plus the odd praying mantis (that's right) were just too large for our small comical lizards to tackle. So for the larger varieties; step up to the plate a species of vivid green salamander which I'd spotted on rare occasions. One I'd managed to grab was almost forty centimetres in length. I was sure they were a match for anything I'd seen, except for larger reptiles like grass-snakes; which were harmless and an attractive green colour. Vipers, however were poisonous, and a hazard to be wary of. Oh yes, nature was rampant in our sheltered valley.

Mindful of possible dangers, I picked some shallots; *un petit cadeau* for Véronique. We'd nipped over to wish François *bon voyage* on his drive back to college. We arrived to find Anna holding court. This usually meant goodies. In anticipation we sat down when asked, whereupon Véronique served us a delightful little ice cream cake with *rosé* wine, followed by sips of *eau de vie* and *quarante-quatre*. Oh dear, what a pity François had to drive. Never mind – more for us then.

After a while our young hero made his move. Following a teary farewell from Véronique and Anna, he shot off down the drive in his Peugeot. Meanwhile, we adjourned to the kitchen for much needed coffee.

Our visit lasted for an hour, before we excused ourselves and left. It was my grandson Dylan's christening that afternoon, and we needed to find out how it'd gone. We'd been mortified that neither of us could get leave to attend. To do so, we'd have had to resign from our jobs; impossible in our dire financial situation.

I'd asked Michael some weeks before, could he book the service near the end of October when our contracts ended. He said they couldn't, and though understandable it was a hard blow for me. Unfortunately, with our project hanging in the balance we couldn't leave. After the difficult phone call we needed to lift our spirits; so grabbing baskets we headed up to the woods to collect chestnuts.

The weather the next morning was particularly foul. First, I missed my lift and got soaked walking to work. Then I was picked for *lavage* duty, which was normally a joy. However, it rained stair-rods all day long. Though I was wet, my heart went out to Diane driving by at eight am. Her day would be even *more* miserable in the orchards. Depressing days like those seemed to affect the collective temperament, and loss of focus often resulted in things going wrong. This day was no exception.

After a series of problems with the tipping unit Armand was sent for. He tried fixing it, but for once it was beyond him so he called out the electrician. Huddled together in the equipment shed we sat out the storm; and to help pass the time, Armand asked me about life in England. He wondered why we'd moved to France, then was surprised when I said we rarely socialized with other expats. He'd noted our TV antenna, and asked if we watched English TV. I said our aerial couldn't pick up a UK signal, so we watched videos. Surprised, he asked why we didn't watch French TV, as a licence payment was automatically taken as part of the *Tax d' Habitation*. I said, that would mean buying a French TV, so maybe later. Actually, what we *had* seen had been puerile rubbish, but I couldn't tell him that. However, he seemed okay with my explanation. Then thankfully, cries of *midi* saved me.

Luckily Diane picked me up as I trudged home; and resembling two drowned rats we towelled ourselves off. After a change of clothes, a hot cuppa and a snack though, it was almost time to return.

As the rainstorm continued to worsen, Diane finally got her own back. Late in the afternoon she pulled up to the *lavage*, windscreen wipers clicking furiously. As the rain poured off me, she shouted above the wind, that they'd been sent home due to the appalling weather. With a concerned look, she asked when *I'd* be finished. Gritting my teeth, I said I'd been asked to work late. 'Oh that's really tough,' she said, tongue in cheek. 'Never mind, have fun. I'll see you later.' And off she drove tooting the car horn.

By the time I clocked out at six forty pm, I found myself walking home alone in the dark, the biting wind and rain lashing me furiously as I bent into it. *Touché* Diane.


The next morning I was feeling dog-rough, head aching and shivering. But even feeling like crap I daren't take time off. Diane was up anyway; and as it was raining in torrents, she felt sorry for me and drove me to work.

'Steward, cross-over panniers,' Christine shouted, as I stepped into the office. Crap, just what I didn't need. Thankfully, I was working with Alain, a guy with a leg disability. Despite his handicap though, he was irrepressible and always laughing. I thought, pull yourself together mate. If *he* can manage, then so can you. At least he wasn't lying around at home claiming benefits. He'd rather work.

Once started, we were put through the wringer; but we still managed to have some laughs. At one point, nodding and winking, he announced that Jacques-Noël was gay; which surprised me, as a tougher looking bloke would be hard to find.

All in all time passed quickly, and the morning flew by. Actually, we both got on so well that I almost enjoyed it.

However, as I was still feeling rough, I prayed for a half day off. Now there must be a God up there; as due to a shortfall of harvestable mushrooms we were sent home at eleven. My prayers had been answered.

Walking out into a sunny day, I waved to the guys on the *lavage*. For once I wasn't envious of them. I felt like skipping home. Though when Diane came in for lunch, she wasn't happy to hear I'd another half day off. For her, conditions on the terraces were worsening daily, as the pickers worked furiously to save the harvest. But when the job was finished she could relax, as no work was available in the packing sheds.

Guilt set in when she'd gone back after lunch; so I did housework, then spent the rest of the afternoon cutting logs. As it was, it was after six pm when she returned. And she wasn't in the best of moods when she did. Her fine new waterproofs had split 'from arsehole to breakfast time,' as the saying goes. Having no choice she'd continued working, with the French poking fun at her thermal underwear, on display to all and sundry.

A much calmer Diane emerged from the shower towelling her hair. Carrying a glass of wine in one hand and the phone in the other, she caught up with Helen and Nadine. After venting her spleen at the apple growing industry in general, she gradually chilled out. Later; with our meal ended and calm restored, we shared another bottle watching Billy Connolly, the renowned *master* of spleen venting. Striding on-stage yet again, he held his audience, including us enthralled.

Sentenced to the cross-over *panniers* the next morning, I sweated out my cold. Stepping out of the gloom at eight am, Armand inspected the pitifully small mushrooms on the conveyor; and with a look of disgust, he shut down the line. The remaining trays were taken away, and I began helping Joël sweep out the galleries, the dust doing my cough no good at all.

Later, Joël was sent off to load a *camione* at the surface, leaving me with the hapless Jacques Plombièr. The area had to be swept out irrespective of dust or colds. Safety masks? Maybe they were available, but I never saw one. If it bothers you carry a handkerchief, one guy told me.

Somehow we got through the morning; and leaving at noon I managed to score a lift. When I arrived home Diane was waiting, a sandwich and cuppa ready at hand. She'd been sent home early, but told to return for a big push at one pm. 'This could be it.' she said. 'We could be finished tomorrow.'

She drove off soon after in heavy rain, leaving me to follow later on foot. No lift this time, and the rain was coming down in sheets. As I walked along the rain-swept road, I remembered Chris saying a while ago, 'Dad, you're living the dream!

The afternoon was spent collecting *panniers;* then after trudging to the surface at six pm, Jacques gave me a lift home. I arrived to find the house in darkness and the car missing. Diane appeared soon after I'd lit the fire. She'd nipped to Le Lude straight from work to buy me cold remedies. What a woman!

After parking the car in the barn she came in, and we got settled before discussing our day. In the twilight that morning, her friend Cecile had spotted what she thought was a *sanglier* on their terrace. However, as it emerged eerily from the mist, it evolved into a huge hare, almost the size of a whippet. Feeding off fallen apples (and probably half-pissed,) it refused to move; loping off only when it was good and ready.

Then even more surprising to Diane, was witnessing Céline display a hitherto unseen emotion – concern. Somehow she'd gotten the idea that Diane was colour blind. Suspecting the girls had set her up, Diane kept a straight face, saying her eyesight was fine; otherwise, how would she recognize her green car in the parking area? Since everyone knew that Diane (*Madame la Pompière*) drove a red Peugeot Céline's jaw dropped. She then heard sniggering behind her and realized she'd been had. She'd actually laughed, Diane said.

With the pressure off, and the picking almost done, the atmosphere was much more convivial. Even Dominic was seen to crack a smile on a rare visit to the site.

By the time Friday rolled around, we were both desperate for the weekend. The walk into work was cold and dreary, the stars hidden by low, scudding cloud. But at least it wasn't raining. Walking out onto the *lavage*, I thanked God for my guaranteed early finish. However, my heart bled for Diane, who was in for another full day on the terraces. As she drove past and flashed me (now I've told you before) I hoped the rain would hold off for her.

The morning flew over as we cracked on, finishing earlier than expected. Diane was in when I arrived, having passed me as I *'lavaged.'* Sadly, she knew that I'd finished for the day; whereas she had to return soon. Trying to lighten the atmosphere, I said my workmates had wished me *'Bonne Anniversaire'* for my birthday on Saturday. However, bearing in mind her relationship with most of *her* workmates, I don't think it helped.

To cap it off; when she finally got home later she was soaking wet. But just as she was about to dive into a hot bath the phone rang. It was Nadine with an update on her problems. Then soon after, there was a call from Kay with more issues. By the time Diane had her bath, then ate her meal, a night of wine-induced oblivion was pretty much a given.

# Chapter 35

## Birthday boy

'Happy Birthday to me, Happy Birthday to me.' Another birthday, and here I was being treated to breakfast in bed while reading 'A year in Provence' for the umpteenth time. This book and certain TV travel programmes had been instrumental in us moving to France initially. And now, less than a year later we were part of a French community. I lay there for a while, reflecting on what we'd achieved since moving here. Then mentally shaking myself I put work plans on the back burner, thinking, let's get ready and go somewhere for the day.

And what a beautiful day it was; with a clear blue sky and not a wisp of cloud to be seen. The sun shines on the righteous, they say. Let's hope that today it included us.

My collection of cards had been laid out on the kitchen table by Diane, alongside presents which had survived the gauntlet of the UK and French postal services. Impatient to get out, I skimmed quickly through the cards. The one from Chris was scurrilous as usual, and contained a £20 note, which I'm sure he could ill afford right then. Setting the banknote aside, I decided to spend it on *him* when we next visited the UK. Some cards however were conspicuous by their absence!

As the clock struck noon Jorge drove up to Le Lavendu, delivered, then drove on by. There was no second post, and no-one had rung. 'Billy no-mates,' I thought, feeling a little peeved as I set off on the drive to Saumur. Detoured through woodland by road-works, we passed many cars lining the roadside. Their drivers were hunters out roaming the forest; hounds coursing ahead of them followed by runners blowing trumpets. Bedlam had come to our commune.

We drove cautiously past groups of men, most of them relaxed and chatting, guns broken open. Passing warning signs marked *attention chiens*, we swung back onto the main road before entering the suburbs of Vernante. As usual my mood lightened when nearing the pretty little village; possibly because its main attraction for *me* was the classic car garage on its outskirts. We often visited Saumur, but I rarely passed through Vernante without stopping to ogle the classic vehicles in 'Automobilia.' Being a very wise lady, Diane listened cynically to my latest excuse for a visit.

'Look,' she said, 'we both know we're going in. Let's just make it part of your birthday treat.'

With the collection drooled over yet again, I drove on to Saumur, my mind awash with Art Deco styled vehicles adorned with walnut, chrome and leather. As I drove onto the deserted riverside car park it began drizzling; so donning rain-wear we strode briskly towards the centre ville. With the downpour growing heavier, we ducked into an *Antiquité Brocante* on the Rue de Nicholas, making our escape as soon as the rainfall eased. It was divine intervention, as buying anything in *there* would have required a second mortgage.

However we'd promised ourselves a celebratory meal. After perusing the menu posted outside, we entered 'La Bourse Brasserie,' where a waiter showed us to a window table overlooking the marketplace. While composing our order we noted our dining companions; a cosmopolitan group comprised of a Foreign Legionnaire eating alone, a group of rowdy French sailors, and a scattering of traders and business people. A motley crew indeed!

In the packed eatery the atmosphere was raucous; the babble of the boisterous clientele competing with the clatter of a busy kitchen. While, wafting throughout the room, the aromas from rich food blended with the tang of blue tobacco smoke hanging in the air. Ah, remember those days?

We enjoyed a fine meal, complimented by a full bodied cote-du-rhone wine, efficiently served and reasonably priced. Appetites satisfied, we watched through misted windows as dispirited market traders packed up their wares.

With *l'addition* settled, we left during a brief lull in the weather. Firing up the car, we drove to Aldi then *Brico*, for food and materials. Then, with headlights on full beam we headed home. Even another cloudburst couldn't dampen my spirits. My birthday had gone down a treat.

Arriving home we unloaded quickly, dashing indoors through the rain, I lit a fire while Diane unpacked. I then checked phone messages. Chris had rung shortly after we left for Saumur. Wishing me Happy Birthday, he said he'd catch up soon. I returned his call but he'd gone out. It was Saturday after all; a busy time for an unattached young guy and his mates.

Once we'd dried out, we toyed with the idea of a Status Quo night, but then decided against it. We were both too tired, and my developing cold required an early night.

During the early hours I visited the kitchen for a glass of milk; and spotting a flashing red light in the lounge, I checked the messaging service. Michael's disembodied voice told me my card would be late. He'd been so busy it'd slipped his mind.

The early night worked wonders, and we awoke to a bright sunny day. Ah well, another birthday over; now what? Diane proposed spending *her* morning making preserves; so leaving her to it I decided to inspect the roof. But when I dragged out Monsieur Renard's rickety old ladder, I thought better of it. I was stupid to hang onto it really. It was only fit for firewood, so the inspection was put on hold until I could buy a much safer one. Thursday was tool day at Aldi, and a variable position ladder was advertised at a bargain price. But what could I do until then?

I began by refitting the toilet seat. Well I had to start somewhere. And no, I didn't sit down on the job. What next though? Ah yes, I'll get the mower out. But, unhappy at being dragged out of the tool-shed, it refused to start. I was so annoyed that I just pushed it back in again. Instead, I loaded rubbish into the trailer – including both best buy sun-loungers!

After stacking away the patio furniture, and thinking not a bad morning's graft, I strolled into the kitchen towards the kettle. But somehow I got hijacked on the way. I ended up peeling onions while Diane shelled walnuts. Hang on – what happened there?

Shortly after tea Chris rang, and as usual we had a hilarious chat. He'd landed an interview at Nissan's car plant near Washington. I could tell he was relieved, so we both wished him luck. And with his 21st birthday looming, I asked what he'd like as a present. Then with a call from Nadine due around nine pm, we bathed before our meal.

Towelled off and nursing a glass of wine, Diane decided to give her mum a call before Nadine rang. She and Dale had just returned from a holiday in South Africa with Rob and Nicola. Reading their postcard, they'd had a great time.

Riding shotgun in Joël's old Citroën the next morning, my birthday seemed a distant memory. But on the *lavage* later, my spirits soared as a spectacular sunrise unfolded. Soon it was coats off and sleeves rolled up, as the temperature began to climb. While changing I'd missed Diane driving by, and it was lunch-time before I caught up with her at home. She pulled up as I took a call from Nadine. Passing her the phone I went to make tea. Returning with two mugs, I heard that a conciliatory meeting with Nick hadn't gone well, and she was definitely moving out.

There was more drama to follow; this time Durham- based, as Stewy told us Helen's waters had broken. They'd rushed off to hospital, but after tests, they'd been told she wouldn't go into full labour for some time. Disappointed, they'd been advised to go home and return at nine thirty pm. He'd update us later. What a carry-on eh?

At six thirty pm Stewy rang from the hospital. Apparently, Helen was climbing the walls (metaphorically speaking,) and unable to bear the pain she'd been admitted. Given a bed, she was high on pethidine. It was a waiting game, and we were in the lap of the Gods.

Our wait was alleviated by a visit from Bertrand and Véronique, who'd popped in to drop off a belated birthday card. Cobbled together from François' English dictionary, it gave 'Franglais' a bad name; but at least they'd tried. Maybe in the future they'd understand the problems *we* have, and be more understanding about our French grammar.

However, as an unexpected bonus, I persuaded them to say 'Happy Birthday.' Now for many foreigners, 'th' is difficult to pronounce. And for the life of them my neighbours couldn't pronounce either that or the letter 'H.'

So sitting there captivated, I enjoyed a ragged chorus of, *'appy birsday veux vous,'* over a shared bottle of *rosé*.

Though we'd all hoped that François could make it, his plans had changed. He'd been invited to a boy's weekend in Spain with friends. He sent his 'best regards' though; with an apology, and wishes for a *'appy birsday.'*

Over our wine we discussed English and French recipes, as Diane was making quince chutney in her kitchen laboratory. As the wine took hold, someone (me) thought it'd be a good idea to give the quince tree a damned good thrashing, Basil Fawlty style. After being bombarded with falling fruit, we staggered around collecting it. Then bruised and battered, my neighbours staggered off home; carrying a box-full of quince as if it were fine bone china. I hoped they'd remember inviting us over on Sunday for a belated birthday tea.

Not long after they'd left the phone rang. It was Nadine, hospital co-ordinator for the family. There was no sign of a baby yet, so we decided to spice things up by having a £10 bet on the newborn baby's weight. With work in the morning, Diane bedded down on the settee near the phone. Leaving her tucked up, I went off to bed.

At one forty am the phone rang. 'It's Nadine,' Diane shouted, 'Helen gave birth at eleven-forty pm UK time.'

Nadine had waited until she knew all was well before ringing. She was off to peel Stewy from the ceiling, she'd said. He'd been strutting around the ward like a farmyard cockerel; new dad to a son called Aaron. Left in peace Helen was recovering nicely – from both the birth, and a hyped-up Stewy.

So, all was well with our world – for the time being anyway. We went off to bed and collapsed. A fitting end to my birthday celebrations, I thought.

# Chapter 36

## Things are looking shaky

Groggy from sleep deprivation I set off for work. Approaching Le Lavendu's drive, Véronique pulled out and offered me a lift. Though it was only a short distance to work, I never refused a lift, especially now that the weather had worsened. Besides, it gave me the opportunity to tell her about the baby. She was delighted at the news as I knew she'd be, and I promised photos soon. All too quickly though we'd arrived, and were absorbed into the flow of workers streaming underground.

Arriving home for lunch, I found Diane brewing up. She said her job was on its last knockings; and though great news for her personally, it was bad news for us financially. On a lighter note Stewy rang. Helen and Aaron were both doing well; and due for discharge eleven hours after the birth.

With lunch ended Diane dropped me off at the *cave*, before shooting off to the orchards. Waving her off, I headed in to my own purgatory. Entering the noisy office, I was sneaking off to the back of the room when a voice hit me like a body-blow.

'Ah Stewaard; you are on cross-over *panniers*,' shouted Christine. 'And you work with Christopher Borelle,' she added like a kick in the teeth. Girding up my loins – which seemed to have shrivelled somewhat, I followed my nemesis to the conveyor belt; my heart plummeting into my boots.

Luckily, Véronique was basket feeder that day; offering some light relief, and acting as a buffer between me and the Iron Man. Taciturn at best, he had no time for *me* at all.

With the line running flat out, I endured eighty minutes of Hell. Believe me; I counted every second. But as the saying goes, it's like hitting yourself on the head with a hammer. It's great when you stop. I often wonder where these quaint old homilies come from. I mean to say – who tried *that* one out.

Anyway the shift finished early, after a back-breaking finale on the *lavage*. Stowing away my waterproofs, I set off wet and weary on the long trudge home.

Walking past the workshop yard, I spotted Armand, Christine, Yves and Joël, gathered around a large hydraulic ram. Swearing and sweating, they were attempting to loosen a huge nut with an extended wrench. Stopping to watch the action it suddenly struck me. Oh joy! My mood soared stratospherically, as I anticipated sweet revenge on my French team-mates for their 'know it all' attitude.

After savouring a few precious moments, I shouted to Armand. 'You know that there's an English manufacturer's plate on that ram, don't you?'

'What has *that* got to do with anything?' he replied irritably.

Shrugging, I replied, 'Oh nothing – except British bolt threads are machined opposite to European, so you're actually tightening the nut.'

A stunned silence followed as he interpreted, and they stared at each other mouths agape. Then Yves began frantically hammering against the wrench in the *correct* direction; and with the nut finally loose Armand thanked me profusely.

Now nobody likes a smart-arse; but as a lifelong chancer, I thought this might be a good time to negotiate some time off. Reminding him that my second contract ended the following weekend, I said we'd promised to visit Helen and Stewy to see the baby. With a note of apology, he said there may not be a third contract, as work had slackened off recently and he'd been sending French workers home. He'd have to look at logistics. Not good; especially following Diane's news.

I got home around five pm, just before Diane. When I told her Armand's thoughts, she said fatalistically, 'Well at least we know where we stand. But let's talk later.'

After changing, we drove off to Le Lude to buy a congratulations card for Helen. On our return, Diane took a call from the new mother, which was mostly baby talk. But during our meal later, we discussed our imminent job losses and what it could mean to us.

Wednesday dawned cold and cheerless. Arriving at the *cave* I was quickly drafted into a 'flying squad,' thrown together to process an urgent order. It was brutal, exhausting work, clearing tunnel after tunnel at a frantic pace. And to add to my joy, Iron-man rolled up on a tractor. His mission was to work flat out (sweating like a pig) taking full *palettes* to the surface.

Finally, with all *panniers* shipped it was almost lunch-time. But what was this? Iron man appeared from nowhere, and pointing to a *brouette* and *palette* he beckoned me to follow him. I looked at my watch. It read 11-50. Now, not only was I looking forward to my lunch, I'd been hoping for a half day finish. I was absolutely knackered. What was this lunatic up to *now*? Maybe it was a change of plan arranged by Armand or Christine, and we'd work another hour then finish early. It'd happened before.

Sighing, I grabbed my equipment and followed him towards *chambre treize,* the deepest tunnel of all. Pointing into the darkness, he said '*Marche,*' and before I could assemble a question, he strode off leaving me bewildered.

Just then, a group of pickers appeared from a side tunnel on the way to clock off. Seeing me stood there, Véronique pointed at her watch, shouting, '*Midi.*' I wondered, should I ask her what to do regarding Iron man.

'To hell with Monsieur Borelle,' I muttered. Parking up my equipment, I joined the stream of bodies heading to the surface. Putting my lamp on charge I spotted Christine. Maybe *she'd* tell me Iron Man's plans, or better still, say I was finished for the day. But she moved on. Ah well, you can't win them all, I thought, emerging from the gloomy *cave* to an equally dismal day outside. It was raining hard; and even though I was given a lift part of the way, I staggered into the house drenched to the skin. In the kitchen I found Diane, who'd been released early due to the downpour. However, she'd been told to return quickly, as Dominic predicted a clear spell later. He'd reduced lunch-breaks in a bid to maximise production. So after a brief interlude together and a peck on the cheek – avoiding my sandwich, she was off again.

At one fifteen pm a toot signalled Véronique's arrival; the welcome lift saving me getting my change of clothes wet.

'*Peut-être ceux sont les pannieres pour tou maintenant,*' she said while driving.

Damn; she thinks I'll be collecting *panniers*. Maybe I'll *still* end up in Chamber 13 with Iron Man. Assembled in the office we awaited our fate. Nerves jangling, I expected Iron Man's shovel-like hand gripping my shoulder at any moment, before steering me towards the tunnels.

Mercifully, Christine said, 'Stewaard; you work with Alain on cross-over boxing.'

Normally this news would sound like a death-knell; but this time I'd no problem with it. I liked Alain, and we worked well together. Arriving at our station, we set up as the rest of the team got organized. Then, as we discussed our weekend the conveyer belt started up. Pressing our ready buttons we waited. Suddenly a cry rang out, '*Les Gros,*' or the large ones.

Looking at each other, we said the same word in two languages at exactly the same time.

'Shit,' I groaned.

'Merde,' croaked Alain.

*Les Gros* were huge flat mushrooms, destined for Parisienne restaurants. After stuffing then cooking them, I'm sure diners think them divine, but to us poor sods on the front line, they meant an afternoon of torture. Because of their size, *panniers* filled twice as quickly, meaning we had to work twice as hard to keep up with the volume, even on the lowest speed setting.

*Don't panic,* I told myself. Often it was only a small order of one or two trays, before switching back to normal mushrooms. Maybe it would soon be over. Glancing at each other like gladiators of old, I spoke those immortal words.

'Those who are about to die salute you.'

I doubt whether Alain understood me, but he got the message. As belt rollers clattered and squealed, a shadowy mass could be seen lurching towards us. Reflected on the aluminium side-plates it rounded the corner, materializing into a large pile of mushrooms.

Within seconds we were swamped, and very soon ankle deep in overspill. It was just impossible to stem the flow, or slow down the machine enough to handle it.

Then a clanking noise signalled the next load dropping.

The afternoon turned into a nightmare with no end in sight. But at five thirty pm, the thumping and screech of machinery stopped abruptly. The silence was stunning. It was over.

By six pm we'd tidied up, trudged back and clocked off, after a four hour work-out that would test the most ardent gym member. Staggering wearily up the road, I stopped occasionally to pick up sweet chestnuts. Using my jacket as a tote-bag I arrived home around six twenty pm. Crashing into the kitchen with my bulging bag of nuts (hey, I only *write* this stuff) I threw them onto the work surface. 'Get the booze out, I'm getting plastered,' I croaked.

'Yeah right! That'd be fine if you were off *work* tomorrow.'

The guilty look on my face said it all.

'Oh you lucky bugger,' she cried, 'you *can't* be!'

As I left, Christine said, '*Travail bon. Reposez* à *demain, et retournez* à *sept heures le Vendredi*. Or to Diane's despair, 'Good work. Rest tomorrow, and return at seven am on Friday.'

My well-earned day off began with me making Diane breakfast, before guiltily seeing her off to work. I hadn't gotten wasted last night after all; but somehow she *still* wasn't happy about my rest day! I assured her that I wouldn't squander the time. I had enough to keep me occupied.

Once she'd gone, I did the breakfast dishes then consulted my check-list. Most of it was electrical, so I got out the appropriate tools and began.

Diane arrived for lunch at twelve forty-five pm as I was filling the kettle. Sitting down with a grateful sigh, she pulled off her boots. While I massaged her feet, she said Céline had sent a Polish guy to help her because he spoke English.

'Well that was good of her.'

'I suppose so,' she agreed.

Unfortunately, after weeks of abuse, she was suspicious of *any* act of generosity. Sad, but that's how it was.

Her morning had been a breeze, she confessed; with nice weather and no Dominic. Also, having survived his meltdown, Céline too was in a better mood. Telling the team to blitz the last rows, she predicted a Friday finish if the weather held. She'd then shot off in her van; probably for a 'liquid lunch' with friends according to the girls. She'd re-appear later, much redder in the face, they said. It'd happened before – often.

'Anyway I'm off,' Diane said, squeezing unwilling feet back into unforgiving boots.

Waving her off I had a thought. When Bertrand ploughed the bottom field he'd unearthed lots of field-stones. It would be useful to collect them, as we both used them on projects. Diane and I normally followed Bertrand's tractor, throwing them into the rear-mounted bucket. This time I decided to walk the furrows with the barrow. After all, who knew when the weather would turn?

The afternoon passed pleasantly enough, though the barrow became bogged in the furrows as it filled. But the *real* killer was pushing it up the steep drive to the rear garden.

Occasionally I'd stop to ease my aching back. And during one welcome break, I glanced across the valley at the guys on the *lavage*. Then I imagined the others working underground like moles. I knew where *I'd* rather be.

Setting off again, I managed to collect six barrow-loads, before my back screamed enough. Relaxing with a coffee on the terrace, I gazed across the bottom field with its crop of golden corn. Even aching from head to toe, I thought how lucky we were to live here.

But this was no time for complacency, what else could I do? Eyes sweeping the garden they settled on the quince tree. Standing there gnarled and twisted, (like I felt) it looked malevolent, as if saying; 'Come and have a go if you think you're hard enough.'

This damned tree often seemed like a malignant entity. Only recently, a wilful branch whipped across my face while I was strimming around its base. It was time for action. However, feeling vengeful I got a bit carried away with the loppers. Oops! Never mind, it would produce healthier fruit next season, I told myself. There'd be nowhere near as many of course, but they'd be healthier. I mean, these trees have to be taught who's boss right? Besides; look at the extra light we have in the bathroom now!

Excusing my hatchet-job, I reckoned there was just enough time for another task. Averting my gaze from the traumatized quince tree, I cleared away the rubble after Diane's sledge-hammer rampage. See – nobody's perfect.

Though Friday was a lovely day I wasn't at my best. Stupidly, I'd done too much on my day off, and standing in the office my shoulder was on fire. Wracked with pain, I focussed hard, projecting telepathic thoughts to Christine. Maybe she'd go easy on me. Was it too much to ask? I only needed to survive half a shift, then I could rest up over the weekend.

'Stewaard,' she shouted over the crowd. 'You will wash this morning.'

Hey, I wasn't about to correct her grammar, I was just pleased to get off lightly. But maybe there was something in this mind control thing. The possibilities scrolled through my mind. 'Naaah,' I thought. 'Don't go down *that* rabbit hole.'

Paired up with Jean we marched off to the *lavage*. After suiting up, he pressed the start button on the tipping unit. However nothing happened. And nothing we tried could *make* anything happen. Armand had just passed by whistling loudly, and I'd remarked, 'You must be happy.'

'Yes,' he'd replied, 'At this moment I am.'

Catching him at his desk five minutes later, I reported the breakdown. 'I am no longer whistling,' he said.

Dropping his paperwork he walked back with me. Producing a screwdriver from his top pocket, he leaned over the engine and touched a contact. Bingo, we were in business!

Grinning, he said, 'This machine is like a woman. You just need to touch the right spot.'

'*Oh puleeeease,*' I said, pretending to retch.

At eight am Diane passed by in the twilight, totally oblivious to my waving spray. Of course she could have been asleep at the wheel. Who knows?

As the sun rose our water-proofs were discarded, and we worked under a cobalt sky. And since Jean was no Jacques Villeneuve on the forklift, I had time to watch Bertrand ploughing the corn stubble into the field.

When we'd caught up later I spoke to Armand, who by now was singing out loud. I told him about my revised ferry booking for 30th October. He then told *me,* that dwindling orders meant a third contract would be unlikely. He thanked me for telling him my plans, saying most French workers wouldn't bother. He then suggested I contact him on my return. Maybe I could work the odd shift here and there. Asking me how I'd fill in my time when finished at the *cave*, I told him about my workload on my day of *repos*. Rubbing his jaw, he said, 'Working in the *cave* won't seem so bad to you now, I think.'

Christine appeared soon after; and unhappy at Jean's progress said, instead of one-thirty we'd probably finish at four pm. '*Non, un heure,*' Jean protested indignantly.

This seemed wildly optimistic to me, as after an earlier bollocking he was driving even slower. But then the forklift ran out of gas.

Our saga eventually ended at two pm. Not bad considering. And it was still a great day; sunny and unseasonably warm. The thermometer read thirty-one C, so it was on with shorts, and out with a handsaw cutting up quince branches.

Around four pm Bertrand roared up on his tractor. With a hearty '*Ca va,*' he shook my hand, saying, he was impressed at what I'd achieved the day before. It felt really good that he'd noticed. Whilst discussing work that needed doing before winter, he said François our translator was visiting soon, which would be a relief for us both to be honest.

He'd just left when our Peugeot appeared on the bottom road. Pulling up, Diane said she had a headache. Although the sun was welcome on the terraces, it brought its own problems. Squinting through the branches into direct sunlight caused apples to be missed. While filling the kettle, she said the packing shed supervisor had lectured her against stacking apples in pyramids. It'd actually been Cecile; but as the job was almost finished and Cecile was a precious friend, she just sucked it up and said, '*Oui, okay.*'

Then Céline had announced that picking would continue into the next week. 'Well done – another week's wages,' I said. 'Every little helps.

She agreed, but said after that the job would be finished. Showered and changed, she then praised *my* endeavours, which pleased me no end. Unfortunately, after this orgy of mutual gratification we blotted our copy book. Well actually it was me. It was the classic mistake of having a wee celebratory drink after our evening meal.

Oh, we started *off* sedately enough, tapping our feet to the Gaillic rhythms of *Riverdance*. But as the sixteen percent proof *grenache* worked its soporific magic, I found my hands reaching for the rock section in the video rack.

Oh no, not again!

The next morning, Diane said Status Quo had vied with Bon Jovi for centre stage at my latest 'gig.' I don't know who ended up as headline act; but by the end I'd played solo performances on all the instruments – when I wasn't fronting as lead singer of course. Apparently I'd also developed an insatiable appetite for snacks 'mid-session.' After watching me scoff maybe a quarter of them, while some ended up on the settee or floor, she realized that another Status night was spiralling towards its inevitable conclusion.

But now a *new* group had been added to the mix, I was in Dire Straights. (in more ways than one) As the group finished their set, I'd staggered off to rewind the tape, dead-set on a grand finale. Sadly it was not to be. 'Tripping over,' I fell onto the settee, where a nifty Diane threw a duvet over me like a poacher netting a fish. Moving anything breakable she switched off 'the concert.' The show was finally over.

I woke up in bed the next morning head thumping. How I'd gotten there I forgot to ask.

# Chapter 37

## The end grows nigh

With work almost ended we planned our UK trip. But first we drove to La Flèche, seeking Christmas presents for family. Finding a parking space near the river we strolled through the market, enjoying the kaleidoscope of fruit, veg. and flowers. Having satisfied our market receptors, we drove to *Noz*, then on to *Gifi*. Those cheap and cheerful stores held a surprising range; and during a pleasant rummage we found some uniquely French toys for the grandkids, and a cute baby present for Aaron. Being a collector of classic automobilia, I couldn't resist a boxed 1956 Chrysler sedan; while Diane, not to be outdone found three tapestry kits she'd been searching for. All in all then it was a good afternoon, made all the sweeter later, when Diane discovered she'd been undercharged on two of the items.

Crossing the *Route-de-Sable* roundabout we called into the huge *Bricomarché*, where a guide to renovating old French properties took my eye. Sadly it was printed in French, and was just too hard to decipher. Something for when my language skills improved perhaps.

By then it'd blossomed into a gorgeous day, and driving past a quaint old church on the outskirts we were intrigued; so we turned back to look around it. Being admirers of ecclesiastical architecture it proved worthy of the visit. Gallo-Roman in design, it was restored by monks in the early 17th century, some of whom sailed off to establish a new order in Montreal Canada. Its cemetery was way over the top, featuring ornate marble headstones and imposing mausoleums. Unusually, there was not a blade of grass to be seen anywhere, just gravelled pathways between tightly-packed plots.

After this sobering end to the day, we arrived home at five pm. Passing Le Lavendu, we waved to Bertrand and François out working in the garden. But we didn't hang around, as we needed to eat. While I built a fire Diane prepared the meal; and after dinner we closed the shutters and enjoyed a bottle of wine while watching a video. Though pretty soon we were yawning, so we headed off to bed at ten thirty. But of course we should have known better.

Reaching the bedroom, we'd just hit the mattress when the phone rang in the lounge. Thankfully we'd taken François' advice, and were using a downstairs bedroom for warmth. Jumping out of bed, I stumbled around in the dark cursing. *I must remember to connect up the bedside lamps*, I thought, rubbing my shin. Anyway; making it to the lounge more or less intact I snatched up the phone. It was Nadine. After a few words, I cupped my hand over the offending instrument.

'Diane dearest, it's for you,' I shouted sarcastically, feeling a twinge of sadistic pleasure as I heard a groan from the bedroom. 'Who is it?' she whimpered.

'Oh, just one of your darling daughters wanting a chat,' I smirked. Filling the kettle, I heard expletives floating along the corridor from a ruffled Diane. Thankfully it wasn't anything serious, I'd already checked with Nadine. She just needed some advice. Nick had taken Ben out for a kid's party, but it was now ten pm in the UK, he hadn't returned, and his cell-phone had gone to voice-mail. Barely awake, Diane doled out soothing advice, while accepting a cuppa from me gratefully.

'Kids,' she said, 'who'd have them?' Ah – *that* old question.

She'd just put the phone down when it rang again. As phone answering had become *my* job in France, I picked it up and heard a frazzled Helen. 'Number two daughter for you,' I said, turning to Diane.

Passing over the phone, I headed back to the kettle. Aaron wasn't feeding properly, was crying non-stop, and both she and Stewy were worn out. Nothing was working. They'd had conflicting advice, and were at their wits end. Over her second cuppa, and almost comatose by then, Diane dispensed *more* motherly wisdom. 'First off, one of you needs to sleep. Yes you're worried, but you can't *both* stay up, you'll be wrecked.'

Blindingly obvious you might think, but not always to concerned parents fresh to the game. After passing on more nuggets mined from a lifetime of domestic and professional child-care, Diane carefully set down the phone. Oh the joys of parenthood we reflected, as we tip-toed carefully off to bed.

While I sorted out electrical problems the next morning, Diane whipped up a cake. Hearing mournful howls echoing across the valley, I went to the kitchen window. Our tranquil morning was then suddenly blown apart, as a group of men and dogs erupted from the woods. Coursing ahead, the hounds were followed by handlers blowing bugles; while sweating and cursing hunters struggled to catch up. But hot on a scent, the baying pack outstripped the main group, leaving them floundering in their wake. 'Well isn't *this* fun?' I said.

We watched helplessly as they ran past the house, up the track and across our top field, aware that in rural France, *la chasse,* or the hunt is paramount. And trashing your property in the process? Well that's par for the course.

Changing into a red tee-shirt, I went outside, hoping they'd see me and move on. Not the best idea, as *chasseurs* often drank from hip-flasks as they stumbled about. It wouldn't be the first time one of them had been shot by accident, I'd heard.

Anyway, the day's drama went off without a hitch – or indeed a shot, as any deer had fled the scene long ago. With the pantomime fading away into the distance, peace returned to the valley once more.

Then at twelve noon precisely, something 'spooky' happened, making my hair stand on end. Beginning with a low moaning sound, an unearthly wailing increased steadily in volume, until it reached an ear-splitting crescendo. What sounded like an air-raid siren sent the hunters scurrying back to their vehicles. In a matter of minutes hounds were caged, vehicles started up, and soon everyone had vanished for lunch.

It was *midi,* so the deer were probably safe for the day, I learned later. After a two hour boozy lunch then a nap, the hunt was often abandoned.

While pondering the vagaries of the French psyche, I remembered something I needed to ask Bertrand. Before the hunt arrived, an old French guy had driven up in a Peugeot 406. Pulling up, he spoke to me in English, which was unusual as our GB plated car was hidden way back in the barn. But news of our arrival had spread it seemed.

He asked if he could drive up the track to the next village. While allowing that maps still showed this byway, I said it was now overgrown and impenetrable. Unperturbed, he said he'd like to see for himself. He then asked if I planned re-opening it in the future. I said no, as only Bertrand or E.D.F used it. He was unshakeable though, even when I said he could damage his car. But it was a public right of way so I couldn't stop him.

Off he drove, his car wallowing up the rutted track. When he reached the wall of undergrowth, he got out, looked around, then climbed back into his vehicle. After a difficult three-point turn he drove back, trundling slowly past us, his eyes noting everything. I wasn't happy with that, so I wrote down his licence number. Unable to do more I finished chopping wood.

Going in to shower before our visit next door, I entered the bathroom, switched on the lights, and click – the fuses tripped. Damn! What was causing this rash of electrical faults? Something must be wired up incorrectly. Like the previous owner, I thought wryly.

While pondering this mystery, François arrived, wearing riding boots. He'd popped over to say they may arrive a little late. His 'fazzaire' said rain was due soon, and he thought it best to sow the bottom field beforehand. That sounded like a good idea, I replied, but I thought *we* were visiting *them*. Nonetheless, Bertrand, François and Lupé appeared soon after, criss-crossing the field on the tractor. Well at least the seed was going in. That much I *was* sure of.

We finally agreed they were visiting us, so I lit a fire. The thermometer outside may show eighteen C, but inside, with tiled floors and high ceilings it was only twelve. Leaving Diane engrossed in one of her tapestry kits, I filled the log-basket, then put some *rosé* in the fridge to chill. Not that it needed to!

The family arrived at four pm, Véronique carrying a belated *anniversaire* cake, and François clutching a bottle of *rosé* from a friend's vineyard. Not to be outdone, Diane brought out her big guns, (calm down now) a home-made walnut and maple syrup cake, topped with whipped-cream. Bertrand looked like he'd died and gone to Heaven, while Véronique nibbled a tiny bit, before saying graciously, '*Delicieux.*' Was that a touch of cake envy I detected there?

After the cake cutting, a belated 'Appy Birsday' was sung enthusiastically for the benefit of François. Then swallowing a delicious mouthful, I mentioned our morning visitor to Bertrand. He too was baffled, but said I'd done well in taking the car registration.

The conversation then switched to outstanding jobs. We compiled a list to be tackled while we were away, and agreed on finishing some the next day. Bertrand would inspect the lawnmower and leaky roof, while I drove François to the dealership to check out my strimmer's warranty.

Before leaving, Bertrand asked to see the crumbling bathroom plasterwork. Maybe it was due to rain seepage behind the wall, he said. Whatever the cause, Madame had left two years ago, and since the damage wasn't serious, it could wait until we returned, I said.

We'd sorted out some problems and agreed a work-plan; so we felt we could head off to England knowing the property was in safe hands.

Passing the woodland culled during the summer, I walked into work. Returning at midday, I saw a grappler stacking the timber at the roadside. Leaving the *cave* at five pm, I found it'd all been trucked away, leaving us a denuded hillside as a view from our dining room window. But that was of no interest to the landowner of course. To him it was just a cash crop.

What I *didn't* expect to see however, were two guys with chainsaws cutting into *my* trees. Dressed in cover-alls and helmets they could be anybody. Angry but wary, I set off to tackle them, rehearsing what I'd say in French. This could be very tricky, I thought, striding up to them. Seeing me approach, they stopped sawing and lifted their safety visors. Phew! It was Bertrand and François, dressed unusually for them in safety gear. They were cutting back overhanging branches and a couple of dead trees. Did I mind?

Well normally I wouldn't. And though relieved that it wasn't two strangers stealing wood, I was peeved that they hadn't asked first; especially after François' high moral stance regarding other people's property. Following a chat about the fencing I left them to it. Making my way home through the paddock however, I still felt a little annoyed.

Shortly after getting home Diane arrived. In a pseudo-surprised voice, I said, 'Hey look, there's two guys up there cutting our wood.'

'Yeah it's Bertrand and François,' Diane replied. 'They asked me if it was okay when you were at *Brico* yesterday. They're cutting it for *us*.' (Oh bugger.)

Arriving later with a full trailer, they asked where I wanted it tipped. And of course, I felt lower than a snake's belly for not trusting them. To make matters worse, François then asked when I was next off work, as they had to take a saw in for

266

repair. They could introduce me to their mechanic, and help me select a good chainsaw. (Double bugger!)

Changing the subject swiftly, I asked, 'Where are your beautiful white ducks? I haven't seen them for some time.'

'*Dans le congélateur,*'or in the freezer, François said – his tone suggesting, '*Where do you think* they are, *on holiday?*'

Providentially, Diane stepped in to save me, saying. 'The goose won't be happy at losing her friends.'

'She will make new friends next year,' he shrugged. ... End of conversation!

Thankfully Bertrand then changed the subject. Rampaging across our hillside the other day, hounds had 'put up' a *sanglier* which ran into our field. The hunters had called off the dogs and let it escape. Looking mournful, he said if he'd had his gun he could have shot it. We could have butchered it together and shared the meat. As part of a learning curve it would have been interesting I suppose.

'Another time perhaps,' I offered.


An uneasy crowd stood assembled in the *cave* that morning. Amid an undercurrent of murmuring, Christine struggled to find work for us all. Then Armand came in and began a spirited talk. Oh-oh, this didn't bode well.

On the *lavage* later, Jean Ives said work was tailing off, and it could mean cutbacks. Further signs soon became apparent, as Armand strode around with a face like thunder. Ah well, I thought, I was only meant to cover sick leave, so I can't really complain. But some of the others would *really* feel the pinch.

We soldiered on, with Diane passing me in the pre-dawn twilight. Though not appearing to see me, she tooted her horn anyway. Then at nine am François drove past and waved, by which time it'd turned into a dank, chilly morning. The weather was immaterial anyway, as Christine appeared at ten-thirty telling me to leave, but return at one thirty pm. I didn't mind being utilized in this way though, as it probably wouldn't be for much longer. Clocking out at 11-00, I strode home in glorious sunshine.

Arriving at the kitchen door I couldn't find my keys. Strange, I thought I had them with me. Still, Diane would be home in an hour then I'd check inside the house. Now how could I pass the time? Well, if I'd been retired, a *petit somme* on a sun-lounger might have been nice. However that wasn't an option, there was too much to do. Let's see now. The tool-shed was locked, but I could always check out the fallen tree in the bottom field. Maybe even without a barrow, I could collect some broken branches.

As it was, I managed to drag six huge branches up the field. It took three trips, before exhausted I reverted to plan B – lying sprawled on the sun-lounger gasping for a drink. I checked my watch. It was only fifteen minutes until Diane arrived.

The temperature by then read twenty-eight C on the wall thermometer, but it would be considerably less in the shade. As I pondered dragging the sun-lounger into the barn, François appeared; chainsaw in one hand and a can of fuel in the other. Not wishing to look stupid by admitting I'd mislaid my keys, I strolled over for a chat. He was off to finish hedging on the top field, he said, striding off up the field. Ten minutes later I heard him fire up the chainsaw. It roared into life then stopped again, just as Diane zoomed up the drive.

'Why are you standing outside in the sun,' she asked?

She'd just finished laughing, when François appeared; the chain hanging off his chainsaw and a scowl on his face. With the right tools it was an easy fix. But with the gung-ho attitude of youth, he'd gone up the hill without any. Which was why I always took everything I might need to do a job, in either the trailer or barrow. 'I bet you don't do *that* again,' I thought, while trying to appear sympathetic.

My smugness at François' deflation was short-lived however. When Diane opened the door she checked the key-rack. 'Your keys aren't here. Have you checked properly? Maybe they're in another pair of trousers,' she suggested.

'No, I'm sure I had them at work,' I said, patting my pockets. 'I hope I haven't lost them.'

Puzzled, I headed off to fill the kettle. Reaching into a high cupboard for coffee I heard a clinking noise. Feeling behind me, I found the keys in my back pocket – the one I never used. How the hell hadn't I felt them while I was working? 'Oh boy, I'm losing the plot,' I thought, switching on the kettle.

'Guess what,' I said, as Diane came from the bathroom.

'Don't tell me. You've found your keys right?'

Dammit, I hate it when she does that.

During lunch on the terrace, she explained Dominic's latest plans, but all too soon, it was time to go back. 'You head off and I'll lock up,' I said.

Turning around, she looked pointedly at the keys I was holding. 'Don't say a word,' I suggested, as she walked towards the car smirking.

On the cross-over boxes with Jacques that afternoon, there were mushrooms scattered everywhere. Shaking her head when she came over, Christine sent Jacques into the *cave*, before asking me to sweep up then go home. That'll do me, I thought.

I'd just left the works yard when François and his friends rode past. Reining in, he asked if I'd like to go to Jaman's. He and his 'fazzaire' were taking their saws in. I jumped at the chance and headed off to change.

Arriving at the workshop we were met by the owner, a young guy sporting a pony tail. Trapped in a time warp, fashion had passed him by. Still, he was helpful and looked honest. Hearing us talking, his heavily pregnant wife waddled over smiling. 'Good afternoon,' she enunciated, 'I speak a 'leetle Eenglish.'(A bonus, as she did the accounts.)

She was fascinated by the UK, saying she loved Scotland after a past visit. Suffice it to say, I was shown a wide range of saws and given valuable advice. And while Bertrand's saws were serviced, 'the missus' and I chatted. Arriving home at seven pm, I found Diane, wondering where the hell I'd been.

# Chapter 38

## Freedom – but at what cost?

The tension at the *cave* was palpable, with rumours of lay-offs growing daily. Being last man in and *Anglais* to boot, I was under no illusions as to my position – especially after my chat with Armand. Therefore, when I was sent into the *cave* with Jean-Luc and Christopher Borelle I was in a stoical mood, thinking I wouldn't be doing this for much longer. Maybe it was the best attitude to adopt, as when Jean-Luc nodded towards a *brouette,* saying, '*Chambre dix avec moi,*' it didn't faze me at all. I just trudged off towards the flickering lights in the distance. Where Iron Man went, I neither knew nor cared. I was just happy he wasn't with me.

Finished in chamber ten by eleven twenty-five am, I took the girls unused *plaquets* to the office. In that tense atmosphere I'd hoped for a half-day off; but with no sign of Christine I turned back into the chamber. With no-one to naysay me, I thought, to hell with this. So using my initiative (yes that's what I said,) I made an executive decision. Pushing the *brouette*, I headed towards chamber nine, the next to be worked. Strangely, I'd never worked in there before; and staring off into the darkness I felt uneasy. With tunnels branching off on both sides it seemed endless. I checked my watch which read eleven-forty. 'It'll be noon before long, and you've got to start somewhere,' I reasoned.

Mentally tossing a coin, I pushed off into the left hand tunnel. It couldn't have worked out better. Rounding the corner,

I saw that the tunnel ended about twenty metres in, and contained only eight beds. Better still, Deni then trundled in. Filling our *palettes* quickly, we pushed them to the entrance to await the tractor. It was lunch-time.

Emerging from the *cave,* I met François and Philippe walking Lupé; and as usual the stupid mutt went for me. It was evident from the beginning that we'd never be bosom buddies, so we'd settled for an uneasy truce – well most of the time. Cresting the head of the drive together, the boys headed towards Le Lavendu, waving to Diane as she pulled up in the car.


It'd threatened rain during lunch, and was tipping down when we drove back to work. I couldn't possibly repeat what Diane said, but the air was blue when she dropped me off. Sprinting through the downpour, I caught up with others heading in; and after clocking on, we crowded into the office to learn our fate.

The afternoon's plans had changed. They'd set up the cross-over box loading during lunch, and guess who was one of the lucky duo picked for the run? Yep! Alain was the other.

We began with Jacques-Noël driving the forklift, and the conveyor belt delivering button mushrooms at a sensible speed. Then without warning, a mound of *gros* trundled around the bend, catching us completely unawares. It then alternated between both, causing us to adjust the belt speed at irregular intervals. Cursing heartily, Alain blamed our problems on bad tray selection. Eventually he said, '*Suffissament,* 'or enough; and pressing the red button, he stopped the belt. Striding over to the forklift he started on Jacques-Noël. A slanging match then ensued; almost coming to blows when Alain called him *un petit merde.* This caused the outraged Jacques to storm off to Christine, who in turn came over to reprimand Alain. Oh this was priceless! With the line at a standstill, everyone watched as a red-faced Jacques-Noël and an outraged Alain shouted at each other. The words *petit merde* featured often in the exchange as I remember it.

271

With them both refusing to back down we set off again, this time with Christine presiding over us. It was farcical, as different sizes continued coming at us whatever she tried, forcing us to alter the pick-up speed continually. However, we eventually finished the order by five pm.

It was cold and drizzly when I left the *cave*. But re-playing the earlier fireworks in my mind, I walked home glowing inwardly, with a smile plastered on my face.

Climbing the drive I thought, I'll dry off then light a fire for Diane coming in. She'll probably be drenched and need a hot soak. Rounding the corner though, I was surprised to see the car in the barn. When I dragged my sorry ass into the kitchen Diane had the kettle on, having seen her sodden hero (yes me) walking up the drive. Apparently, after a manic afternoon spent picking in the rain, when even his wife was roped in, Dominic had finally called a halt. Magnanimously, he sent everyone home early, (unpaid of course,) as all viable apples had been picked. He said he'd contact them when a final pick was required. Diane was then completely stunned when he suggested she go home and rest. She should enjoy her UK visit, he said, as family is important. I didn't begrudge her a break, she richly deserved it. After initially swearing she was going to get 'lashed' though, she relented later, saying she'd pack for our journey instead.

Thursday dawned, and as a novelty I drove to work. Little did I realize, this would be the hardest day I'd ever work at the *cave*.

It started off normally enough, with me partnering Yves on the cross-over boxes. But we had a time limit, as he had a truck to load for an urgent delivery. It was chaos as usual, with mushrooms covering the floor when we'd finished. Christine seemed happy enough though; asking Jean-Claude to help me clean up when Yves hurried off. Then turning to me, she said, 'You can now go home.'

Eleven o'clock, great. I began planning a trip out with Diane. We could drive somewhere nice; maybe stop off for lunch at some bistro. Then the body-blow landed.

*Retournez à après midi, à quinze heures et demi.*' Return at three thirty? What time was *that* to go back? Arriving home puzzled, I told Diane.

'Well at least we can have a long lunch-break together,' she sighed.

Following a relaxing three hours, I reluctantly changed back into my work-clothes; walking to work while Diane drove to Le Lude for shopping. Stiff joints protesting, I wondered what surprise was in store for me this time.

When I arrived, Christine looked up from her clipboard, told me to grab loading equipment then follow Marie who stood waiting. I did just that; and after a long trudge we reached the far end of a tunnel. Here we met a team of girls working furiously. Leaving me she walked off again. Not a word was exchanged on the long walk over, or when she left me. The old adage never applied more than then. 'Treat them like mushrooms. Keep them in the dark and feed them shit.'

Never mind, I'll be finished by five thirty I thought – maybe six at the latest. Yeah right!

Checking my watch later, I was surprised how quickly time had passed. Apart from one brief visit by Jacques-Noël on a tractor, I was alone. The girls had vanished into the gloom and it was deathly quiet. Gritting my teeth, I worked on; painfully aware that a five thirty pm finish was now a pipedream. There was just too much work for one person.

Then help arrived at last. Jacques-Noël had returned. Great I thought, *now* we're getting somewhere. Alas no! My fussy helper began segregating *panniers* onto different *palettes*. What the hell was he up to? We hadn't time for all that. They'd be unloaded and checked against orders at the weighbridge. I tried explaining this, but ignoring me he plodded on.

At seven pm it was finally cleared. I stood up stretching. Thank God *that* was over. I was feeling elated. Friday was officially my last work-day, but Christine said I could finish tonight, as I'd worked hard and done all I was asked since I began. Obviously the message hadn't reached Jacques-Noël though. Parking his tractor he grabbed a *brouette* and *palette,* and striding off towards another chamber, he said, '*palette, champignons.* 'A man of few words, he marched off into the tunnel. 'When's this nightmare going to end?' I thought.

Finding a *brouette* and *palette,* I followed him. As we neared the tunnel's end, our lamps picked out the women doing a crash clearance. Pointing to them, he mumbled, '*Non ouvert.* 'Fantastic! '*Non ouvert,* or button mushrooms were swept off the beds by hand, and needed less *panniers*. With us both working flat out it shouldn't take long.

Then to an imaginary fanfare of trumpets Iron Man arrived. With a cigarillo jutting from his determined jaw, he dived in, making short work of the *panniers* and leaving both Jacques-Noël and I trailing in his wake. Finally, at eight pm the cry rang out. '*Bon, finis!*'

After a gruelling thirteen hours it was finally over. I trudged out for the last time bone weary. And since none of my work-mates knew I was leaving that night, they went their separate ways oblivious, leaving me stood there alone. And that's just how I wanted it, no fuss. I'd call by and see them soon.

Looking around, I hung up my lamp for the final time. Donning my waterproof coat I set off. Oh, didn't I mention it? On my final walk home it was teeming down.

As I walked out Armand appeared from the office. Shaking my hand he wished me well, thanking me for my hard work and reliability. He said he'd seen me struggle at first, trying to match the furious pace set by the others. Then he'd heard about my shoulder injury and decided to cut me some slack. His decision had been justified, he said, as I'd become faster, fitter, and stronger as time passed.

I then thanked *him* for taking a chance on *me*. He said we'd both benefitted, but now I must enjoy visiting family in the UK. When I returned I should call in for my cheque. There would be five days holiday pay added, plus two kilos of mushrooms. Work was still slack, he said, but when we returned, who knows?

Hunching my shoulders I left the *cave*. Trudging up the unlit road, rain whipped into my face. It stung like needles until I turned into our drive, where the hedge sheltered me from the worst of it. I'd finally made it. Stumbling gratefully towards the brightly lit kitchen, I was met by Diane's dulcet tones. 'Where in God's name have you *been* all this time? You look like a drowned rat.' And with that cheery welcome I stepped inside.

We were now both unemployed, with our UK visit imminent. But right then it was essentials first. My priority was to get out of my wet clothes and into a hot bath. Then warmed through, I needed a drink and a meal – in that order.

After dinner we settled down in front of the fire, watching rain stream down the French windows. Feeling no pain, I thought, maybe a comforting brandy might be nice.

As music played softly in the background, it slowly began to sink in. By then Diane had gone off to bed, so finishing my drink I switched off the music. The party was finally over.

# Chapter 39

## Journey home – and a safe return

I woke up feeling strange. Something seemed to be missing. What was it? Oh yes, work. What'd taken over our lives completely had ended. And though it'd seemed like ages, it'd been just a couple of months – but what a couple of months. Anyway, onwards and upwards; it was Friday and we had a trip to prepare for.

First stop was Noyant, where we enjoyed a stroll around the market; something we'd missed out on for ages. We did a food shop, bought last minute presents and filled the fuel-tank. Home again, I checked the car over thoroughly, then went in to help pack. After making sandwiches and a flask of coffee, we showered and dressed quickly. Booked on the evening ferry, we needed to avoid rush hour traffic around Le Mans and Rouen.

While loading the car the Charpentiers arrived to say goodbye. Handing over our keys to them, we explained what they needed to do in our absence; our main worry being our fridge and freezer going off during a power cut. But I also had to explain the security lights and timer adaptors we'd rigged up. With information imparted, kisses were given and received, hands shaken, and they left. Finally, with the house locked and shuttered we drove off.

The fickle finger of fate struck just after we passed the crossroads. A speeding Renault Espace hurtled around a corner on our side of the road. To avoid a collision, I swerved towards the ditch – then braked hard before plunging into it. Our freshly prepared flask of coffee, essential on the long journey crashed to the floor. Oblivious to the situation, the Renault driver careered off around the next bend. Cursing heartily, I picked up the leaking flask. Shaking it, I heard the inimitable rattling of a shattered thermos. Like Victor Meldrew, I growled, 'I don't *believe* it.'

Now I despise people littering the countryside, and can be quite vocal on the subject, but right then I was past caring. I slung the flask angrily into the ditch – after flinging more expletives at the disappearing Renault.

The rest of the journey passed without incident (and coffee) until we joined the Périphérique encircling Caan. Unable to find the exit we drove around it twice; then just as we were about to panic, we spotted a tiny white finger sign and made our escape.

On board the ferry at last, we strolled around the deck to stretch our legs, before heading for our pre-booked seats. Unfortunately they were occupied by a sleeping couple. It wasn't worth making a fuss though, as there were many others to choose from. And, as we always found them uncomfortable anyway, we chose to sleep on the floor yet again.

Docking at Portsmouth at six thirty am UK time, we drove, bleary-eyed, to Nadine's. She was still living at Maldon with Nick, who was fortunately at work. We enjoyed a relaxed visit; and after a filling breakfast, we headed north for our stop-over with Jill and Dale. They'd advertised their house for sale, and with a viewing that morning, we'd timed our arrival for lunch.

After our meal, Jill (aka Granny Schumacher) drove us into Grantham. Having a heart problem, Dale didn't drive much then, so we were at her mercy. Shooting off briskly she got up to speed, berating the odd driver who dared impede our progress. And after parking up we enjoyed a pleasant afternoon wandering around town. The evening was spent catching up, before we all turned in early to bed.

We headed off at nine forty five the next morning, our shiny new flask filled with coffee. Hoping it would fare better than its predecessor we joined the A1 north. Passing Durham by one pm we arrived soon after at Burnhope, where we met Stewy, and a smiling Helen holding baby Aaron. He was like his dad, she said, feisty and overactive; and he was having trouble feeding and sleeping. Roll up Super Granny Diane, who'd volunteered our services for a few days. Using old school methods we intended establishing a routine; giving them a break by taking on the night feeds.

The next day we visited Michael, where I spent a boisterous time with *my* grandchildren. As usual I wound them up; and when we left they were 'hyper,' which was normal after one of my visits. 'Thanks for that Dad,' said Michael ruefully.

Luckily, we also caught the elusive Chris. Enjoying a day out with him at the Metro Centre Shopping Mall, we picked his 21$^{st}$ birthday present, before returning for a house-party at Burnhope. Being well-served, Chris slept over; and when I drove him home the next morning he gave us Xmas presents, including Michael's which had been left with him in case of time constraints. I'd asked them not to buy us anything, but as usual they had anyway.

When we first moved to France, I'd kept in touch with a work colleague, an I.T geek who'd been building a computer for us. He lived in Washington New Town, and navigating its urban sprawl, we arrived and were introduced to Diane's new baby. (*Definitely* metaphorical) Back in France it would become our lifeline to the UK. After drooling over it she was given operating instructions, money changed hands, and it was carefully loaded before heading back to Burnhope.

Our last duty was to our faithful Peugeot 405, which had endured a tough life for quite some time. It was booked in for a full service, at a garage appropriately named 'The Peugeot Clinic' which specialised in the marque.

The finale to our week was a bonfire night party hosted by Stewy's parents. Food, booze, kids whooping it up, and the sky ablaze with pyrotechnics. What more could you ask for? Well not the fireworks Diane got dragged into; a political argument with Stewy's brother Duncan on leave from the army. But as Duncan soon found out, she's more than capable of handling herself, in that or any other situation.

The final leg of the tour was to Northumberland, where we collected the final items from our ex-neighbours Matt and Maria. On the way we called into The Riverside Garage Bellingham. Mark the owner, was a lover of Cote de Rhone wines, so we'd bought him a mixed selection as a gift. He'd gotten us out of a few scrapes in the past, and sold Diane's car for a modest fee when we moved. It was a pleasure to do *him* a favour for once. Then, with the trailer loaded we headed for the A1 south. First stop Grantham.

We arrived for a pre-arranged lunch, before loading yet more 'stuff' and heading off to Essex. This time we were aiming for Nadine's new flat in Burnham-on-Crouch. We'd visited it the previous week; but this time we'd be searching for it in the dark. Without sat-nav. to help us, Nadine suggested we meet in Safeway's car park. Nick was taking Ben and Lewis to a firework display then having them for a sleep-over. It would make things easier, as we needed to find the flat urgently. The trailer lights had died; so with hazard-lights blinking we limped into the car park, to be greeted by Nadine's flashing headlights. With her window down she drove over. 'Just follow me,' she said, then shot off.

Parked behind her flat later, we had a meal, a drink and a hot bath. After our tiring drive, I left them to it and crashed out upstairs. However, Diane stayed up chatting to Nadine until two am.

When I woke her at five am she was shattered; and once underway we misread Nadine's detailed directions. On Finding the A12 though, it wasn't long before we reached the M25 motorway. Known cynically as the largest car park in Europe it was running freely for a change, and soon we'd arrived at the Dartford crossing. Next, the final run into Portsmouth.

With little traffic we arrived early, giving bored customs officers something to inspect. Behind us vehicles arrived and were segregated; trucks and coaches being directed to their own lanes before loading began. Half an hour later, with the car and trailer taking a well earned rest below-decks, we picked up our cabin key, opened the door and flaked out.

Two hours later I lay wide awake. I'd had a full night's sleep already, and had just needed to rest my eyes before driving through France. However Diane was comatose. Snoring like a buzz-saw she was totally wiped out; a victim of her late night with Nadine. The noise in that confined space was phenomenal, so I dressed and went for a walk around the ship. Buying a newspaper at a kiosk, I relaxed in a window-seat, reading, and occasionally watching other sea traffic.

Thirty minutes before docking a tannoy message requested cabins be vacated, so I descended to find Diane coming to. After a quick shower we were once again ready for action, joining crowds assembling near the exit doors.

Docking at three thirty pm local time I re-set the car clock, and soon we were trundling down the gangplank onto French soil – on a murky day requiring lights! I was painfully aware, that despite attention our trailer's electrics weren't working. But at least it was daylight, so we'd just have to risk it. Pulling into the first garage we came across we filled up with fuel, which at that time was much cheaper than in the UK. We were off and running.

With hot coffee still in our flask, we drank as we drove. Naughty I know, but we had to make up time. It was the kind of day when dusk fell suddenly, and we didn't want to run into any police. We reckoned we'd pass through Le Mans before dark, and gambled on the local *gendarmerie* being lax, allowing us to get home without 'a pull.' With an on the spot speeding fine of 90 euros; God knows what driving with dodgy lights would cost us – without anything else they might find.

Fortunately everything went fine, until we reached the outskirts of Le Mans in twilight, where we missed the turn for La Flèche. Realizing our error we turned back, took the correct route, and I put my foot down.

After a hairy drive along unlit country roads, we eventually crept through La Flèche towards Le Lude. I'm sure The Hippo would have tip-toed if it could. Sneaking through the deserted town, we arrived home at seven thirty pm in total darkness. Wound up like clockwork we un-hitched the trailer, pushed it into the barn, and switched on the power in the boiler room by torchlight. Opening the house up we flicked on lights. Then after unpacking the car I lit a fire, and we had a cuppa while we settled in.

As the lounge warmed up *we* chilled out; and opening a bottle of wine we celebrated another successful mission. Totally wired on coffee and wine by then, I picked out a music video and hit the play button. Oh yeah, we were back!

Throwing open the French windows I stepped out into the velvet night. Gazing up at the star-studded sky my heart sang. This was the life we wanted; and despite the hardships we'd endured it was worth fighting for. We'd come a long way on this crazy journey so far, but we still had much to do.

'I'm off to bed now,' said Diane yawning. 'Lock up, will you?'

Stepping back inside I closed the shutters. Tomorrow was another day.

The follow up to 'Hippo in a hairnet' is titled, 'If only we'd known', and will be available shortly.

For an exclusive excerpt, please turn to the next page.

# If only we'd known

# Chapter 1

## Home is where the hearth is

'What do you think it'll look like? I asked a sleepy Diane, as we approached the village. I reckon we'll have a job on our hands, don't you?

It was a surreal experience driving through that lush wooded valley, then pulling up the drive to the farm. We could have been returning from a shopping trip. On the other hand, it felt as if we'd been away for months. And though everything was comfortingly familiar, much had changed in the relatively short time we'd been gone.

November 2004, and we'd taken a break from renovating our French farm, to visit Diane's daughter Helen and her husband Stewy. Spending time with them and their new baby Aaron had been great; and catching up with other family members had been long overdue. But it was time to get back to reality. Before we left France, Diane had promised to return to the orchards for the late apple picking. But with that promise fulfilled, we had decisions to make. We were past the tipping point with our project. If we worked hard through the winter and finished the house, we could possibly rent it out next summer. It all depended on how far our money stretched. Though whatever we decided, the next season might prove to be a deal breaker. But right then it was late at night, we'd arrived on the last ferry, and we weren't relishing the long drive ahead of us.

Once we hit the autoroute though, the miles rolled by metronomically; and as dawn smudged the sky, we pulled up outside the farmhouse. After opening up and dumping our luggage, it was time to uncork the Merlot. I agree, it's not your normal breakfast, but after a long hairy drive, we felt we deserved it. Out came the glasses and on went the music. We were back!

Considering the home coming party the night before, we arose surprisingly early that first morning. It'd gotten kinda wild at one point, as our old friends dropped by to welcome us back. Status Quo, Bon Jovi, Meatloaf and Tina Turner had all made it. Yep, you've got the idea!

Given the circumstances, waking up should've been an absolute nightmare; but miraculously we both felt fine. Bursting with energy after one of Diane's legendary fry-ups, we began making plans. Skirting the orchards the previous evening, Diane had spotted *balloxes* on the terraces; so leaving me to unpack, she drove off to pick up her outstanding wages and check out the work situation.

Handing Diane her cheque, the *secretaire* said, unfortunately picking was on hold due to bad weather. She'd ring when things changed. A frustrated Diane returned home and loaded the washing machine. We then set off to the *cave de champignons* to collect *my* cheque. After handing it over, the supervisor suggested I return the next morning for my bonus – two kilos of freshly picked mushrooms. Driving off to Noyant we banked the cheques, before heading back to Le Lude for supplies.

Noticing that we were back, our neighbours popped over, handing back our bunch of keys like a hot potato. Véronique had been reluctant to take it at first, as it's apparently not the done thing, except with family. Business taken care of, the ladies drooled over Aaron's baby photos, whereupon Betrand magically produced an opened bottle of *rosé* to 'wet the baby's head.' I *still* don't know how he does that.

When they left we finished unpacking, before airing Michael Flately's *Lord of the dance* video. It wasn't a patch on Riverdance in ou humble opinion, but hey, what do *we* know? Feeling the effects of the journey, Mr Flately was switched off in mid-leap, as we crashed out for a nap.

During the week, the temperature took a nosedive, which was a cause for concern. Sure we had logs for the lounge fire, but with no central heating as yet, our situation was dire to say the least. In a bid to remedy this situation, we visited Saumur mid-week, looking for some additional form of heating. Settling on two oil-filled radiators, we prayed they'd boost the lounge temperature. Then at least we'd be comfortable in the heart of the house. The rest would have to wait for funds.

On the way back, I called in at the *cave* office, and found Armand the boss at his desk. Welcoming me back, he asked about our UK visit; then we discussed business, which he said was still in the doldrums. With no work on offer, we shook hands and I left; Armand promising to call if the situation changed.

Home again with the heaters connected, we began feeling the effects immediately. Combined with the log fire, the lounge was moderately comfortable at a steady 17 deg C. Diane even suggested cutting back on wood burning, which she suggested might cure the cough I'd developed lately. Lets not jump the gun here!

With it being a smidgin warmer, I decided to remodel the fire surround. But outside scrubbing the stones I'd collected the heavens opened. Returning to the kitchen drenched, I found Diane wrestling with two huge pumpkins. Our *cave* was piled high with these monsters – the progeny of two plants Véronique had given us. Triffid-like, they'd taken over the garden, giving birth to twenty enormous orange offspring.

We'd given some away, but were stuck with the rest. It seems everyone around here grew them for the festival of *Toussaint.* Not wanting to waste them, Diane consulted her recipe books.

Dicing them, then blending them with spices, she simmered them in pans. On the kitchen worktop, rows of gleaming Kilner jars stood at attention, awaiting the metamorphosis to follow.

After tea we chilled out beside a glowing fire; a hint of wood-smoke blending with the aromas seeping through from the kitchen. Projects taken care of we chatted contentedly. Clutching glasses of full-bodied red wine, no entertainment was needed.

Printed in Great Britain
by Amazon